WILEY
EXECUTIVE
MBA
Strategies, Skills, Solutions

MASTERING BUSINESS IN ASIA

ENTREPRENEURSHIP

WILEY
EXECUTIVE
MBA
Strategies, Skills, Solutions

MASTERING BUSINESS IN ASIA

ENTREPRENEURSHIP

Chris Boulton
Patrick Turner

John Wiley & Sons (Asia) Pte Ltd

This publication is designed to provide accurate and authoritative information with regard to the subject matter covered. It is sold with the understanding that the Publisher is not engaged in rendering professional services. If professional advice or other expert assistance is required, the services of a competent professional person should be sought.

Other Wiley Editorial Offices
John Wiley & Sons, Inc., 111 River Street, Hoboken, NJ 07030, USA
John Wiley & Sons Ltd, The Atrium, Southern Gate, Chichester PO19 BSQ, England
John Wiley & Sons (Canada) Ltd, 22 Worcester Road, Rexdale, Ontario M9W ILI, Canada
John Wiley & Sons Australia Ltd, 33 Park Road (PO Box 1226), Milton, Queensland 4046, Australia
Wiley-VCH, Pappelallee 3, 69469 Weinheim, Germany

Library of Congress Cataloging-in-Publication Data:

0-470-82138-8

Typeset in 11.5/13.8 point, Berkeley by Paul Lim
Printed in Singapore by Saik Wah Press Pte Ltd
10 9 8 7 6 5 4 3 2 1

This book is dedicated to

[Chris]
My wife, Caroline and sons Alex and Nick

[Patrick]
My daughter Catherine, who as this book goes to press is embarking on her own first entrepreneurial venture in London.

Contents

Acknowledgments   ix

Preface   xi

Section I Introduction   1

  1   Entrepreneurs and the Asian Context   3

  2   Top-of-mind Issues and Other Themes   21

  3   Entrepreneurs and Opportunity   35

Section II The Entrepreneur and Cash   57

  4   Case Study: Start-up in Bangalore   59

  5   Raising Start-up Capital   79

  6   The Check is in the Post: Managing Cash   117

  7   Government and Entrepreneurship   149

Section III Growing Pains   167

  8   Managing Growth   169

9   Raising Expansion Capital   187

10   Going International   215

11   Let's Go IPO   239

Section IV Themes of Maturity   265

12   Handling Succession   267

13   Releasing Entrepreneurial Potential: MBOs   287

Section V Conclusion   327

14   A Look Forward   329

     Index   343

Acknowledgments

We would like to thank several groups of people who in their different ways have made invaluable contributions to this book:

- Nick Wallwork, Selvamalar Manoharan, and Janis Soo at John Wiley & Sons for creating the initial opportunity and subsequently for their ongoing patience and guidance;
- Cassandra Cheung, whose initial research provided a strong boost to the project;
- Robyn Flemming, whose experience as an editor has contributed immensely to shaping and smoothing our finished product;
- The many entrepreneurs and advisers who patiently answered our questions, provided comments, and suggested ideas; and also those who completed our online questionnaire as part of the initial research for this book;
- The directors and shareholders of MeritTrac Ltd who very kindly agreed to be the subjects of and help construct the start-up case study in Chapter 4;
- The Global Entrepreneurship Monitor, the UPS Asia Business Monitor, and the Deloitte Technology Fast 500 Asia Pacific programme for permission to quote extensively from their survey results.
- Several of Patrick's INSEAD colleagues for their generosity in allowing us to quote from their work. Individual acknowledgements will be found in the appropriate places in the text.

Finally, our close families and colleagues who have been living and breathing this book along with us for the past year!

Preface

Entrepreneurship in Asia is both an exciting and a huge topic! Our aim with this book is not to provide a comprehensive coverage in terms of either issues or geography but to give the reader a flavor of a selection of key themes and issues relating to entrepreneurial activity in the region today.

We tried to imagine a typical reader, and one of the images that seemed particularly appropriate to us was that of a businessman or woman reading the book on a plane on the way here. We wanted to provide them with bite-sized topics to take in between films, work, food and dozing so that by arrival time he or she would have gained a basic background and understanding of some of the key issues.

Our early preparation for the book was to pull together a selection of potential topics. To do this we drew on a wide range of experience, discussions with businessmen, and advice. We also carried out an online survey of Asian entrepreneurs and their advisers. As was to be expected we were faced with a significant number of likely topics, all of which to some degree or other are important to Asian entrepreneurs. Narrowing down the pool of likely themes was a challenging task, but we feel the ten included in this book not only represent some of the more pressing issues, but also will provide the reader with a good basis and taste for the entrepreneurial scene in Asia today.

As you read, you will discover that we do not confine the scope of our book just to the early stages of the entrepreneurial process. Entrepreneurs don't stop being entrepreneurial once their business idea gets some traction, they just meet an ever-changing set of issues and challenges as their businesses develop. For example, an entrepreneur starting up a business is more likely to lose sleep over attracting seed capital than managing the growth of the business. In the same way, the CEO of an established business may be far more concerned about succession than on raising further capital for expansion. All these themes have their seasons, but their importance can be understood better in the relevant context.

To this end, we have divided the book into sections which will track the growth path and changing issues facing entrepreneurial businesses in Asia. Section I sets the scene, identifies key themes and also looks at innovation and opportunity – the mother and father of entrepreneurship – in the region. Section II covers the turbulent albeit necessary relationship between entrepreneurs and cash. A case study from India sets the scene for this section and is followed by chapters on raising capital, managing cash, and the role of governments in funding entrepreneurs and promoting entrepreneurship in general. Section III covers themes relevant to businesses which have progressed through the start up phase and are looking to expand the business further. In this part we cover the development issues around growing companies, the challenge of expanding abroad, and the financial aspects of growing a company including raising expansion capital, and raising public funds through IPO. Section IV looks at two themes related to more mature businesses. First, the growing issue of succession in family businesses and second the increasing adoption of a method to re-invigorate and restructure some of the more mature Asian economies – the management buyout (MBO). Finally, we take a macro view and identify some of the themes which will be relevant going forward.

So as you take your seat for the long-haul flight, we hope that the film selections are beaten into second place by the passion, insight, and commitment, of Asian entrepreneurs, and the emotional, rollercoaster world that is entrepreneurship in Asia.

Chris Boulton
Patrick Turner
February 2005

SECTION I

Introduction

Entrepreneurs and the Asian Context

*E*ntrepreneurship is a societal phenomenon as well known and deeply rooted in the Asia-Pacific region as anywhere else in the world. However, different speeds and patterns of political and economic development have created a patchwork across the region, with widely differing degrees of entrepreneurship from country to country.

After a brief look back to get a historical perspective, we look at the degree of entrepreneurship in Asia today through the figures gathered by the most recent Global Entrepreneurship Monitor report, and in the light of these, offer some reflections on the kind of parameters that seem to influence the degree of entrepreneurship in any one country or community.

We conclude by looking at how easy or difficult it is to become an entrepreneur in the various countries that comprise the region, from which it is clear that some countries are infinitely more entrepreneurship-friendly than others.

SETTING THE SCENE

Mumbai, India: April 2004. A hundred or so young men and women have assembled for a talk on the pitfalls to avoid when planning the launch of a new business. They range in age from 25 to 45, and they are members of the young entrepreneurs section of the local TiE group chapter.[1] Only a handful have ever launched a business before, and so most are aspiring entrepreneurs. There are many questions at the end of the talk. One is: "Can you please explain to us what break-even means?" Another is: "What is the difference between a business model and a business plan?"

Beijing, China: April 2004. One of the authors of this book sits in a smart boardroom chatting with Linan Zhu, chief executive officer (CEO) of Legend Capital, one of the most high profile, most experienced, and best known of the native Chinese venture capital (VC) firms. The question is asked: "What is the major headache that Chinese VC firms have right now?" The answer is given without hesitation: the majority of entrepreneurs submitting business plans for funding have no idea of how to run a business, much less any experience in doing so.

Shenzhen, China: April 2004. A VC conference has attracted over 700 delegates, including a strong non-Chinese contingent from VC strongholds such as Silicon Valley and Israel. After one of the panel sessions, a young man asks: "How can we start up a new company if we are always expected to put in our own money?"

Entrepreneurship is bubbling all over Asia – even, as improbable as it may seem, in North Korea, where since July 2002, citizens have been allowed to open small businesses such as restaurants and bakeries. In March 2004 the authorities introduced markets where licensed individuals and companies can trade goods. Over the first three months of operation, this measure produced some 300 markets across the country, and they were quickly becoming an essential part of daily life.[2]

In some places – China, for example – the atmosphere isn't unlike that which prevailed around the world during the build-up to the dot.com bubble. Everybody, it seems, wants to become an entrepreneur. It should perhaps be hastily added that the similarity in atmosphere ends there, as the phenomenon is not being fueled by a seemingly free flow of funding as was the case during 1998/99, and funders are being infinitely more cautious. A repeat of the dot.com boom and bust is therefore unlikely.

DRIVERS OF ASIAN ENTREPRENEURSHIP

There appear to be two main reasons for this region-wide enthusiasm: the rapid economic rise of the region's two biggest countries, China and India; and active government encouragement.

Rapid rise of China and India

With the rest of the world beating a path to the doors of these two countries in search of low-cost manufacturing (China) and services (India), countless new business opportunities have opened up in response to the much-increased demand. This has attracted the interest of two groups of entrepreneurs: locally resident would-be entrepreneurs, anxious to seize the chance of launching a company of their own; and already successful entrepreneurs from abroad, often from the entrepreneurial hotbeds on both coasts of the United States, who see new opportunities appearing back home. This latter group are the returning diaspora – people who left their native country in search of education and greater opportunity, who are now attracted back home, but who bring with them the education, experience, and often personal wealth they acquired abroad. The combination of these two groups is a potentially powerful teaming up of ideas, experience, and funds that is already producing success stories.

Active government encouragement

The second reason behind the enthusiasm is the deliberate attempt on the part of many governments to actively encourage a higher level of entrepreneurship. The degree to which this is being done varies from country to country, as we shall see later in Chapter 7, but in all cases the result is an increased level of awareness of what entrepreneurship is all about, and a growing level of interest in actually doing it.

Some countries – such as Singapore, for example – are going out of their way to make the country an attractive place for foreign entrepreneurs to come and set up shop, the rationale behind this being that such foreigner-launched new businesses will not only provide new employment opportunities for Singaporeans, but will also help to build up a cluster of role models and success stories more rapidly than could be achieved by depending solely on the growth of home-grown entrepreneurship. These efforts appear to be having the desired effect, as in the first six months of operation, the streamlined residence permit scheme for foreigners with business plans (EntrePass), introduced in October 2003, had attracted 800 applications.

But as we saw in the sketches that opened this introduction, there is a gap between the desire to become an entrepreneur on the one hand, and the availability of the requisite skills, experience, and funding on the other. The bridging of this gap will, of course, take time. As one young Japanese entrepreneur we talked to put it, "You cannot spend years telling people that the work ideal is lifelong service in a big corporation, and then tell them to become entrepreneurs and expect the mindset to change overnight."

A HISTORICAL PERSPECTIVE

Human memory is notoriously short, and there is a tendency in some quarters to talk about entrepreneurship as though it was a phenomenon that started sometime in the early 1990s in Silicon Valley. While it is true that what might be termed the "Silicon Valley model" is something that many other parts of the world, including Asia, would like to emulate (there is a group of office buildings in Singapore that calls itself "Asia's vertical Silicon Valley", and Penang is referred to as Malaysia's "Silicon Island"), entrepreneurship in Asia goes back a long way.

The Indians, for example, have always had the reputation of creating entrepreneurial communities wherever they have settled, be it the UK or, longer ago, East Africa.

In Singapore, private-sector entrepreneurs were dominant before independence,[3] creating companies that are in many cases the backbone of the country's small- to medium-sized enterprise (SME) fabric today. However, much of this entrepreneurial activity was based on trading, and at the end of 1963, there were only 548 small manufacturing companies, producing low value-added products that were sold in the local market. After independence, the government sought to accelerate industrialization by attracting multinational corporations (MNCs) to invest, and those MNCs that did so helped to nurture local industrial entrepreneurship by providing a ready market for the output of locally manufactured products.[4]

In Korea, big business groups, the *chaebol*, have historically dominated the economy, and in the past, many observers noted that Korea and Taiwan were examples of two extremes, since the former relied very much on big business and the latter relied heavily on SMEs.[5] With regard to Taiwan's SME development, the following passage from a paper by Rong-I Wu and Chung-Che Huang[6] vividly describes what has been the process:

> During the last four decades, the successful development of Taiwanese small- and medium-sized enterprises (SMEs) has become the most important part of Taiwan's economic legend. The key players are the many Taiwanese businessmen, sometimes called "black-hand bosses," who were once machinists and apprentices but eventually became successful employers. They embody the dreams and stories of blue-collar workers who may be undereducated and short of capital but can gain fortune through hard work in untidy and uncomfortable factories. The spirit of entrepreneurship among skilled employees has led to the establishment of millions of SMEs that fulfill this dream. This process has become a reality over and over again across the island. These SMEs exhibit flexibility, vigor and ambition, providing the unique characteristics of Taiwanese entrepreneurship.

In Thailand, industrial development really started in the early 1960s with a Western-style economic development. In contrast, with the previous regime's policy founded upon public enterprises, the government turned to private enterprises as an engine for growth. This policy contributed to the transformation of Thailand from an agricultural-based country to an industrial and service-based economy with a market-led and open orientation.[7]

One very important point that is often overlooked when Westerners talk about Asia is the varying influence of different ethnic and religious factors across the region. For example, it is impossible to understand entrepreneurship in Malaysia without being aware of the Bumiputeras. Literally "sons of the soul," the term is used to designate ethnic Malays as distinct from the immigrant Chinese or Indian sectors of Malay society.

In order to remedy the economic inequalities that existed within the country, it was agreed among representatives of the three major ethnic groups that upon independence, the Malays would be granted certain "special rights" in the realm of religion, economics and politics. The main reason for this "positive discrimination" was to elevate the status of the economically disenfranchised Malays, and thereby create a more equitable society.

Embedded within these larger policies is the issue of creating a Bumiputera Commercial and Industrial Community (BCIC), which involves fostering Bumiputera entrepreneurs, professionals and creating a Bumiputera middle-class (Economic Planning Unit, 2001). This has become the backbone of Malaysia's strategy for strengthening national entrepreneurship, and all related policies and strategies have to take this into consideration. Non-Bumiputera entrepreneurs have not been totally neglected however. The government continues to nurture the business community through a variety of entrepreneurial support services.[8]

However, there are signs that this policy may be relaxing somewhat, as, for example, it was not applied to the high-tech Multimedia Super Corridor established in 2000 (see Chapter 3).

Entrepreneurship in Thailand has been permeated by the hard-working values of Confucianism. In this context, attitudes toward failure and success appear to be irrelevant as long as the momentum of the working spirit prevails over the outcome. Failures have been viewed as a learning process on the entrepreneurship road map. Buddhist values also contributed to the attitude of tolerance toward failures among the entrepreneurial class.[9]

TRACKING ENTREPRENEURSHIP IN ASIA

The creation of the Global Entrepreneurship Monitor (GEM)[10] in 1999 represented the first concerted attempt to provide a regular annual review of the state of entrepreneurship around the world, and this section refers extensively to the work done for the GEM, and in particular for its 2003 annual report,[11] which covered 31 countries.

The most significant elements in the compilation of the report data are the surveys of representative samples of the adult population in each of the countries. The surveys are carried out by locally based commercial research firms, using local languages, and the sample size varies from 1,000 up to 22,000.

The principal measure of entrepreneurial activity developed in the GEM is the Total Entrepreneurial Activity (TEA) index, which is simply the number of individuals active in the start-up or early growth phase of a new business, expressed as a percentage of the total working population. The higher the TEA, the higher the level of entrepreneurship:

Figure 1.1 shows the TEA index for the Asia-Pacific countries covered by the survey. The following initial comments can be made:

- The region's countries are symmetrically positioned around the US figure, with five above and five below.
- Among themselves, these countries split quite clearly into three groups, with Thailand and India detached at the higher level of entrepreneurial activity; Korea, New Zealand, China, and Australia close to the US level, with all above the overall global figure; and then Singapore, Taiwan, Hong Kong, and Japan forming a group trailing some way behind the rest.
- Only two countries in the report had a higher TEA level than Thailand's. These were Uganda at 29.3 and Venezuela at 27.3.
- At the other extreme, Japan's TEA of 2.3 is actually the lowest 2002/03 figure of all the countries covered by the study, although it is only a hair's breadth behind France (2.4) and Russia (2.5).

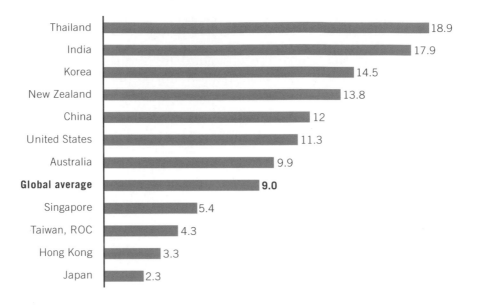

Note: The figures for India, Thailand, Korea, and Taiwan are from the 2002 report.
All others are the average of the 2002 and 2003 reports.

Figure 1.1 Total Entrepreneurial Activity in Asia-Pacific, 2002/03

This index, although revealing, is all-encompassing and includes all kinds of motivations for becoming involved in a start-up or early-stage company. So, in order to refine the analysis somewhat, the GEM study makes a distinction between two types of entrepreneurship – necessity-based and opportunity-driven. The former group includes everybody who has launched their own economic activity through the lack of any alternative revenue-generating possibilities; while the latter group are those entrepreneurs who have spotted a specific opportunity and have foregone alternative earnings possibilities in order to pursue it.

In this book, we will be almost exclusively concerned with the latter group. Figure 1.2 shows the opportunity-driven TEA index for the countries in the region. Here again, various observations can be made:

- As would have been expected, the proportion of necessity-based entrepreneurship is rather higher in those countries that can still be considered as "developing." For example, nearly 60% of Uganda's overall entrepreneurship activity is necessity-based.

- That said, the figures still leave India and Thailand ahead of the rest of the region, and indeed the United States, in terms of opportunity-driven entrepreneurship.
- Although still last on the list of Asia-Pacific countries in terms of opportunity-driven entrepreneurship, Japan has two countries – Croatia and France – behind it on a global basis.
- In terms of relative positioning, the major change compared with the overall TEA index is that the heavy weight of necessity-based entrepreneurship in China moves it into the trailing group.
- On the other hand, the very low level of necessity-based entrepreneurship recorded in Japan moves it closer to the other three countries in the trailing group.

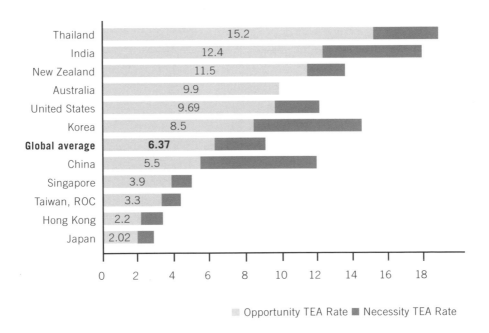

Note: The opportunity TEA rates for Thailand, India, Korea, and Taiwan have been taken from the GEM 2002 report.

Figure 1.2 Total Opportunity-driven Entrepreneurial Activity in Asia-Pacific, 2002/03

The fact that the GEM studies have now been running for some years, although with a varying selection of participating countries, enables the tracking of the TEA index over time, and thus gives an idea of how stable or volatile this measure is. Table 1.1 shows the TEA figures since 2000. (The first year, 1999, is omitted because only one Asia-Pacific country was covered.)

Table 1.1 TEA Index Levels, 2000–03

Country TEA rate	2000	2001	2002	2003
Thailand	n/a	n/a	18.9	n/a
India	6.3	11.2	17.9	n/a
Korea	13.7	15.0	14.5	n/a
New Zealand	n/a	15.6	14.0	13.6
United States	12.7	11.7	10.5	12.1
China	n/a	n/a	12.3	12.0
Australia	n/a	15.6	8.7	9.9
Global average	**n/a**	**9.9**	**8.0**	**9.0**
Singapore	2.1	5.2	5.9	4.9
Taiwan, ROC	n/a	n/a	4.3	n/a
Hong Kong	n/a	n/a	3.4	3.2
Japan	1.3	5.1	1.8	2.8

Note: n/a signifies data not collected for that year.

It can be seen that in most cases the index levels remain relatively stable over time. The most significant exceptions to this are:

- Australia, where the level of 15.6 in 2001 had dropped to 9.9 by 2003; and
- Japan, where there is a jump to 5.1 in 2001. Singapore shows a similar jump.

In all of these cases it can be reasonably surmised that the worldwide jump in interest in entrepreneurship that accompanied the dot.com boom had an effect on the 2001 figure. In Japan the level has since fallen back to earlier levels, while in Singapore the improvement has largely been sustained.

The only country that really shows a surprising degree of volatility is India, where the 6.3 of 2000 grew to 11.2 in 2001 and to 17.9 in 2002. It could well be that this is a reflection of a dramatic increase in entrepreneurial activity fueled possibly by the sharp rise in information technology (IT) and business process outsourcing (BPO) activity.

FACTORS INFLUENCING ENTREPRENEURSHIP

The fact that there are such wide variations between entrepreneurial activity in different countries, even taking into account the distinction between necessity-based and opportunity-driven entrepreneurs, inevitably prompts the question, "Why should this be?" This, in turn, opens up the whole subject area of what factors influence people to become entrepreneurs and stimulate entrepreneurial activity.

Producing entrepreneurs

There have been many attempts to shed light on this issue, some of them arriving at fanciful conclusions suggesting, to take an artificially exaggerated example, that you are more likely to be an entrepreneur if you are the second child of an immigrant family whose parents divorced before you were 12, and so on. In fact, the only recipe that seems to stand up to critical examination is that you are more likely to become an entrepreneur if someone in your environment is or has been one – your father, for instance, or some other family member.

However, your environment includes more than just your family, and so it can also be said that if there is a strong entrepreneurial community where you are brought up – your home town, or even a cluster of towns in your area – then this can also encourage you to think of becoming an entrepreneur yourself. It's not just a question of icons, or role models; it's more a matter of entrepreneurship appearing to you, in those you see around you, as a perfectly normal and widely practiced way of pursuing a career.

In this context, in the GEM study one of the three statistically significant contributing factors to high levels of entrepreneurial activity was provided by people who said they knew an entrepreneur. Such people were nearly three times as likely to start a business as the rest.[12]

This mechanism can be seen reflected in the GEM TEA index figures. Nobody will be surprised that the US figures are consistently high and above the global average in view of the "can do" pioneer spirit that that country prides itself on. By extension, the acceptance that mistakes will be made, and that entrepreneurial failure is in some ways a positive if painful experience, also contributes to the overall environment influencing future generations of entrepreneurs.

Precisely the opposite phenomenon can be observed in Japan, Singapore, and Korea, for instance, where over the years, children in school have been taught to think inside molds, and have basically been told that professional happiness consists in working hard in order to get a good lifelong job in a large company. These are also societies that traditionally haven't looked kindly on failure.

The lack of an entrepreneurially active environment also leads to misconceptions about what an entrepreneur is, and the kinds of people who become one. For instance, there is still a widespread idea that entrepreneurs are, by and large, people who drop out of school when they are in their teens, and then go and invent something in the shed at the bottom of the garden, and this leads them on to fame and fortune. There is even a considerable number of people who believe that entrepreneurs are born rather than made, and that by extension, the idea of teaching and learning entrepreneurship is absurd.

Can entrepreneurship be taught?
(aka Are entrepreneurs born or made?)

The answer is that, of course, the principles of entrepreneurship can be taught. If they couldn't, that would make entrepreneurship the one and only human activity impossible to teach, which is an absurdity. In fact, entrepreneurship education can help people to understand how to go about validating an idea to determine whether it is a viable commercial opportunity, how to go about planning and launching a new company with all that this entails, and then how to run it, including the pitfalls and danger areas and how to avoid them.

But it can do much more than this. It can positively influence an individual's perception of the risks entailed in becoming an entrepreneur so that he realizes that the risks he perceives can be managed in such a way as to radically reduce them. This on its own is enough to make many people consider becoming an entrepreneur, whereas before they would have been afraid to do so.

There is, in fact, empirical evidence of this, which demonstrates that education and training in entrepreneurship can help entrepreneurs to increase their firm's chance of survival, and to a lesser extent, it can help make the resulting business more profitable.

According to a Kauffman Center study,* compared to other business school alumni, entrepreneurship graduates:

- are three times more likely to start new businesses;
- have annual incomes that are 27% higher and own 62% more assets; and
- are more satisfied with their jobs.

The annual incomes figure being greater than that for non-entrepreneurs is in line with the 20% more found by an INSEAD internal study of its alumni carried out in 2001.

* Alberta Charney and Gary D. Libecap,
Impact of Entrepreneurship Education
(Kauffman Center for Entrepreneurial Research, 2000).

Clearly, there are entrepreneurs who don't complete their education and do move on to fame and fortune, but these are very much in the minority. The GEM report found that those with post-secondary or graduate education are twice as likely to be involved in an entrepreneurial firm as those with less education.[13] This figure is identical with the findings of a 1998 study of the fastest-growing entrepreneurial companies in Europe, which found that 67% of the CEOs of the 500 companies studied held a university degree, and nearly half of these additionally had some form of postgraduate degree.[14]

These figures, taken with another factor looked at in the GEM report, raise the topic of entrepreneurship education. The GEM report found that another of the three statistically significant contributing factors to high levels of entrepreneurial activity was a belief on the part of the individual that he or she possessed the skills necessary to start and manage a new business. People who believed this were on average five times more likely to be engaged in entrepreneurship.[15]

This finding can be taken together with the third of the three significant favorable factors, which was perception of business opportunities; those who could see good opportunities were three times more likely to be an entrepreneur than the rest.[16] The significance of this in terms of education is twofold. First, one of the basics of any entrepreneurship education program is the whole area of opportunity recognition and validation – training people how to develop ideas and, once developed, how to distinguish those that represent real business opportunities. Second, education obviously includes the universities and other institutes of higher learning, many of which have research laboratories out of which come new ideas, techniques, and products, which become the basis for new businesses.

Level playing fields

So far in this section, we have looked at the question of why people become entrepreneurs. Another major factor influencing the level of entrepreneurial activity is how easy or difficult it is to become an entrepreneur – in other words, the level of official and administrative burden that an entrepreneur has to cope with. Also in this part of the equation are the costs an entrepreneur has to face, both at start-up and during the operation of the business, and the availability of funding for entrepreneurial activities.

There are still wide differences between countries in these areas, as shown in Table 1.2.

Table 1.2 Indicators of Administrative Burden in New Business Creation

Country	Number of procedures	Time (days)	Flexibility Hiring (The lower the index, the better)	Firing	Cost (% of average income per cap)	Total
United States	5	4	33	5	0.6	47.6
Singapore	7	8	33	1	1.2	50.2
Australia	2	2	33	13	2	52
New Zealand	3	3	33	20	0.2	59.2
Hong Kong	5	11	58	1	2.3	77.3
Japan	11	31	39	9	10.5	100.5
Mongolia	8	31	33	25	12	109
Malaysia	8	31	33	15	27.1	114.1
Papua New Guinea	7	69	17	4	26.4	123.4
Korea	12	33	33	32	17.9	127.9
China	12	46	17	57	14.3	146.3
Sri Lanka	8	58	33	40	18.3	157.3
Thailand	9	42	78	30	7.3	166.3
Taiwan	8	48	81	32	6.1	175.1
Pakistan	10	22	65	33	46.8	176.8
Bangladesh	7	30	33	32	75.5	177.5
Vietnam	11	63	43	48	29.9	194.9
Philippines	11	59	58	50	24.4	202.4
India	10	88	33	45	49.8	225.8
Indonesia	11	168	76	43	14.5	312.5
Cambodia	11	94	33	49	553.8	740.8

Source: Doing Business in 2004 (World Bank, the International Finance Corporation, and Oxford University Press, October 2003).

Notes:
• The overall total in this table is purely a mechanism for establishing some sort of ranking. Given that in all cases, the lower the value the better, in theory the overall lowest total represents the most favorable administrative environment for new business creation, although clearly this is a simplification that ignores any relative weighting between the individual indicators.
• The data is accurate as at January 2003.
• In order to establish comparisons and benchmarks that are valid across countries, the same standard assumptions are applied in the data collection. However, the data often focus on a specific business form – limited liability company – and may not be representative of the regulation on other businesses – for example, sole proprietorships.

As far as availability of funding is concerned, when this subject is mentioned the tendency is to think in terms of venture capitalists. In fact, classic VC companies only finance a small fraction of new companies, and all of these are potentially high-growth firms concentrated in an area usually connected in some way with new technology. It's the classic Silicon Valley model that many other countries have tried to emulate. In fact, the absolutely crucial element for the creation of new firms is non-institutional financing – family, friends, and business angels – estimated to be responsible for nearly 92% of all funding in the countries covered by the GEM report.[17]

▶▶ CONCLUSION

The overall picture that emerges from this introduction is one of a region encompassing both high and low levels of entrepreneurial activity; both active efforts to encourage entrepreneurship and no efforts at all. The two most populous countries in the region (and indeed, in the world), are in fast developing mode, thus opening up a whole new era of entrepreneurial opportunity, while the other countries of the region are still figuring out how they can best adapt to the China/India phenomenon in such a way as to protect and develop their own economies, and this, too, is increasing interest in and encouragement of entrepreneurship.

But much still remains to be done. Those young professionals from the Mumbai TiE group we spoke about at the beginning of the chapter need to find ways of acquiring skills to open the doors of entrepreneurship to them. The same can be said of the many would-be Chinese entrepreneurs busily working on ideas to present to Linan Zhu and his fellow investors in China. Remember that the GEM report found that people who believed they had such skills were on average five times more likely to be engaged in entrepreneurship than the rest of the population.

So, we will certainly see an increasing level of entrepreneurship across Asia through these early years of the 21st century, and the following chapter takes a look at some of the key themes involved in this growth.

ENDNOTES

[1] TiE, a not-for-profit global network of entrepreneurs and professionals, was founded in 1992 in Silicon Valley, California. Although its birth name, The Indus Entrepreneurs, signifies the ethnic South Asian or Indus roots of the founders, TiE has come to represent Talent, Ideas, and Enterprise. It has grown to more than 40 chapters in nine countries. See www.tie.org.

[2] *BusinessWeek*, July 26, 2004, p. 23.

[3] See Kwok Bun Chan and Claire Chiang, *Stepping Out: The Making of Chinese Entrepreneurs* (Prentice Hall, 1994).

[4] Ben Chan, "Vibrant Entrepreneurial Spirit in International Markets – New Possibilities for Singaporean-Owned Small and Medium Enterprises," USASBE Annual National Conference, Entrepreneurship: The Engine of Global Economic Development, 1997.

[5] Ku-Hyun Jung, "An Upsurge of Entrepreneurship in Korea and its Possible Reasons," unpublished paper prepared for Expert Workshop on Entrepreneurship in Asia: Creating Competitive Advantage in the Global Economy, held in Hong Kong, July 8–11, 2002.

[6] Rong-I Wu and Chung-Che Huang, "Entrepreneurship in Taiwan: Turning Point to Restart," unpublished paper prepared for Expert Workshop on Entrepreneurship in Asia: Creating Competitive Advantage in the Global Economy, held in Hong Kong, July 8–11, 2002.

[7] Phagaphasvivat Somjai, "Entrepreneurship in Thailand," unpublished paper prepared for Expert Workshop on Entrepreneurship in Asia: Creating Competitive Advantage in the Global Economy, held in Hong Kong, July 8–11, 2002.

[8] Mohamed Ariff and Syarisa Yanti Abubakar, "Strengthening Entrepreneurship in Malaysia," unpublished paper prepared for Expert Workshop on Entrepreneurship in Asia: Creating Competitive Advantage in the Global Economy, held in Hong Kong, July 8–11, 2002.

[9] See note 6.

[10] Coordinated by Babson College and London Business School, and sponsored by the Ewing Marion Kauffman Foundation.

[11] Paul D. Reynolds, William D. Bygrave, and Erkko Autio, *GEM 2003 Global Report* (January 2004).

[12] *Ibid.*, p. 43.

[13] *Ibid.*, p. 41.

[14] Juan Roure (IESE Barcelona), *Towards a European Model of Entrepreneurial Growth; Lessons from Europe's 500 Most Dynamic Entrepreneurs and their Companies*, unpublished.

[15] *GEM 2003 Global Report, op. cit.*, p. 42.

[16] *Ibid.*

[17] *Ibid.*, p. 57.

Top-of-mind Issues and Other Themes

U sing the findings of two parallel and complementary surveys, this chapter takes a look at the issues that entrepreneurs in Asia-Pacific say are "top of mind" for them in 2004. It shows that, like entrepreneurs the world over, they have cash and cash flow management at the very forefront of their preoccupations, although problems concerning the recruitment and retention of staff, and issues arising from new product development are also well to the fore.

However, the further the chapter drills down into the detail of the surveys, the more localized and purely topical the issues become, touching on subjects as diverse as the current difficulties over obtaining a US visa and, perhaps counter-intuitively for this part of the world, environmental worries.

Overall, the surveys find a high degree of optimism among Asian entrepreneurs.

ENTREPRENEURS' HOPES AND HEADACHES

When we started thinking about this book, we decided very early on that it would be a fascinating exercise to try and determine what are the issues that especially concern entrepreneurs in the Asia-Pacific region at this time. What are the things that get them most excited, and what are the problems that keep them awake at night?

Accordingly, we undertook an informal and small-scale online survey, the responses to which we complemented through a wide range of personal conversations. In parallel, one of us was serving as advisor for a survey of SME attitudes being carried out on behalf of UPS, part of which specifically addressed the same questions.[1] The UPS survey was based on telephone interviews around the region and was carried out at virtually the same time as ours but using a much larger sample, and so we have a double spotlight, so to speak, focused on the subject.

In general terms, we found a very high degree of optimism – 97% of our respondents described themselves as "somewhat" or "very" positive about prospects for their business over the next five years.

MAIN ISSUES

In order to get an initial "feel" for the sorts of issues that matter to entrepreneurs around the region at this time, we gave them a series of topics to consider and then rate as "Not important," "Somewhat important," or "Very important." The figures corresponding to the "Very important" rating are shown in Figure 2.1.

> " The most important issue... centers around cash management... "

The clear result of this is that – surprise, surprise – the most important issue, rated as "Very important" by over 80% of all respondents, centers around cash management, exactly as you might expect it to be for most entrepreneurs no matter where in the world they are. This is mirrored exactly in the UPS study, in which cash flow was the

Percent respondents rating "Very Important"

Figure 2.1 Current Issues Rated as "Very Important"

issue most often spontaneously mentioned as "keeping entrepreneurs awake at night."

In our survey, immediately following cash management in terms of importance came the issues of new product development and gaining new customers, followed by managing company growth, and issues relating to management and staff recruitment and retention. UPS's spontaneous responses also put hiring and retaining qualified staff near the top in order of importance, but they put government policies second in line, whereas our prompted responses put them toward the bottom of the list, and nearly a third of our respondents considered that they weren't at all important at this time.

In terms of differences across the countries included in our survey, in general terms, we didn't find any major inconsistencies in outlook. However, we did find one or two interesting localized differences. For instance, the only country where most respondents considered government policies an important issue was India, rating it even higher than recruiting and retaining key staff.

THE ISSUES THAT KEEP ENTREPRENEURS AWAKE AT NIGHT

We also invited our respondents to indulge in some crystal-ball gazing, and we invited them to do this in two

" The only country where most respondents considered government policies an important issue was India... "

parts – first, by rating a series of possible future developments according to the impact they expected from them over the next three years; and second, by focusing in more closely on issues with a potentially negative impact. The results are presented in Figures 2.2 and 2.3.

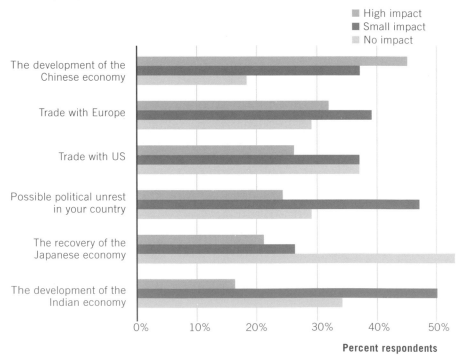

Figure 2.2 Issues Rated by Expected Impact over the Next Three Years

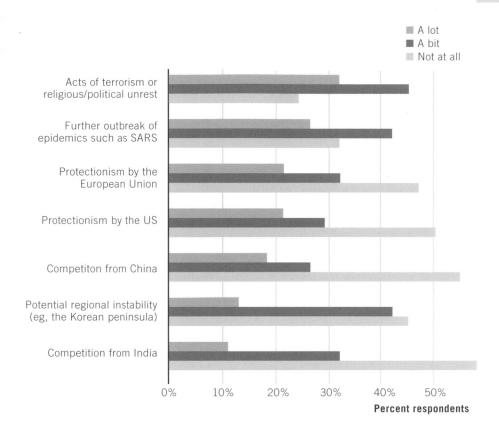

Figure 2.3 Level of Concern at Potential Negatively Impacting Issues

Unsurprisingly, of the range of issues we invited our respondents to choose from, the development of the Chinese economy is the one that most people (45%) expect to have a high impact over the coming three years, although at the same time it is clear from Figure 2.3 that most respondents (55%) don't fear that competition from China will negatively affect their businesses over this time frame.

The UPS study devoted a special section to the whole question of what they called "the China factor" (see the following box for highlights).

The China factor

With the rapid emergence of mainland China as a dominant economic force and a manufacturing base for the world, the *UPS Asia Business Monitor* explored the country's impact on the region's SMEs in depth, with opinions differing sharply across the 11 markets other than China that were surveyed. South Koreans are the most wary of their neighbor, with two out of three (65%) respondents rating China a threat. Significant proportions of respondents in the Philippines (44%) and Thailand (39%), countries that traditionally have provided low-cost manufacturing labor, also believe that China poses a threat.

Irrespective of their views on China, few SMEs have a business presence in China, with only one out of five respondents setting up joint ventures, wholly owned operations, or distributorships in the country, and only one-third (36%) of those who have no presence planning on creating one. Of those with no presence in the country, 58% do business with it. Across the board, respondents agree that working with China is fraught with potential pitfalls. Topping the list of perceived dangers is the protection of intellectual property (a concern for 69% of the region's SMEs), followed by transparency (68%), government intervention (65%) and a lack of trust in business partners (65%).

> ❝ It came as a surprise to us that our respondents thought that trade with Europe is likely to have a greater impact over the next three years than trade with the United States. ❞

It came as a surprise to us that our respondents thought that trade with Europe is likely to have a greater impact over the next three years than trade with the US. Even those that considered these issues as having a small impact ranked Europe higher. A glance at Figure 2.3 will show that this is clearly not the result of a higher feared risk of protectionism on the part of the US, as the risk of protectionism was ranked at nearly the same level for the US and the EU.

Political unrest was considered by nearly a quarter of our respondents as likely to have a high impact over the next three years, and this response is mirrored in Figure 2.3 where it can be seen that nearly a third of all respondents (32%) consider that acts of terrorism, or religious or political unrest will have a negative impact going forward. As might have been expected, there was considerable difference between the responses from different countries on this issue, with in general Australia and New Zealand much more relaxed than other countries. Singapore was the country where the highest percentage of respondents (55%) feared a high negative impact on this issue.

For a region hard hit by SARS in 2003, and still suffering sporadic occurrences of avian flu, it isn't surprising to see that over a quarter (26%) of our respondents are very concerned that a further epidemic-like outbreak of a disease such as SARS will have a strong negative impact on their business over the next three years. Equally unsurprisingly, the highest responses came from China, Hong Kong, and Singapore.

Like UPS, we included in our survey an open-ended question inviting respondents to tell us, unprompted, about the issues that keep them awake at night at this time. Issues pertaining to the recruitment and retention of appropriately qualified staff were the most frequently mentioned (26%), followed closely by issues related to cash flow management (21%). This latter figure is very close to the 23% that UPS found for this issue in their survey. Other topics mentioned by various respondents, although with nothing approaching the same frequency, were issues concerning strategic partnerships, the need to develop new products, market volatility, and just simply managing the growth process.

A few isolated individual concerns emerged, such as the Pakistani respondent who told us that the current stance adopted by the United States on the issuance of visas is causing him a real problem with his business. And one or two of our respondents were obviously happy to have the opportunity to give expression to their concerns – for instance this, also from Pakistan:

In Pakistan the following issues can potentially hinder business:

1. The internal law and order situation.
2. Political strikes which make it impossible for our engineers to get to work.
3. The US market's backlash against outsourcing given that this is an election year.
4. Infrastructure issues mean that we have to invest in our own from connectivity to power generation, etc.
5. Bribes to all and sundry.

Or this cry from the heart from Singapore:

No support from banks (they have no clue about how to fund and support entrepreneurs at all — very stubborn, so many ideas are lost in Singapore).

Other various concerns that surfaced in the UPS survey were as follows:

- Pollution and the environment ranked the highest among a number of potential concerns prompted during questioning. Of the 1,200 respondents, 81% agreed that this was a concern, led by those in the Philippines (94%) and Hong Kong (92%).
- Health also ranked highly in these two markets (93% in Hong Kong, 91% in the Philippines, 79% overall).
- Crime fears featured strongly in the Philippines, Indonesia, and Japan (93%, 90%, and 90%, respectively).

A LOOK ON THE BRIGHTER SIDE

We also wanted to find out what our respondents considered to be the exciting developments going on in their business at the present time, and we got a wide range of answers. Some of these were excellent illustrations of the well-known half-empty/half-full glass syndrome, reflecting excitement about opportunities stemming from what others perceived as potentially negative issues – new product development, broadening of the customer base, a good management team working hard together. Here are three of our favorites:

There is an ever increasing business pie because of thirst for knowledge and information and customisation of it; and the exponential interest in Asia and what's happening here – which we specialise in. (Singapore)

Big orders piling up (China)

Salary increase for the employees and watching them be happy. (South Korea)

WISH LIST

We also thought it might be fun to play genie of the lamp with our respondents, giving them the opportunity to formulate wishes for the future. The specific wording of our question was: "What key factor do you think could significantly make you more optimistic about the future?" The responses were wide-ranging, from the general –

Political and economic stability. (Hong Kong)

Government regulations and support; access to funding. (Singapore)

Better government macro economic policies. (Thailand)

– to the very detailed and specific:

Investors finally start pumping money back into South East Asia. Indonesia stabilises. Malaysia unpegs the ringgit. (Singapore)

Less dependence on the US; greater development of inter-regional markets. Better political and corporate governance leading to less corruption and cronyism. Returning citizens with academic, technical and linguistic skills. (Sri Lanka)

> Resolution of political issues: N. Korea; HK–PRC; Taiwan–PRC; Muslim insurgency in Indonesia and Thailand. More transparency and growth in ASEAN. (Hong Kong)

However, most of our respondents opted simply for wishing for more growth, several of them singling out China. One of these, from Singapore, very neatly encapsulated what may well be the over-arching pattern of the next decade or more

> China is driving. More focus on branding = moving upstream away from pure OEM [Original Equipment Manufacturer(s)] = owning more IP [intellectual property] = value concepts. India just behind, driving too.

EXPECTED GROWTH

An idea of where the crystal-ball gazing and wish lists are expected to lead over the next 12 months is given in Figure 2.4, which summarizes how respondents to the UPS survey described their feelings with regard to the anticipated growth prospects of their own companies.

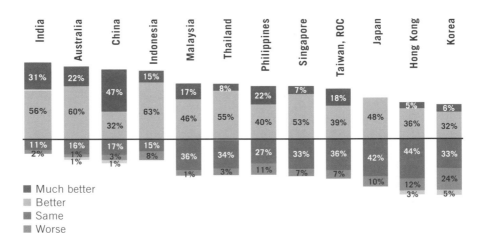

■ Much better
■ Better
■ Same
■ Worse
■ Much worse

Figure 2.4 Expected Company Prospects over the Next Year

The UPS survey went a step further and asked respondents what they felt about other people's business prospects. The result was that in every market surveyed, China was singled out as the country with the strongest prospects, with 88% of the 1,200 respondents expecting to see growth in the People's Republic in the following 12 months. Following in relatively distant second and third places were India and Hong Kong, with 58% of all respondents predicting growth for India and 56% for Hong Kong.

At the opposite end of the scale, only 24% of respondents expected growth in Indonesia in the next year, while the figure for the Philippines was only 19%. Predictions for economic growth in specific markets were relatively consistent across the region, with a few exceptions. Most notably, while 53% of respondents across all 12 countries included in the survey[2] expected growth in South Korea, only 7% of respondents in South Korea share this view for their own country.

This relative pessimism among South Korean SMEs may at least partly be explained by the large proportion (42%) of South Korean respondents who report that their business prospects are currently worse than they were 12 months ago, by far the largest proportion of businesses to see a decline in the past year. By contrast, only 2% of Indian SMEs consider their current prospects to be worse than a year ago, while 83% believe that things have taken a turn for the better. Overall, with the exception of South Korea, there are more respondents who report that business has improved than those who say that it has worsened. The same is true when looking ahead to the next 12 months. Across the region, most SMEs believe that their businesses will improve in the next year, with India (87%), Australia (82%), and China (79%) leading the way.

BUSINESS PRACTICES

To round off their interviews, the UPS survey asked their respondents a series of questions about their business practices, intended to ascertain the degree to which various initiatives to make the workplace more pleasant have taken hold around the region. A summary of what they found is set out in the following box.

Business practices and executive insights

At the top of the list is the deployment of internal communications initiatives, practiced by 74% of SMEs around the region (90% in India), with a smokeless environment now offered in 68% of Asia-Pacific SME offices (84% in the Philippines and 83% in Australia). Casual days are popular in Taiwan and Hong Kong (85% and 81%, respectively), while flexible hours are most widely provided in Taiwan (62%), Australia (61%), and India (59%). After-hours socializing is particularly common in China (87%), as are company outings in Taiwan (78%).

Japanese SMEs trail the pack in implementing these initiatives, with less than half offering a smoke-free office environment and just 26% providing casual dress days or flexible hours – which is understandable given that only 20% of Japanese SME employers believe that flexible hours contribute to employee retention. On the other hand, two-thirds of SMEs (66%) in Singapore and 61% in Australia and in Thailand, agree that flexible hours help to keep staff happy. Training and education, and company health insurance are the most valued initiatives in retaining employees overall, rated as worthwhile by 74% and 73%, respectively, of respondents at the regional level. Taiwanese SMEs believe off-site team building to be particularly important.

Clearly, the ability to hire and retain staff is considered valuable, as difficulties in this department were most commonly cited spontaneously (49%) in response to the question, "What are the least pleasant aspects of your job?" Other commonly mentioned problems include too many meetings (39%) and long working hours (39%).

Unsurprisingly, many respondents in all of the surveyed markets found themselves working longer hours since they took on their current roles, with 45% saying they spend more time on work and only 10% saying that they manage to spend less. This situation is particularly common in China, Singapore, Australia, and India, where more than half of all respondents work harder in their present role than in the one they held previously.

Notwithstanding the high degree of commitment and personal sacrifice that it takes to run a small business, there are a number of tangible and valued rewards as well. Chief among these are a sense of achievement and personal autonomy, cited by 85% and 77% of all respondents respectively. Recognition from others, higher income, flexible working hours and freedom from the corporate rat race also play an important role in motivating a majority of SME leaders across the region.

▶▶ CONCLUSION

One of the issues associated with writing a book on entrepreneurship in Asia is that it is such a broad subject both in content and geography. We used the findings of our research to help guide us to appropriate topics to include in the book, and we have focused on the topics highlighted as important by entrepreneurs.

However, as might have been expected, the entrepreneurs gave more weight to operational-related topics such as managing cash, innovation, gaining customers, and so on, and less weight to others, which may be important, but which entrepreneurs prefer to ignore in the short term. A good example of this is succession. It was interesting to see that while many young and growing companies saw planning succession as not important, the more established businesses and also members of the finance community (for example, corporate finance advisors, accountants, investors, and so on) certainly did.

Accordingly, in order to accommodate the diversity of issues experienced by businesses as they grow, we decided to pick a selection of key issues from each stage of business growth, beginning in the following chapter with the start of it all – the business idea.

ENDNOTES

[1]   The inaugural UPS Asia Business Monitor, published in January 2005, is based on information gathered from 1,200 interviews with SMEs (companies with 250 or fewer total employees) in 12 Asia-Pacific countries. Respondents were comprised of company owners, proprietors, CEOs, managing directors, and other top management in charge of key business decisions. Interviews were conducted by telephone from August 16 through September 28, 2004 by the independent market research organization TNS, using the respondents' native language. Findings are reproduced with permission.

[2]   Australia, China, Hong Kong, India, Indonesia, Japan, South Korea, Malaysia, Philippines, Singapore, Taiwan, Thailand.

3

Entrepreneurs and Opportunity

*I*n this chapter, we look at the sources that provide the opportunities *that are developed as new ventures. After some reflections on the nature of entrepreneurial ideas, and historical patterns in Asian entrepreneurship, we consider an illustrative sample of the multiple initiatives that exist region-wide to foster innovation through the establishment of tech parks, in many cases attempts to emulate the Silicon Valley model, and then go on to identify some current problems with innovation practices in Asia. After a look at the topic of new venture spin-offs from university research, the chapter ends with a survey of franchising activity in the region.*

IDEAS

The road to becoming an entrepreneur starts with an idea. In fact, that isn't strictly speaking always true, for it sometimes happens that it starts with the decision to become an entrepreneur. In these cases, this gives rise to the search for an idea. In both cases, the idea is the genesis of the entrepreneurial activity. However, the idea on its own is not enough, as the identification of ideas is possibly the easiest part of the whole entrepreneurial process, and indeed there exist well-tried techniques – brainstorming, for instance – for assisting this process.

> " A business opportunity has the qualities of being attractive, durable, and timely, and is anchored in a product or service that creates or adds value for its buyer or end-user. "

What has to happen after the identification of the idea is the determination as to whether it constitutes a sound opportunity, which raises the question, "What constitutes a business opportunity?" Many definitions have been put forward over the years, but our favorite one is this: a business opportunity has the qualities of being attractive, durable, and timely, and is anchored in a product or service that creates or adds value for its buyer or end-user.[1] In other words, if there isn't a market for your idea, then it isn't an opportunity, as it isn't capable of being exploited commercially in such a way as to profitably sustain an enterprise.

This reflects the principal underlying truth of all exploitable ideas, and that is that they are anchored in some sort of unsatisfied need, thus providing the latent demand that can be turned into a market. Following on from this are further observations that are key for the would-be entrepreneur to keep in mind:

- The landscape is constantly changing, thus opening the way for ideas that weren't feasible yesterday. Similarly, what constitutes a great opportunity today, may not do so down the road; hence the need for all enterprises to reinvent themselves as they go forward.

- Whenever anybody expresses dissatisfaction with the way something works or how something is done, that signals a potential need to be filled.
- An opportunity may simply involve taking something that is successful in one part of the world and introducing it in another.

All these points are basic, unalterable truths that entrepreneurs ignore at their peril. One of the main reasons for so many company failures during the dot.com euphoria was the simple fact that all too often the attitude was that there would be a market; all you had to do was provide the service, an attitude that was summed up in the phrase "Build it, and they will come."

The prevailing belief was that the Internet would change all the rules of buying and selling. At the same time, not many people were asking consumers if they were going to make a mad dash to the Internet to buy items like dog food, plants and furniture. As a result, many pure-play e-tailers selling such items ended up on the dot-com scrap heap. Demand simply did not materialize. Look at all of the business-to-business exchanges that people were touting as the end of business as we know it. It didn't happen.[2]

Many young people were dazzled by early dot.com success stories, and there was an immense rush worldwide to get into the act and not be left out. True, some companies did survive, but all those who did were either serving a clear need right from the start (for instance, eBay), or had to reinvent themselves in order to identify a need they could serve, sometimes metamorphosing out of all recognition from their origins (for instance, Chemdex).

We should, perhaps, make one point clear at this juncture: our purpose is by no means to make light of, still less to deride, the emergence of what has been termed the "knowledge-based" economy. We simply wish to underline two crucial points:

- New business ideas stemming from a "knowledge" or high-technology root still need customers in the good old-fashioned way.

- Not all new businesses need to stem from a "knowledge" or high-tech root. If what you want to do is open an exotic ice cream parlor and there are customers willing to buy from you, then go for it.

What is indubitably true is that tomorrow's high-growth, globally active firms with the potential to change the world are more likely to be "tech" companies. Having said that, we have a suspicion that there will always be room for the McDonald's and Starbucks of this world.

Entrepreneurship in Asia was for many years rooted in trading – bringing new products to the country where the entrepreneur lived; selling abroad products from his or her home country; and, progressively, exploiting trading opportunities between third countries. Support activities, such as banks and transport companies, grew up around these activities. Such opportunities still exist today, and probably always will, but it is now already a long time since they constituted the bulk of entrepreneurial activity.

The Industrial Revolution in Europe in the 19th century set the stage for a new breed of entrepreneur to emerge, moving away from a purely buying and selling activity, which essentially adds little or no value, to more value-adding activities, such as engineering or manufacturing. The famous engineers of the period were in many ways archetypal entrepreneurs, of which two of the best known are Isambard Kingdom Brunel and Gustave Eiffel, who had created his own company specializing in metallic structures in 1864, 25 years before the construction of his famous tower in Paris.

In the early part of the 20th century, entrepreneurial activity accelerated in the Western world, thus providing the subject matter and inspiration for Joseph Schumpeter's seminal theoretical work on entrepreneurship during the 1930s and 1940s.

However, in Asia, entrepreneurial activity remained dominated by trading activities for much of the last century; for example, as we saw in Chapter 1, as recently as 1963 there were only 548 small manufacturing companies in Singapore.

There were, of course, exceptions. In Japan, for instance, the company that was to become Sony was founded in 1945 by Masaru Ibuka, who was joined later by Akio Morita. And long before then, in 1911, Masujiro Hashimoto founded one of the companies that would eventually find themselves fused to become Nissan, already in 1915 manufacturing and selling a vehicle called the Dat Car, predecessor of the Datsun.

However, it wasn't until toward the end of the 20th century that entrepreneurial activity in Asia really caught up with the rest of the world, not necessarily in terms of quantity, but in terms of focus. The emergence of Silicon Valley as an entrepreneurship powerhouse had a galvanizing effect on most of the countries in the region, with the result that in many cases, attempts have been made to emulate the Californian experience. In dozens of places, innovation centers have been created in attempts to emulate the cluster of businesses created out of the "networking, trusting, collaborative, nurturing, supportive, resilient, resource- and opportunity-rich 'habitat' for innovation and entrepreneurship"[3] that is Silicon Valley.

> " It wasn't until toward the end of the 20th century that entrepreneurial activity in Asia really caught up with the rest of the world... "

We look at some of these in the following section.

"DOZENS OF POTENTIAL SILICON VALLEYS ACROSS ASIA"[4]

In this section, we look at a representative sample of the many clusters and technology parks around the Asia-Pacific region. The list has no pretension to completeness – it is merely intended to give a flavor of the range of initiatives that exist.

Malaysia: The Multimedia Super Corridor

The Multimedia Super Corridor (MSC) is Malaysia's initiative for the global information and communication technology (ICT) industry. It is a dedicated 15 x 50-kilometer corridor, stretching from the Petronas Twin Towers to the north to the Kuala Lumpur

International Airport in the south; and encompasses Cyberjaya (the technology core) and Putrajaya (the new administrative capital of Malaysia).

Conceptualized in 1996, the MSC has grown into a thriving dynamic ICT hub, hosting more than 900 multinationals, foreign-owned, and home-grown Malaysian companies focused on multimedia and communications products, solutions, services, and R&D.

Implementation of the MSC is divided into three phases from 1996 to 2020.[5]

China: Haidan Science Park, Beijing

With its high concentration of China's intellectual resources and technical personnel, the Haidan Science Park (HSP) has been described as China's Silicon Valley. Set up in 1988, the HSP was China's first large-scale high-tech park. The next 12 years witnessed a rapid but healthy annual growth of over 30%. Now regarded as the home of China's burgeoning high-tech industry, the HSP has had some impressive achievements and is gaining more and more global attention.

The park not only has 56 universities, including China's two premier institutions, Peking University and Tsinghua University, but also 232 research institutes of various kinds led by the Chinese Academy of Sciences. Backed by this cluster of universities and institutes, the HSP has a solid foundation for its high-tech industries which now number over 6,000, nearly 80% of which are IT industries.

Taiwan: Hsinchu Science Park

Established in 1980, the Hsinchu Science Park (HSP) in north-western Taiwan stretches over 1,500 acres. It has strived to develop a favorable environment for investment, to attract high-tech talent, to introduce advanced technologies, and thus to promote domestic industry. Over the past 22 years, the government has invested approximately US$1,006 million in the Park's infrastructure.

At the end of December, 2002, the HSP accommodated 335 companies, including 282 domestic companies and 53 foreign ones. These firms achieved a total revenue of US$ 20,453 million, representing an annual growth of 4.2%.

Additionally, the government is actively developing the bases of the Park at Chunan, Tungluo, and Duhsin, together with the development of the Southern Taiwan Science Park, Luchu Base, and the Central Taiwan Science Park, hoping to duplicate the success of the HSP.

It is worth noting that the HSP was scored 4.35 out of a maximum possible of 5 in the ratings of "tech hotspots" compiled by David Rosenberg in his book *Cloning Silicon Valley*. This was the highest score in Asia, and higher even than Cambridge in the UK and Tel Aviv in Israel.

Singapore: Biopolis

Biopolis is envisioned to be a world-class biomedical sciences R&D hub in Asia. This facility is dedicated to providing space for biomedical R&D activities, and it is planned as an environment that fosters a collaborative culture among the private and public research communities.

Biopolis Phase 1 is a 185,000-square-meter biomedical complex of seven buildings completed in 2004 at a cost of US$500 million. Several key government agencies, publicly funded research institutes, and R&D labs of pharmaceutical and biotech companies have already located there, and the site will eventually house upwards of 1,500 scientists.

India: Genome Valley, Hyderabad

The government of the state of Andhra Pradesh has set up a "knowledge" park for pure research and an adjoining biotechnology park for manufacturing in Genome Valley, an ambitious 600-square-kilometer site.

As of March 2004, over 100 biotech companies are located in this, India's first state-of-the-art biotech cluster. Presently, 17 companies have taken space in the SP Park, while in the ICICI Knowledge Park phase one is fully occupied, phase two is 90% booked, and phase three is in the planning stage.

Vietnam: Quang Trung Software Park, Ho Chi Minh City

This 43-hectare park was established in 2000 as the country's leading center for software development, trade promotion, and international cooperation. It is also an incubator for new IT entrepreneurs.

As of July 2004, 68 companies had contracted to operate in the park, which aims to attract hundreds of companies and employ up to 20,000 people by 2010.

Bangladesh: High-tech park, Kaliakoir

In April 2004, Bangladesh announced the first step toward establishing the country's first high-tech park with the allocation of 232 acres of land at Kaliakoir, near the capital, Dhaka. The US$43 million priority project, aimed at promoting and encouraging public- and private-sector investments in the high-tech industries, is expected to take two years to complete.

Pakistan and China: Cross-border collaboration

Pakistan and China recently signed a joint declaration under which it was decided that they would guide and encourage their departments, scientific research institutes, universities, and high-tech enterprises to conduct broad technological cooperation in areas of mutual interest. As part of this agreement, China agreed to help provide guidance and technical assistance for the development of a high-tech park on an already identified site in Islamabad.[6]

More recently (May 2004), it was reported that the Pakistan Software Export Board had signed a Memorandum of Understanding with the Dubai Internet City to set up a modern high-tech park in Pakistan.[7]

SOME PROBLEMS OBSERVED

In spite of the intense activity there has been around the region in establishing knowledge/tech hubs, centers, and so forth, the exercise hasn't been without its problems.

INSEAD's Professor Arnoud de Meyer and Research Associate Sam Garg recently carried out a research program to take a close look at the way innovation in Asia has developed over the past few years, and the results (to be published early in 2005[8]) are revealing.

Broadly speaking, they identify five problem areas.

Ineffective market input

Innovation in Asia suffers from ineffective market input. Rarely did they find sophisticated marketing experience. Many of the people they talked to complained about the lack of trend-setting local customers who would be willing to partner with an innovator in order to experiment. And the most sophisticated markets are either far away, as is the case for the United States, or rather closed, as is the case for Japan.

> Innovation in Asia suffers from ineffective market input.

This point echoes what some academics have been saying about university research, suggesting that research agendas should be at least partly tailored toward market needs, rather than continue as pure research unrelated to anything except the scholar's research interests. Thus, for example, Dr. Su Guaning, the president of Singapore's NTU (Nanyang Technological University), said:

> Our technology transfer effort is focusing on identifying novel technology with quality, commercial potential. And to add commercial value through technology development and refinement of economic objectives. We are developing a proactive technology transfer process to facilitate generation of more investment-ready technologies. The goal is to have more commercially attractive technologies for startup companies.[9]

Strong but inappropriate role of national governments

Governments have traditionally played an important and heavy-handed role in the development of East and Southeast Asian economies. This appeared to be a successful formula in a period where the basic industrial network needed to be developed and the objective was clear: catching up with the industrialized world.

But the environment that is required to let innovation blossom requires different regulatory environments (such as for intellectual property rights or the management of knowledge workers) than the ones currently in place. It also requires more risk-taking by governments, which often remain one of the most important economic actors through their own procurement.

Inadequate human and financial resources and skills

While the absolute number of engineers and scientists, or experts in general, in this part of the world is high, in relative terms it is quite low. De Meyer and Garg foresee very soon a shortage of technical skills, both in terms of quantity and quality, leading to inflation in R&D costs.

Furthermore, one often hears the complaint that there is barely any sophisticated risk capital in Asia. This leads to a higher capital cost for innovators. If you need to look for real venture financing in the US or the UK, you end up paying a risk premium that puts you at a disadvantage compared to your competitor in Europe or the US (see Section II, "The Entrepreneur and Cash").

Lack of appreciation for intangibles

Many of the research managers De Meyer and Garg worked with had difficulty appreciating the value of intangibles such as brands or intellectual property.

The widespread stories about counterfeiting (which is obviously not exclusive to Asia), or the limited success (and commitment) by Asian companies in building strong local brands (notwithstanding a few exceptions such as Samsung or Singapore Airlines), illustrate this sufficiently.

An underdog mentality

De Meyer and Garg found that many Asian companies suffer from an underdog mentality, which becomes a self-fulfilling prophecy. Companies perceived themselves to be good exclusively for low-cost/low-value production. (This was a point that also emerged when we talked to people and companies about the problems Asian companies face when they try to internationalize their business. See Chapter 10.)

> " Many Asian companies suffer from an underdog mentality, which becomes a self-fulfilling prophecy. "

UNIVERSITY SPIN-OFFS

An entrepreneurial seedbed that has been the subject of increased attention in recent years is the potential for new start-ups deriving from university research. Efforts have been made not only to "market" patented new technology from this source, but also to encourage and make it easier for university faculty to actually participate in start-ups themselves.

India has been particularly active in this respect. Vijay Chandru, a computer science professor at the Indian Institute of Science (IISc) in Bangalore, was one of four professors who in 1999 made a request to the Council of IISc for permission to commercialize through entrepreneurial ventures technologies developed in the laboratory. The result was a holding company called MetaString Pvt Ltd., within which was created Strand Genomics, a bioinformatics company with a focus on developing advanced data-processing, annotation, and visualization software tools and services for the global bioinformatics industry; and PicoPeta Simputers, a solutions company to build on the Simputer platform for handheld computing and communications, notably a personal digital assistant (PDA) device to run on Linux.

In 2003, Chandru and Venkat Chandrasekhar, a professor of entrepreneurship at IISc, wrote an article[10] in which they set out their ideas on entrepreneurial academics in the light of the MetaString experience. Here are some excerpts:

In the current "knowledge economy", by nature, academia will become the largest asset holders, and it will be in their interest to exploit these assets for their own growth, and entrepreneurship promotion gives the opportunity. However, universities need to change and adapt their objectives, structures and teaching programmes and note that:

- Knowledge is now the key determinant for competitive advantage in businesses and economies
- Universities are principal builders of knowledge
- Universities have a responsibility to apply that knowledge to the economy, businesses and the community

Historically, the university involvement has been low. Our universities have produced great discoveries and inventions but very few new businesses. To a graduate from the university till a few years ago, entrepreneurship was not a relevant career option. However, the university was important in passively contributing to manpower, adding and enhancing skills, knowledge and capabilities. It has been a provider of facilities and a creative cauldron of intellectual property.

But the changing role requires that apart from teaching and research, the universities should also engage extensively in the application of its knowledge repository. Universities have a huge asset base of knowledge worth millions that is currently unexploited/under-exploited. They have a responsibility to get value from these assets to support existing university teaching and research, economic performance and growth, employment, and wealth creation.

The good news is that there are winds of change blowing across the Indian academic landscape. Incubation centres have come up on several campuses, alumni who have been successful entrepreneurs in the US and elsewhere are providing seed capital and networking for ventures emerging from their alma maters.

One of these incubation centers, and probably the most successful, is the one at the Indian Institute of Technology (IIT) Bombay (IIT(B)).[11] The first pilot IT business incubator was started in 1999 in a makeshift facility. It was formally inaugurated in January 2002 with capacity for eight companies. Restricted to IT companies, it offered typical incubator facilities: about 300 square feet of office space, PCs, Internet connection, phone, and common facilities such as laser printer, fax machine, coffee machine, and so on, as well as mentoring support and business networking. In return, companies pledged a specified percentage of equity for the services provided to them.

The incubator was open to all IIT faculty, students, and alumni, and indeed to outsiders. The key criterion was if IIT-developed research was being commercialized.

As of May 2004, 13 companies had been incubated. Of these, three had succeeded in obtaining VC finance, one had reached commercial viability without venture finance, while three companies had closed down.

The main challenge incubator management faced was that of recognizing the peculiarities of operating in an academic environment, and then working to achieve changes in attitudes, mindset, and simply in ways of doing things. In this respect, their experience is totally applicable to any academic institution anywhere in the world, with the possible exception of the United States.

Among others, they were faced with the following issues:

- Openness in knowledge dissemination. It is in the very nature of academic research to share it with others, notably in the peer review system. However, this openness is in conflict with the notion of protection of intellectual property.
- Emphasis on fundamentals and basic algorithms with low priority given to "bells-and-whistles" features, and scant attention paid to documentation and user manual support. This derives from the traditional fundamental characteristic of academic research for the advancement of knowledge, rather than for any commercial use; hence the scorn some entrepreneur academics sometimes earn from their peers. Academic reward, the purists hold, is measured in terms of Nobel prizes, rather than Nasdaq listings.
- Laxity on delivery times and deadlines, and lack of feel for "window of opportunity," again deriving from a mentality not accustomed to being subjected to the pressures and demands of the business world.

So the IIT(B) incubator management found that it had to build what they call a separate and distinct ecosystem within the institute itself. This involved the following:

- Mindset change – customer orientation. This, they found, takes a long time.
- Student movements – entrepreneurship cells, e-clubs. Also the provision of formal research and education in entrepreneurship.
- Alumni involvement – many IIT(B) alumni are successful entrepreneurs (including, for example, Romesh Wadhwani of the Wadhwani Foundation).
- Networking relationships with VCs, other non-profit organizations, and professionals outside campus – being connected and networked, they found, is as important as being innovative.
- The raising of an early-stage venture fund to promote incubation.[12]

This whole topic of academics as entrepreneurs was the subject of a two-day conference held at the National University of Singapore in July 2004.

FRANCHISING

A piece of advice often given to aspiring entrepreneurs is: if they cannot find a suitable opportunity to develop themselves, then they can gain some very useful experience by going to help someone else develop theirs. Franchising takes this notion a step further, as it fundamentally involves launching yourself into an entrepreneurial career using someone else's tried-and-tested idea. It is a thoroughly well-established practice – the figures are, in fact, mind-boggling. For example, a recent study carried out in the US showed that franchised businesses are the cause of US$1.53 trillion of annual output and 9.5% of all private-sector output in the US, and directly or indirectly provide over 18 million jobs.[13]

Before we look at the development of franchising in Asia, it is worthwhile to have a brief look at what franchising is. It is basically a distribution system in which two business entities agree to carry on a marketing relationship on a contractual basis, creating economic value for both parties. The franchisor licenses the franchisee to use his know-how and/or business model in return for an entry fee and a specified level of royalties, usually calculated as a percentage of sales. The basic difference between franchising and licensing lies in the degree of control of, and influence exerted by, the licensor or franchisor over the licensee or franchisee. A franchisor will specify in minute detail by means of an operating manual exactly how the franchisee must run his business.

When thinking about franchising, most people would probably think immediately of the very successful and visible fast-food chains such as McDonald's, but it is used in a wide variety of business link-ups. Examples include:

- manufacturer/retailer – e.g. car dealerships, petrol stations;
- manufacturer/wholesaler – e.g. soft drink bottlers;
- wholesaler/retailer – e.g. hardware chains, grocery groups; and
- trade name/retailer – e.g. fast-food chains, hotels, car hire.

The exact details of what services the franchisor offers and what duties the franchisee is expected to perform will vary from franchise to franchise. To take location as an example to illustrate this point, McDonald's, for instance, handles everything, including site selection, lease/purchase negotiation, and so on. Some other franchisors are happy to let their franchisees do this, although all will usually give guidelines.

On seeing the golden arches and Colonel Sanders' beaming face absolutely all over the region, one might conclude that Western franchises had stormed through the Asia-Pacific like some massive invading force. This, however, would miss various key aspects of the franchising phenomenon in the region.

The first of these was that, by and large, and totally understandably, Western franchisors approached Asia with some caution, and tended to look for partners who could demonstrate proven financial solidity. This had two effects: the first was to create an intermediate level of "master franchisees" with broad, often national, sometimes international territorial rights; this in turn left a lot of unoccupied space at the individual franchisee level into which new local regional franchise chains moved. In at least one case – Jollibee in the Philippines (see box) – a local franchisor pre-empted the arrival of the universally known rival Western chains.

If McDonald's is the Goliath of fast food, Tony Tan's Jollibee is its Filipino David

The Philippines is a huge embarrassment to McDonald's. Filipinos are as mad about American culture as they are about fast food, and in 1981, when the golden arches first went up in Manila, everybody assumed that McDonald's would rule the Filipino market, as so many others. At the time, Tony Tan was a local entrepreneur who, with his siblings, had just turned a few ice-cream parlors into burger kitchens. He was soon getting friendly advice that he was still young enough to do something else for a living. At best, said his friends, he could buy the McDonald's franchise.

Mr. Tan did nothing of the sort. Instead, he chose to do battle with the invading global giant. And a strange thing happened. Within four years, Mr. Tan's chain, Jollibee, had become the market leader. By the 1990s, Jollibee was trouncing its rival so thoroughly that McDonald's was forced to choose between retreat and imitation. McDonald's denies that it has opted for the latter, but that is how it looks – and tastes – to Filipinos. Even so, they continue to pass it by in favor of Jollibee. Other global heavyweights appear to have no hope whatsoever. Burger King's Filipino franchisee is trying to sell out, but, after over a year, it is still looking for a buyer.

Like many successful entrepreneurs in the Philippines, Tony Tan is ethnically Chinese. His parents emigrated from Fujian, once one of China's poorest provinces, and his father made ends meet as a cook in a Chinese temple. Hanging around the kitchen early in his life, Mr. Tan apparently developed unusually sensitive taste buds. A colleague considers them downright surreal. She remembers witnessing Mr. Tan tasting a chicken and spotting a minor ingredient that he had noticed only once before – years ago, in a Chicago food stall – and which he at once set out to track down.

His palate, indeed, seems to have been Mr. Tan's greatest source of confidence throughout his struggle against McDonald's. Modest in every other respect, he never once doubted that he could make better food – or at least "better" to Filipinos. To this day, he still attends the weekly three-hour meetings of Jollibee's "new products board." The decisions made there find their way into "the commissariat," a top-secret spice kitchen and the nerve center from which Jollibee outlets are supplied.

Describing Mr. Tan's recipes isn't easy. Generally speaking, the Philippines is not famous for its food, and cardiologists consider it downright evil. In their own kitchens, Filipinos tend to cook meat with stunning amounts of sugar and salt, and to soak it in bagoong, a sort of brine. But no matter how poor, they like to splash out every so often on fast food. And then they like burgers that are sweet and juicy, spaghetti that is saccharine and topped with hot dogs (no Italian would recognize it), beef with honey and rice, and, for dessert, variations on the mango theme. All this Jollibee provides, whereas McDonald's, perhaps hidebound by its global standards, never quite seems to get it right.

Nor is Ronald, the Americans' red-haired clown, any match for the jolly bee, a ubiquitous icon in the Philippines. The Tans chose the bee because they thought it epitomized the Filipino spirit of light-hearted, everyday happiness. Like Filipino working folk, explains Mr. Tan, "the bee hops around and produces sweet things for life, and is happy even though it is busy."

Indeed, the corporate jolliness is infectious, and as much a part of Mr. Tan's success as his recipes. Jollibee's staff outsmile McDonald's by a huge stretch. This January, they started greeting customers with a gesture adopted from the sign language of the deaf – a vertical stroke for "bee" and hands shoveling toward the heart for "happy" – which kids have started using in playgrounds. Staff call customers and one another "sir" and "mom", which is at once casual and respectful in the Philippines. From the cleaners to Mr. Tan, who is not above dressing up as a rapper and doing an awful Puff Daddy imitation for the delight of his staff, everyone at Jollibee projects fun.

All this success doesn't seem to have gone to Mr. Tan's head – yet. He refuses to say "I," and habitually deflects credit to "us," meaning siblings and colleagues. But success may be taking a different toll. Of late, Mr. Tan has discovered global ambition. "It's on his mind all the time now," says a colleague. Goliath in the making?

The real reason why he didn't bid for the McDonald's domestic franchise all those years ago, he now claims, was that he already envisioned expanding overseas. That may be true, but it would have been a remarkably long-term vision for a man who was, at the time, a small entrepreneur in a poor country. In any case, the expansion has certainly begun. Jollibee recently opened eight stores in California, and a few more across Asia. It had to close one in China, but it is now regrouping for another push. In time, Jollibee means to be everywhere.

So far, this has been a low-risk strategy, because Jollibee aims mostly at the diaspora of overseas Filipinos. But in order to go global, Mr. Tan concedes, Jollibee soon has to break that Filipino link and reach out to other nationalities. As ever, though, he feels that he can, because "we have an edge over all the American brands in food." His brothers and sisters on the board are less convinced. What an irony it would be if a Filipino David were to become vulnerable to the slings of Davids elsewhere.

© The Economist Newspaper Limited, London,
2 March 2002.

And so the period since 1998 has seen the development of a myriad of local chains, a lot of them in the highly competitive fast-food segment, a handful with genuinely innovative business ideas unseen in the rest of the world (for instance, the Japanese QB Net chain of 10-minute haircut "shells").

The figures are impressive; in China, for instance, it is claimed that there are over 1,900 local franchise chains – 400 more than in the US. According to China's State Bureau of International Trade, fast-food chain revenues in China reached US$9 billion in 1999, up 20% over the previous year.[14]

The following sample list will give an idea of the current development of some of the main Asia-Pacific franchising chains.

- Jollibee in the Philippines (see box), a burger-style fast-food chain, of which around half of the over 900 outlets are franchised, including outlets in other parts of Asia and some in the US.
- QB House in Japan, a 10-minute haircut chain with over 100 outlets in Japan and two in Singapore.
- The Hulian Supermarket Chain in China, which has 11,000 franchised stores.
- The Jim's Group in Australia. Started in 1982, it is now the largest lawn-mowing franchise in the world. In addition, the Jim's brand has been extended to all manner of business systems, from antennas and appliance repairs to wardrobes and window cleaning. With around 2,200 franchisees, the Jim's Group is Australia's largest franchise network.
- New Zealand's Fastway Courier Franchise Network, founded in 1983, is now the world's largest courier franchise, with operations in 15 countries.

So, it is clear that the region hasn't just rolled over in the face of the invading Western chains. Indeed, in one case – the 7-Eleven 24-hour-a-day supermarket chain – the original US franchise owner was bought out by his Japanese master franchisee!

In 1973, the Southland Corporation of Dallas, Texas licensed Ito-Yokado of Japan to develop the 7-Eleven concept in Japan. However, in 1991, Ito-Yokado bought a controlling interest in Southland, thus rescuing it from bankruptcy. Since then, the 7-Eleven concept and brand has gone from strength to strength. As of February 2004, Ito-Yokado and its affiliate Seven-Eleven Japan jointly held 73.9% of the outstanding shares of 7-Eleven, Inc., and the company had over 22,000 units worldwide, around 90% of them franchised.

As far as legislation covering franchising is concerned, the picture around the region is a varied one:

- In China, in 1997, the Ministry of Internal Trade introduced what they called the Measures for the Administration of Commercial Franchising Operations, which establish a framework for franchising activities that closely resembles franchising as we understand it. This legislation was followed in 2000 by a further measure, which stipulates that franchisors who are eligible for having their franchise documents recorded are to be "reputable franchisors." For this they need to have at least one company-owned outlet and three franchised outlets and to have engaged in franchising for more than one year. Further legislation is expected soon.
- Indonesia has also had legislation covering franchising since 1997, while such legislation was introduced in Malaysia in 1999.
- Although the Thai Parliament has considered the adoption of a *Franchising Act*, it hasn't yet enacted such legislation, although there are a variety of laws in Thailand designed to regulate and protect the interests of consumers, local distributors, and franchisees, and which therefore can apply to franchising agreements. The same situation applies in Singapore and India.

MBOS AND MBIS

In addition to starting a new venture, it is possible to become an entrepreneur without having a brilliant idea and without launching a new venture from scratch. This is done by buying an already existing company and managing it to a higher level of growth and value creation by means of a management buyout (MBO) or management buy-in (MBI).

With the notable exceptions of Australia and New Zealand, MBOs and MBIs have never been very important in Asia, with the deals done limited mainly to a few relatively large ones. And yet these activities are a crucially important feature of Western economies, particularly in the UK and the US, providing a ready mechanism for new entrepreneurial talent and energies to create new value in existing companies.

We look at this topic in detail in Chapter 13.

▶▶ CONCLUSION

Asia is buzzing with new IP development activity to the extent that, in some places, there are many more innovative ideas than entrepreneurs to exploit them. Much of this activity is taking place within specially planned innovation hubs, many of them trying to emulate the Silicon Valley model.

At the same time, non-technological start-ups are also burgeoning, sometimes bringing strikingly original ideas to seemingly well-trodden areas – for instance, QB House's 10-minute haircuts in Japan, and the Bed Supperclub in Bangkok.

The overall picture is completed by a high level of franchising development, leaving just one area of entrepreneurial activity still relatively undeveloped in the Asia-Pacific region – the area of MBOs and MBIs.

However, as a recent workshop on this topic in Mumbai[15] showed, it can only be a matter of time before the region makes inroads into this area as well.

ENDNOTES

[1] J.A. Timmons, *New Venture Creation: Entrepreneurship for the 21st Century* (5th Edition – Irwin McGraw Hill).

[2] Bob Woods, TechNewsWorld, June 2, 2003, www.technewsworld.com/story/20685.html.

[3] David Rosenberg, *Cloning Silicon Valley* (Pearson Books, 2001).

[4] INSEAD InnovAsia brochure, www.inseadinnovasia.com.

[5] MSC dedicated website, www.mdc.com.my/msc/msc.asp.

[6] Reported in paknews.com, January 17, 2004.

[7] Government of Pakistan Board of Investment, www.pakboi.gov.pk/News_Archive/2004/May/11-05-2004.html.

[8] Arnoud de Meyer and Sam Garg, *Inspire to Innovate: Management of Innovation in Asia* (Palgrave, 2005).

[9] Speech given at the Singapore Venture Capital Association's AGM on April 30, 2004, reported in *SVCA Venture Journal*, August 2004.

[10] Venkat Chandrasekhar and Vijay Chandru, "Commercial Academics: An Indian Story," unpublished.

[11] Lest we be accused of political incorrectness, or at the very least inconsistency, we ought perhaps to point out that the city name "Bombay" is embedded in the name of the academic institute in that form, in very much the same way that "Peking" is officially a part of the name of the University of Peking.

[12] We are grateful to Professor Rajendra K. Lagu of IIT Bombay for the information regarding their incubator.

[13] "Economic Impact of Franchised Businesses," a report by PricewaterhouseCoopers for the International Franchise Association Educational Foundation, March 2004.

[14] Rae Sheila, "Beijing's Franchise Revolution," *China Brief*, November 2000.

[15] "MBOs and MBIs in India: The Way Forward," an INSEAD workshop held in Mumbai, September 22, 2004.

The Entrepreneur and Cash

*T*his section deals with the very close and necessary, albeit often turbulent, relationship between entrepreneurs and cash.

We are all aware, either from experience or from textbooks on entrepreneurship, that there are two key resources required in starting a business: people and money. However brilliant the entrepreneur or his idea, he is going to need cash to set up and get going. If he wishes to build a new factory, expand abroad, make an acquisition – or indeed buy out a business partner, then the need for cash is present. It is no coincidence that this relationship between cash and entrepreneurs can be a distinguishing factor between successful businesses and unsuccessful ones. However, the next four chapters look at the cash needs relating to early-stage businesses, including the climate in Asia for raising funds, the key sources of capital available, the styles of different investors, and the growing role of governments in helping to drive entrepreneurial activity.

4

Case Study: Start-up in Bangalore

*I*t is difficult to box the study of entrepreneurship into convenient sections of textbooks. This can lead us to believe that there is a set of optimal decisions which can be taken at every stage of a business's life and that the causes of business success, or indeed failure, can be traced back to the decisions or actions taken. In reality, of course, this isn't the case and, quite apart from their competence or incompetence as CEOs, entrepreneurs are hugely affected by the environment they face. In Asia, we may reasonably conclude that the opportunities provided by continuing and strong economic growth must favor the competent entrepreneur. However, while the market conditions may be positive, the Asian entrepreneur can face a more difficult environment in the more practical aspects of implementing their plans, two of the most important of which are raising cash and managing cash. To this end, we feel it appropriate to begin this section with a real-life case study that not only highlights some of these issues, but also demonstrates the passion, drive, and emotion involved in setting up a business.

The business we have profiled is called MeritTrac, based in Bangalore, India. For readers who haven't had direct experience of start-up businesses, the case provides an opportunity for them to taste some of the real issues involved in setting up a business – in particular, the commitment needed and the inevitable ups and downs of the process. For those who have direct start-up experience, this case study will hopefully help to place this in context and perhaps provide some new insights into the process. In either case, it will be a helpful introduction to the subject before we go on to discuss specific related issues in the next few chapters.

We believe MeritTrac provides a rich and interesting case study for the following reasons:

- The business was set up just before the burst of the tech bubble (discussed in the next chapter) *and* survived the 2001–02 recession.
- It was set up to operate in the Indian outsourcing sector. This has been one of the most interesting growth sectors in Asia in recent years, and its development has had far-reaching implications globally.
- It highlights many of the issues facing start-ups, including trying to get the first round of funding, as well as dealing with tough issues such as cash management and survival.

Although much of the teaching surrounding the setting up of businesses concentrates on the technical and analytical side of product development, business planning, and so on, in reality new business creation is a huge emotional experience. Indeed, the setting up of a new business has often been described as an emotional rollercoaster and, to this end, the style of the case study is *involved* rather than *detached*, so that readers may also experience this themselves.

CASE STUDY:
"OUTSOURCING SERVICES TO OUTSOURCING BUSINESSES" – A START-UP IN BANGALORE

Sector background

The strengths of India in the areas of information technology (IT) development and business process outsourcing (BPO) are well known. Many large Western businesses – in particular, financial institutions – are taking the step of relocating back-office functions in India. An example of this is call centers. A customer who buys a product or service in the US or Europe may be re-routed as they call a local helpdesk number to a customer service center in Mumbai, for example. In this way, companies can make attractive savings on back-office functions due to the lower wage rates in India. This trend is deepening, as companies are basing more and more of their back-office and development functions in Asia.

The BPO and IT-related business growth has created a huge demand for employees in India – currently, some 500,000 people are employed in this sector and this is estimated to grow to some 22 million by 2008. For every 100 applicants for these posts, it is normal that fewer than five will receive job offers. This small conversion rate is a reflection of the different and specific needs of the various employers in terms of employee skill sets. To put this in perspective, a new call center needing 100 operators would need to assess some 2,000 candidates. How do these companies manage such a challenging task, particularly when they may need to run assessment centers in different cities or universities throughout India? In the absence of better options, they have tended to perform these tasks "in-house." This can tie up vast amounts of resources. Typically, a company will need to invest in and build up this resource in terms of people and expertise in order to do the job properly. Some have used human resource consultants, which can be a useful one-off solution, but it can be expensive because of the customization required for each project.

As the BPO and IT sectors started to gather pace in 2000, it was clear that the existing assessment solutions were already sub-optimal and, with the demand for assessments expected to grow to some 7.5 million per annum by 2005, there would be a growing need for a better solution.

It was against this background that a small group of entrepreneurs from Bangalore developed a vision for a new business – one which would provide outsourcing services to the outsourcers...

Getting started

In early 2000, Madan Padaki was pursuing his career in international sales and marketing with a multinational software house after having graduated from SP Jain Institute of Management – one of the premier business schools in India. Although he enjoyed his job, it was his dream to set up and build his own business. He was no stranger to the risks of doing this – it was the height of the dot.com boom and Madan had many friends who were either founders of or employed by start-up companies. He had observed the growth of IT and BPO companies in India and felt there was a real need in the market to provide assessment services to meet the enormous expected growth in demand for labor resources.

One of Madan's friends had recently founded a relatively new software development company, Diffsoft, which was developing software to manage the banks of questions used for candidate assessment purposes by large multinational IT businesses. They got together with another friend, Murlidhar, a service operations specialist and graduate from the Indian Institute of Management, Lucknow, and reviewed the whole recruitment-assessment process. After much deliberation and brainstorming, they came up with an outline business plan for a new company that could provide assessment and processing services for businesses needing to hire large numbers of employees.

The team felt very energized and quickly started to carry out market validation in support of their business plan. In particular, they approached those major business processing or outsourcing companies whom the team felt would have an ongoing need to employ large numbers of candidates with particular skill sets. They were greatly encouraged by the interest and response, and felt it was time to find some financial support for their plan. They believed that raising funds of US$1 million would provide the business with the right start to establish a leading position in this new area.

The reality of start-up funding

In mid-2000, the team approached four or five Indian-based venture capital (VC) companies. While they seemed to like the business idea, they had some key reservations:

- *Skepticism about the market*: In particular, this was an entirely new business area.
- *Concern about scalability*: The operational business model was based on an ability to provide testing for large numbers of candidates. The VCs felt that while this could be an interesting niche business, the ability to really grow it and develop a significant business – and achieve the financial returns associated with this – was less credible.
- *Experience of the team*: While the proposed directors, Madan and Murlidhar, had excellent CVs and qualifications, neither had direct experience of recruiting or of setting up a business.

There were also other factors at work. The environment in which the team was trying to find investors wasn't straightforward. It was the era of the dot.com boom and VCs were focused on finding high-growth, tech-based opportunities – MeritTrac was seen as neither. Also, the amount of funding required was relatively small, with VCs typically looking to invest in opportunities that needed at least US$3 million.

In addition, the proposal was at its very early stage – it had no full-time employees or customers. A comment from one of the VCs put the whole process into perspective: "If you think this is such a great idea, why aren't you convinced enough to leave your jobs?"

Shortly afterwards, Madan quit his job and committed himself full-time to the project. All this happened within the first month.

A sense of urgency and anticipation develops

It was now July 2000 and the general fundraising environment was starting to become more difficult. VCs in general were becoming more concerned about future economic prospects, and the tech investment boom was at the end of its honeymoon period. Madan could see that they would need to develop the business quickly if they were to raise the funds they required. Gaining some paying customers to prove the business model would be the key priority.

Madan and Murlidhar, with the help of their friend from Diffsoft, decided to go ahead with setting up the business. They agreed to invest US$10,000 between them, which would be used to establish the business entity and cover initial expenses. Madan worked from home to ensure that these costs were minimized.

Almost immediately, the move from ideas to action and commitment brought some early success. At the end of July the team won two orders in one day. One was a project to test 2,000 candidates across three cities, while the other was to handle a series of walk-in interviews. The projects were worth some US$5,000. This was the trigger for the second team member – Murlidhar – to quit his job and join MeritTrac full-time.

The need to service real customers led Madan and Murlidhar to search for office premises. Still hampered by limited resources, the team struck a deal with another start-up company. They agreed to work for 10 hours a week in exchange for office space and two workstations. A further boost came in the guise of a new team member – Jayanth. A contact at one of their first customers, Jayanth was very excited by MeritTrac's business idea and, although he was keen to re-enter full-time study, agreed to join as a founder director in September. This new member brought much-needed human resources (HR) experience to the team, having worked for an internationally renowned HR consultancy.

October brought two more exciting, albeit small, projects. The first was to design question papers and conduct university campus testing for a multinational customer; the second was to assess candidates to deliver 100 software engineers for a new software development business.

Another attempt at raising funds

MeritTrac had come a long way in six months. By November 2000, the business had:

- four customers, two of which were blue-chip names;
- a founding team with a complementary set of skills and experience;
- office space (of sorts); and
- revenue of US$10,000.

The team re-approached some VCs, again hoping to raise funds of around US$1 million, but found that their interest in start-ups had waned even further. They seemed to have a growing skepticism about the ability of start-ups to generate acceptable returns, and were beginning to focus on later-stage opportunities which already had products, customers, and positive cash flow. The team spent much effort providing the VCs with background information, forecasts, and scenarios. In fact, the requests for more information seemed to be taking up more time than they were actually spending on the business. Even so, all this was to no avail and the VCs seemed no nearer to making a decision either way. In the end, the team realized that the discussions were going nowhere. They felt that proceeding down this path would have little chance of success at this stage, and would just continue to take up a lot of their time, effort, and emotional energy. Instead, they decided to take another look at their business plan to see what they could achieve if they raised a smaller amount of money.

After completing their review, the team calculated that by raising only US$200,000 to US$250,000 now, they could take the business to a point in two years where it could achieve cash break-even. Their experiences of the last few months had given them confidence that sales of US$500,000 would be achievable in the first year of operation, and that this could rise to US$6 million by the third year.

The revised business plan reduced expenditure wherever possible. The following items were identified as the key priority for the smaller pool of money they were now targeting:

- setting up office premises that would be appropriate to service the blue-chip client base the business intended to target;
- hiring employees; and
- developing content.

The team considered the need for working capital to finance the credit they would need to extend to their potential customers. They decided not to include this, as the lower level of funds meant the projected growth wasn't so aggressive and should be manageable. Besides, many of their customers would be well-known international businesses and therefore potentially good payers.

With the new and lower fundraising target of US$200,000 to US$250,000, the team felt that instead of needing to approach VC firms, they could now approach high-net-worth businessmen, or "business angels," who were often on the lookout for this kind of alternative investment opportunity. They contacted second- and third-tier accountancy firms in Bangalore, as these firms seemed traditionally to have strong relationships with the type of individuals MeritTrac was seeking.

They were fortunate to catch the eye of some interested businessmen, but after meeting a few they came away with the impression that although these were savvy businessmen, they were also very aggressive deal-doers who would invest little and ask for a lot. Although they were interested in investing in early-stage businesses, they seemed to have a low risk profile. This manifested itself in their need to control their money once invested and to have the lion's share of the return. One potential investor with whom they had several discussions seemed to sum it up – they gained the impression that he would be extremely worried about his money and would probably want to communicate with them at least on a daily basis. Another potential investor had a very high personal profile, which made the team feel that they would be too exposed as a business to his reputation going forward. They felt they needed more of a longer-term investor who understood their business and would be helpful, rather than become a type of micro-manager.

One of the accountancy firms suggested they approach some agri-businessmen. Agriculture as a sector had been doing well over this period, and many of the businessmen involved had enjoyed a period of sustained personal wealth creation and were beginning to consider alternative investment opportunities. These businessmen had been less caught up in the private investment boom in the cities, and it was thought they might take a more enlightened approach. MeritTrac was introduced to one such businessman, a Mr. Ranganath, who lived in a small town not far from Bangalore. Apparently, he had US$200,000 to US$300,000 spare in cash and was interested in exploring this type of "alternative" investing. The first meeting, which took place in a hotel, proved very disappointing for the team. The only question the businessman asked during the meeting, which included a detailed presentation by the team about their business, was whether they preferred to drink coffee or tea.

The team felt despondent. They were pitching either to aggressive and potentially smothering business angels from the cities, or to apparently less savvy and passive ones from the countryside, and having no luck with either.

Shortly afterwards, though, Mr. Ranganath got in touch again and arranged another meeting. It seemed that the team – used to the quick-fire meetings of the city – had misunderstood his approach to business and relationships. At this next meeting, the team felt that some connection was made, and the chemistry and trust it created seemed both mutual and positive.

Discussions continued over the next two to three weeks. Finally, at the end of November, Mr. Ranganath declared his intention to invest and the discussions switched to how much and for what stake. With no benchmark valuation for the business, this was going to be a difficult discussion. They all agreed to approach a certified public accountant (CPA) in Bangalore to provide a valuation that would be a basis for discussion. The CPA used various methods, including discounted cash flow, price to earnings (PE) ratio, and economic value added (EVA), and eventually came up with a valuation of US$3 million.

The MeritTrac team were elated with this valuation, which seemed a testimony to the hard work they had put into the business over the last six months. This elation, unfortunately, was short-lived. The angel investor was shaken by the outcome. He found it difficult to understand how a business, still at a very early stage, could be valued so highly and wondered how he could get an attractive return if his entry price was US$3 million. He had heard of the high valuations associated with the dot.com companies, but this was a very different business, and even the dot.com businesses were starting to see more realistic valuations. Mr. Ranganath proposed a counter-offer of a US$50,000 investment for 51% of the business – which valued the business at just under US$100,000. This brought the team back to earth very quickly and made them consider a realistic response. They moved away from the benchmark evaluation techniques they had used for the initial valuation and concentrated more on what was really important in terms of the business and their aspirations.

They knew that the business would need another round of fundraising later and were reluctant to use more than 20–25% at this stage because of the overall dilution of management's equity stake. They also argued that over-dilution of management's equity in the business could have a negative effect on their drive to run the business – and this wouldn't be good for the angel investor either. The third key issue for them was the amount to be raised. They had already revised their business plan to accommodate a lower investment and didn't want to reduce this further, as it would start to compromise the viability of the business going forward. To counter these arguments, though, the current lack of other funding options put them in a difficult negotiating position.

After 15 days of intense negotiation, they agreed to an investment of US$200,000 for 27%. This valued the business at approximately US$740,000. Mr. Ranganath agreed to this as long as management also invested another US$10,000 between them.

The structure of this investment was to be as follows:

- *Phase 1*: US$100,000 invested for 27% to be released in tranches. The first was to be US$30,000.
- *Milestones to be achieved*: A number of objectives – both financial and non-financial – were also set to be achieved before the balance of the Phase II US$200,000 could be drawn down. These included:
    - six new customers;
    - setting up of offices;
    - development of content – in particular, a question bank; and
    - commencement of work on an online testing module.
- *Phase II*: After six months, there would be a review of progress, and satisfactory achievement of milestones would

trigger the outstanding balance of US$100,000 – and the injection of US$10,000 from the management team. All this would then be invested over another 18 months.

- *Other conditions*: Mr. Ranganath also wanted other rights and controls, including:
    – a seat on the board of directors of the company;
    – his approval required for any expenditure over US$2,000;
    – a monthly review of progress;
    – tag-along rights (if the management team found a buyer for their shares, then he had the option to be included at the same price); and
    – the right to sell his shares, as long as the board approved.

To balance this, MeritTrac also gained agreement from Mr. Ranganath to the following:

- Mr. Ranganath would forfeit an agreed number of his shares if he was unable to complete phase I funding.
- For the first time, the full-time team members would be able to draw a salary of US$350 per month.

The team engaged a lawyer friend to pull all these terms and conditions together in a shareholders' agreement, which they and Mr. Ranganath signed at the end of December.

The first tranche of US$30,000 was drawn down in January 2001. The team was in a celebratory mood.

Money in the bank

With a very healthy bank account, and more money on its way, the team were able to put their plans into action with some confidence.

Their priority was to rent some suitable office space and begin recruiting key employees. As their office would also double as a testing center, it was important for it to look presentable and professional – both to their high-profile customers and to the candidates they would be testing. By the end of January, the team had found some suitable premises and allocated US$20,000 to US$30,000 to fit it out to a suitable specification. They also recruited clerks to cover administration and finance, and an operations manager. In February, they added a software team to develop their online assessment product. A further US$20,000 was drawn down from the phase 1 tranche, leaving a balance of US$50,000 remaining.

On the sales front, the team also made some good progress. A couple of large orders from two leading multinational corporation (MNC) software development centers in March brought in around US$12,000.

By review time in May, the business had met all the milestones laid down by Mr. Ranganath to release phase II money – but at that point it had used only half of the phase I funds. This meant there was US$50,000 outstanding from phase I, and US$100,000 (plus an extra US$10,000 from management) still to be drawn down to grow the business. The future looked rosy…

Problems from an unexpected quarter

By mid-2001 the economic climate was starting to change for the worse. Despite this, MeritTrac had continued to grow steadily, adding more customers including, for the first time, a business process outsourcing company. This was a breakthrough for the team, who believed that the growth of their business would be driven by the growing demand of the BPO companies that were starting to develop strongly in India.

Unfortunately, the angel investor – like many wealthy individuals at the time – had begun to experience financial difficulties caused by heavy investment in the stock markets. He agreed at review time to release the final US$50,000 of the committed phase I funds, but delayed making the payment. There were continuing promises of money, but it never materialized. Finally, a check was received, but it was returned by the bank due to lack of funds.

The unfortunate events of September 11, 2001 not only worsened the angel investor's financial position, but also started to affect the business.

The final quarter of 2001 saw sales fall rapidly. The business now had a monthly cash outflow (sometimes referred to as its "burn rate") of US$4,000 supported by a monthly income of only US$400.

This quarter also coincided, somewhat unfortunately, with the addition of another key team member – Mohan Kannegal, who was a specialist in technology and content development. Mohan was Madan's classmate from business school and was initially involved in helping to put together the business plan. He chose to join the company full-time in December after completing an assignment in London. Also in December, Mr. Ranganath advised the team that he could only invest another US$20,000 from the remaining undrawn balance of US$150,000.

This was a low point for the team, who saw in New Year 2002 with dread. They felt as though they were staring down the barrel of a gun. With a monthly cash burn rate of US$4,000 and only US$6,000 left in the bank, they had only one-and-a-half months left before they would run out of cash.

To make matters worse, it was at this point that the team saw at first hand the stark reality that sales don't equate directly with cash. The December revenue of US$400 became a bad debt when one of their smaller customers also ran into financial difficulties. The team still had a strong relationship with Mr. Ranganath, who they felt would help them out, but even this avenue became a dead end when he confirmed that he would be unable to help for at least another six months due to his own financial problems.

The team turned to one of the original four shareholders in the company, Diffsoft, which still seemed to be making cash from its own business activities. They asked if Diffsoft could provide them with US$5,000 to US$6,000 to tide them over the next couple of months. However, like many small businesses, the company was focused on conserving cash to ensure its own survival in 2002. Diffsoft made the hard observation that, unless MeritTrac could survive on its own, then it would have no future. This had a profound effect on the team, who were shaken, and it led them to consider their future … their dreams.

Survival plan

It didn't need too much deliberation for the team to decide that their business model was still relevant and they were fully committed to seeing it through, even in the face of their current dire situation.

They felt that the cause of their current problems was mostly external, and if they could ride out the next six months or so then they could embark again on growing the business. With only US$6,000 in the bank and minimal to no cash inflow, the only way for them to survive would be to conserve cash with drastic cost cutting. At this point, their monthly costs were as shown in Table 4.1.

Table 4.1 Monthly Costs

Item	US$
Directors' salaries	1,000
Employees' wages	2,000
Office overheads	1,000
Total	**4,000**

Their plan was simple and potentially effective. They decided they would need to stop all salary and wage payments, leaving only the office overheads of $1,000, for which they had enough in the bank to cover six months of running.

The team called a meeting of all the employees, who numbered eight including the three full-time directors. The employees had been very loyal so far, and the directors felt it was important to tell them exactly what the position was and to be clear about their plan to deal with it. They needed the full support of the employees if their plan was to work. Accepting zero wages for up to six months, with no guarantee of a job afterwards, was a big thing to ask. Losing any of the employees would be a blow for the business. Due to cash constraints, it had only recruited absolutely essential staff and having to re-recruit later would slow up business growth significantly, as well as compromise some of the ongoing customer projects.

To their surprise and immense relief, not one member of staff wanted to leave. All agreed to forego their salaries to help the business survive. The team were greatly encouraged and promised the staff they would pay salaries as soon as the business received revenue. They also pledged a transparent accounting system to support this. In short, any cash from customers would be divided up among all the employees – but if there was no cash, there would be no salaries.

The key objective of survival for the next six months was achieved, but there was also another side effect of the survival plan. Unwittingly, the business now had in place perhaps the most effective employee incentive scheme possible. As salaries now had a direct relationship to cash received from sales, all staff now looked earnestly for ways to drive the business and bring in customers. From January to March 2002, the business embarked on a collective exercise of marketing to an average of 50 companies per week, and also looked at developing aptitude courses to prepare candidates for tests.

During this three-month period, the business was rewarded with sales of US$5,000 – considerably higher than the US$400 per month at the end of 2001. By June, all the hard work really paid off, with sales back up to US$10,000 per month. The business had four new customers, including another from the BPO sector. More importantly, all the salaries were now back to normal.

July turned out to be a record month, with sales of US$15,000. With the worst now over, MeritTrac continued on its steady growth path for the rest of 2002. Celebrating New Year 2003 was a very different affair for the team than the previous year – it brought with it the promise of an exciting year ahead as their business went from strength to strength. By the end of the financial year at March 31, 2003, the business had recorded sales of US$125,000 and a net profit of US$15,000.

Growth brings a different kind of cash problem

The expansion that the business was now experiencing brought a new and unexpected cash issue to the fore. Sales were increasing every month, but cash was getting extremely tight. The team realized that the business was starting to experience the growing pains associated with a lack of available cash to cover working capital.

The working capital dynamics of the business in respect of growing sales were as follows:

- Operating costs were typically 50% of sales. These had to be paid within the month they were incurred and included salaries, overheads, and variable costs such as hire of testing facilities when operating outside of Bangalore.
- Payment terms given to customers were typically 30 days, which meant they were given one month's credit.

February 2003 was a record month with sales of US$22,000, followed by only US$20,000 sales in March. The next quarter got off to an excellent start with sales of US$25,000 in April, after which they continued to grow at a fast rate. Sales doubled to US$50,000 in May and grew by half again to US$75,000 in June. This was great for profitability (see Table 4.2), but it opened up another type of cash problem.

Table 4.2 Operating Profit, First Quarter, 2003

	April	May	June
Sales	25,000	50,000	75,000
Costs @ 50% of sales	(12,500)	(25,000)	(37,500)
Operating profit	**12,500**	**25,000**	**37,500**

With the type of growth MeritTrac was experiencing, the cash flow movements during the month had little resemblance to the profit achieved in the same month. However, with its policy of 30-day payment terms (see Table 4.3), the cash flow seemed to be able to work with a small headroom even when sales were doubling – as long as costs were held fairly constant at 50% of sales.

Table 4.3 Cash Flow, First Quarter, 2003 (Assuming 30-day Payment Terms)

	April	May	June
Receipts +30 days	20,000	25,000	50,000
Payments (Costs)	(12,500)	(25,000)	(37,500)
Net cash	7,500	0	12,500
Cash balance	7,500	7,500	20,000

However, reality proved to be very different. The team learnt that customers typically didn't pay their bills on time – and the idea of paying within 30 days just didn't seem to fit with market practice. Some just asked for longer payment terms – a request MeritTrac found difficult to turn down given their focus on growing sales and a customer base. The team were half-correct in their assumptions about their blue-chip multinational customers: while they proved to be reliable payers, they turned out to be some of the slowest.

Apart from some customers who were deliberately slow payers and stalled with the usual excuses, payments from others were delayed due to the lack of regular payment mechanisms – every payment seemed to require a new process. A further drawback was customers wanting contracts carried out at short notice. The effect of this was that MeritTrac often operated without a formal service agreement in place. This, of course, made it difficult to get payment. The operations teams that placed the work were less interested in the administrative details of organizing payments, and the management team found they had to deal with legal and finance departments before checks would be signed.

With the team keen to grow the business and make the most of the sales opportunities and to grow long-term customer relationships, the cash payment issues were a constant source of potential conflict. MeritTrac's small size also seemed to put them in a weak bargaining position. The problem, however, was very real and the effect of stretching average customer payment terms to 60 days – which itself still remained a challenge – can be seen in Table 4.4.

Table 4.4 Cash Flow, First Quarter, FY2003/04 (Payment Terms of 60 Days)

	April	May	June
Receipts +60 days	22,000	20,000	25,000
Payments same month	(12,500)	(25,000)	(37,500)
Net cash	**9,500**	(5,000)	(12,500)
Cash balance	**9,500**	**4,500**	(8,000)

Overall, the growth in sales the business was experiencing, together with the lengthy and erratic process of receiving payment from customers for work completed, proved a lethal combination in terms of cash management for the business. The whole of 2003 was spent fighting a cash battle, and the team regularly had to temper their euphoria at winning sales orders with the necessity to pay salaries late. At one point, the position became so difficult they were forced to take out personal loans to provide a cash float.

Thankfully, the business survived, and by January 2004 it had grown sales to US$100,000 per month and was moving from strength to strength.

What options lie ahead?

The team had just endured what can be described as a two-year emotional rollercoaster ride with their business. The ride started at the beginning of 2001, when the euphoria of raising their first outside capital and setting up the business properly soon dissipated into gloom when the full amount failed to materialize and the general economic situation quickly deteriorated. With disaster staring them in the face by the end of 2001, a realistic but tough survival plan brought them another six months of trading time and saw them through to a new dawn of growing sales. However, the growth experienced by the business over the ensuing 12 months took the team totally by surprise and they felt as though they had been flung from one survival situation into another just as tough as they fought the cash management battle.

This bright team knew the theory about managing a growing business, but rarely attempted to apply it in 2003. In their own words, they were "just too busy."

By the final quarter of 2004, MeritTrac was a very different business. It had:

- regular monthly sales of US$150,000 to US$200,000 and growing;
- provided services to over 80 customers in the IT and BPO space;
- assessed over 400,000 candidates – the run rate was 15,000 to 20,000 per month across some 15 cities in India; and
- 125 full-time employees with a further 700-plus certified test administrators across India.

In addition, the business faces a buoyant market. The team believe the market for their services is growing at some 200–300% per year and in line with their original expectations. On the downside, however, they still have working capital problems and the cash situation is beginning to feel like a drag on their growth.

This has led them again to look at raising capital to fund the growth. On the one hand, they are daunted by the prospect of starting another fundraising process. The last one had been extremely time-consuming and had been unsuccessful in many respects. This time, they would probably need to raise at least US$1 million, which would be beyond the reach of most private investors. This meant going through a process with a venture capital fund with no prospect of success at the end.

On the other hand, the growth of the business going forward was always going to be constrained by the available cash. The prospect of being overtaken by a well-funded competitor in this new market niche was very worrying. An investment of new cash would enable them to maintain their current position as market leader in their field and be strong enough to take on bigger customers. Overall, they would be able to grow much faster with new funding.

Originally they had thought to approach some VC funds again. Those funds still operating after the recession were well aware of the opportunities the market upturn was bringing and were on the lookout for new investment proposals. More recently, however, there had been a new and interesting development. They had been approached by a small number of their larger customers who were very interested in MeritTrac's business model and keen to discuss some form of strategic investment. In some ways, this seemed an attractive option as the customers were already familiar with the business and the market opportunity. The team were concerned, though, about the potential conflicts of interest that may arise if some of their customers, who were often also competitors, became shareholders.

So, by the end of 2004, the team were facing some tough decisions. The key questions facing them were:

- Should they raise money or continue to grow within their own resources?
- How much should they raise?
- Who should they raise it from?
- What to do about the customers who are interested in becoming strategic investors?

▶▶ CONCLUSION

We are grateful to the directors of MeritTrac for allowing us to share intimately in both their triumphs and struggles. In doing so, we have been able to experience the drive, commitment, and resourcefulness required to set up a new business in Asia. With the progress that MeritTrac has made, management is now blessed with a relatively broad selection of options. However, the biggest challenge for them is that at US$1 million, the amount of capital they are looking to raise is still too small for formal venture capital, but probably too big for individual investors. In addition, while they have the opportunity to grow fairly rapidly, they are still not likely to fall comfortably into the target market of VCs, which are generally looking for fast-growth, technology-backed businesses. In the next chapter, we will explore some of these issues further – in particular, the type of funding environment that faces exciting early-stage businesses such as MeritTrac.

Raising
Start-up Capital

*T*he creation of new businesses is of vital importance to the development of vibrant and growing entrepreneurial economies in Asia. However, this acceptance of the importance of new business creation to Asia doesn't necessarily translate to the widespread provision of practical help for budding entrepreneurs as they pursue their vision, particularly in the area of providing capital. From the viewpoint of the individual entrepreneur anywhere in the world, pulling plans together and setting up a business can provide all the ups and downs of the world's biggest rollercoaster ride... and more. Asia is no different, and indeed can be more challenging. This chapter focuses on the fundraising environment in Asia and the potential sources of capital for entrepreneurs.

INTRODUCTION

It is a well-known and accepted fact that small- and medium-sized enterprises (SMEs) are the main engine of growth and employment of most economies. This is being recognized by Asian governments, where the main thrust of their policy initiatives has been to take measures to stimulate new business creation. In China, for example, the importance of SMEs cannot be over-emphasized. They account for over 90% of enterprises, contribute to more than 50% of GDP and exports, and provide employment for over 70% of the huge and growing urban workforce (see Figure 5.1).

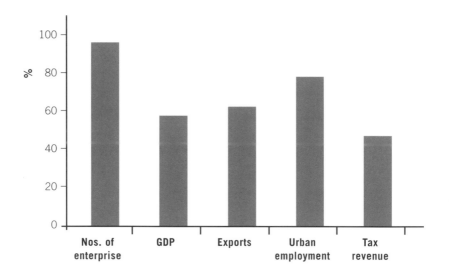

Source: People's Daily, June 23, 2004.

Figure 5.1 Importance of SMEs to the Chinese Economy

Indeed, although China's growth statistics of some 9% per annum are very impressive, since the early 1980s the private sector in China has been growing at a rate nearer 20% per annum. In terms of new enterprises, over 500,000 are believed to have been established in China in 2003 alone. The contribution of the SME sector to China's current and future growth is acknowledged by the Chinese government.

The Chinese Communist Party School's Office for Economic Research estimates that going forward the number of SMEs will rise to 27 million from the current 7 million by 2020, and that over this period they will create 198 million jobs for new and laid-off workers. Despite this, businesses in China find it difficult to gain access to capital and feel that there is a bias toward the larger state-run companies.

Not surprisingly, the picture is fairly similar in India (see Figure 5.2) and its government has recognized the need to develop and unshackle the entrepreneurial sector, which had already grown from 870,000 businesses in 1981 to nearly 4 million in 2003. Next to India's massive agricultural sector, it provides the largest number of employment opportunities.

> " The SMEs have become an essential basis of China's economic growth, market prosperity and employment increase. "
>
> VICE PREMIER ZENG PEIYAN, *PEOPLE'S DAILY*, JUNE 23, 2004

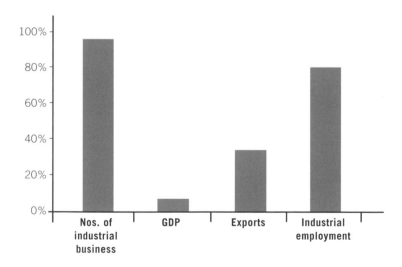

Source: Indian Small Industries Development Organisation (SIDO), 2003.

Figure 5.2 Importance of SMEs to the Indian Economy

SOURCES OF FUNDS

A seemingly large range of funding options faces the entrepreneur in Asia, although in practice, choosing an appropriate source for funds really depends on the stage of development of the business. The range of funding options for early- and later-stage businesses is outlined in Table 5.1.

Table 5.1 Sources of Funds

Early stage	Later stage
• Own money	• Private equity
• Family and friends	• Government
• Business angels	• Strategic partners
• Government	• Initial public offering (IPO)
• Venture capital	• Secured instruments (e.g. bank lending)
• Strategic partners	

Figure 5.3 illustrates specifically the sources of funding for early-stage businesses, which is the focus of this chapter. The shaded boxes represent individuals, businesses, or funds that invest *directly* into businesses, usually in return for a shareholding. The unshaded boxes and black arrows indicate institutions that invest *indirectly* into the investee company. They do this by investing in a tax-efficient and limited liability vehicle such as a venture capital fund, which itself will invest directly into the business. This is an important difference to note when approaching the various sources of funding. There are positives and negatives associated with both types of investors – that is, those that invest their own money and those that invest other people's money – and these are issues we will touch on later.

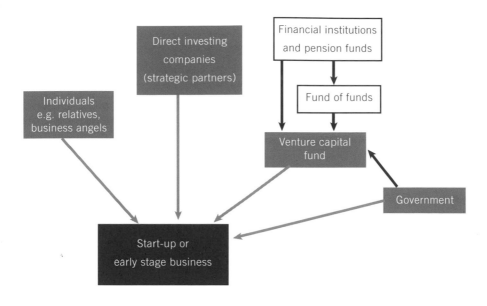

Figure 5.3 Sources of Funds for Early-stage Businesses

The term "early stage" is often used to describe businesses that are not yet able to survive on their own cash flow; in other words, they are "cash flow negative." These businesses need cash to help them get to a situation where they are covering their costs with cash from sales.

Later-stage companies have demonstrated their ability to sell products or services to repeat customers and are generating enough of their own cash to survive and grow steadily. These businesses need cash to accelerate a growth opportunity. We will be looking at this later stage in two subsequent chapters: Chapter 9, "Raising Expansion Capital," and Chapter 11, "Let's Go IPO." For the rest of this chapter, we will be focusing on the early stages of a business's life until it is able to be "cash flow positive."

Each business is, of course, different, and some may only need one more round of funding before they can become cash flow positive and grow to a level where they can attract larger amounts of capital. Other businesses may need more rounds of funding – often termed in investment circles as series A, B, C, and so on. This is particularly the case where research and development (R&D) is significant, in which case business progress may be based on the achievement of milestones rather than growth in sales.

THE CLIMATE FOR EARLY-STAGE INVESTING

> "...since the burst of the tech bubble in 2001, the climate in Asia for early-stage investing has remained cautious."

Most start-ups involve initial investment from the founders and family and friends, with the next most likely investor being a business angel or some form of government grant or loan guarantee scheme. Early-stage businesses with the potential for rapid high growth may attract the attention of venture capital. However, since the burst of the tech bubble in 2001, the climate in Asia for early-stage investing has remained cautious.

The Asian VC World Pre-bubble

In the heady years of the mid- to late 1990s, finding funds for potentially high-growth, tech-related businesses was relatively easy. The number of VC firms and angels entering the market in Asia grew rapidly in these years, fueled by the following:

- Exciting returns were experienced by some of the earlier VC and angel investors in technology businesses.
- There was a perception that Asia was developing as a hotbed of technology development – in particular, telecoms and internet-related start-ups.
- Burn rates (monthly cash outgoings) for Asian start-ups were a lot lower than in the US and Europe, due to lower wage rates. This meant that cash invested would go further, and so returns to those investors could be higher.
- Technology businesses were seen as global, and there was a

healthy appetite for listing of exciting Asian companies on both local and Western stock exchanges – for example, the US Nasdaq.

- The market in Asia for products of technology companies was growing, fueled by the growth in local consumer and infrastructure development demand and by the move of MNCs' operations to Asia.

All types of investors were keen to get a piece of the VC action, and this meant that there was a growing demand for more VC funds, as well as for attractive opportunities in which those funds might invest. Figure 5.4 graphs the annual formal VC funds raised between 1998 and 2004 in Asia. The rapid growth in funds raised from 1999 to 2000 illustrates the growing interest both in Asia and in technology-focused VC funds.

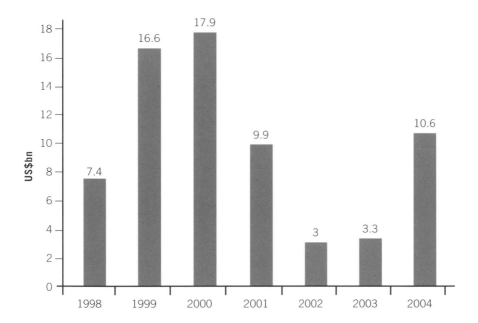

Source: Asia Venture Capital Journal

Figure 5.4 Venture Capital Funds Raised in Asia, 1998–2004

It seemed that entrepreneurs were able to raise money on the back of interesting ideas as long as these had the potential to reach, or create, huge potential markets. Even if these markets and the product were real, the means by which the business would actually implement its production and the credibility of its go-to-market strategy were often not so important at this stage. The objective for investors was to become shareholders as early as possible in order to maximize their returns.

Figure 5.5 is a simple illustration of how this worked. Most of the risk was seen in the R&D phase and initial customer acquisition, rather than in how the real money and profits were going to be made. Well before a cent was made, there may have been several rounds of funding (series A, B, C, and so on) at ever-increasing valuations.

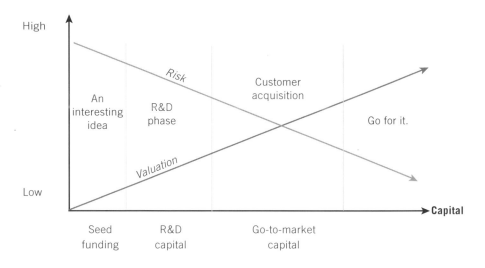

Figure 5.5 The Good Old Days

Justifications for increases in valuation would include:

- meeting certain development milestones – for example, prototype testing;
- hiring of certain key employees; and
- expressions of interest from identified customers.

The new valuations were finally justified and cemented by the completion of a new series of funding which included new investors investing at a higher valuation than the previous round. This created the effect of *bedding down* the VC funds which had invested in previous fundraising rounds and allowed them to record an *uplift* in valuation of their fund. This virtuous circle of value growth for all was sometimes ended by a listing on a public stock exchange. It wasn't unusual at this time for companies to achieve an exciting listing when they were still to make any profits! The style of investing at this time set some dangerous precedents, which were to make coping with the post-bubble future very difficult for the investee companies and VC funds alike. Some of these precedents are discussed below.

> " The style of investing at this time set some dangerous precedents, which were to make coping with the post-bubble future very difficult for the investee companies and VC funds alike. "

High valuations and intricate structures

There were instances in Asia where companies were achieving valuations as high as US$100 million as early as series A. This was often necessary to win the deal, but VC funds would cover themselves by introducing downside protection mechanisms into the structure. For example, it was normal for *liquidity preference* provisions to be included in the investment agreements. These essentially ensured that the VC fund received its original investment (or sometimes a multiple of this investment) before management could receive their return in the event of an exit. New investors at future rounds would generally honor these rights as long as the previous investors also participated in the most recent funding round and the company had been seen to meet its planned milestones. This new round of fundraising would bring a new layer of shareholder rights and preferences, which would be placed on top of the old ones. After one or two rounds of this type, the resultant shareholder structure could be very complex indeed – particularly for a business that probably had not yet sold a product.

Limited capital invested at each round

Companies needing capital were often encouraged to raise only enough funds to enable them to deliver some meaningful milestones. Achievement of these would justify raising the next round at a higher valuation. To use an analogy, these companies were building a bridge to get across to the other side, which promised sales and profits. Instead of raising enough funds to get all the way across, the amount they would raise would only get them part of the way across. At the time, everyone felt that raising the next round on the potential of reaching the other side would be easy as long as the bridge was seen to have extended out further than at the previous funding round. This was fine as long as new funds were forthcoming, but the implication if the climate changed was clear.

Little emphasis placed on implementation skills

Under this scenario, the medium-term capabilities of the management team to reach the potentially huge markets seemed to be less important than being able to meet the identified next set of milestones. It was often assumed that once the final, and largest, round of funding was raised, this would enable the business to recruit strong teams to deliver this part.

Asia in 2000/01: The bubble bursts

The world recession had an immediate and catastrophic effect on the early-stage investment scene in Asia. The combination of the collapse of the world stock markets and the reassessment of the market opportunity for the products of the technology businesses resulted in a major risk adjustment for investors and VC firms alike. The main implications soon became clear and are illustrated in Figure 5.6.

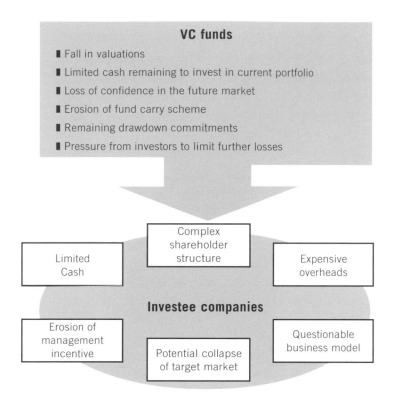

Figure 5.6 The Post-bubble Environment in Asia

The world stock markets, which were the accustomed exit route for technology investments, were unlikely to recover for some time. Moreover, when they eventually recovered it was extremely doubtful if stock-market investors would have such an insatiable appetite again for high-risk technology stocks. Technology stocks that had already listed suddenly lost their appeal, largely due to the collapse of consumer and capital spending – or, in other words, the future market for their products. The long pipeline of technology IPOs which had been building up over the previous two to three years was left high and dry – as were the many institutional investors who had invested in the pre-IPO rounds at high valuations.

Many VC funds entered a state of relative inertia as the implications of the change in environment sunk in. First, the valuation of their funds – calculated as the sum of all the individual valuations of the investee companies put together – had to be readjusted downwards to take into account the fall in share prices of the listed companies in the venture capital funds' portfolios. Unfortunately, it didn't stop there. Many of the non-listed investee companies didn't have enough cash to enable them to survive beyond the next milestone, and unless the existing VC investors were prepared to put in more money it was likely they would run out of cash. In terms of valuations for VC funds, this meant that many of the investee companies would have to be written down at best to the carrying cost, but more prudently to zero. This writing down of the fund value also had implications for the fund carry, the fund managers' ultimate upside financial incentive, which became worthless. All these issues, together with increasing pressure from the fund investors – or limited partners – to limit the damage and preserve cash, meant that VC funds had little appetite for new investments or to support existing ones. Some fund investors, keen to take control of their own cash, withdrew their remaining commitments. The penalties incurred by such actions were relatively toothless in the face of drastic falls in the overall fund valuations.

Hence, the fall in funds invested in early-stage situations after the burst of the tech bubble and subsequent recession in 2000/01 led to a massive overhang in "uninvested" funds not only in Asia, but globally. This, together with the ensuing fall in appetite of investors to place money in early-stage funds, led to a rapid fall in the annual amount of funds raised after 2000 (see Figure 5.4). The more recent recovery in funds raised is due to the interest in later-stage opportunities and management buyouts, rather than to a recovery in early-stage investing.

So, what did all this mean for the entrepreneurs? Some management teams had already managed to list their businesses, but due to the "lock-in" periods that were typical for these companies, management had so far mainly had paper money, which one day had been worth millions of dollars, but the next almost nothing. There were also many who were waiting in the IPO pipeline. They had been serenaded by competing investment banks, which in some cases would have discussed valuations on listing of more than US$1 billion – and who had already arranged and completed the pre-IPO round of funding at a high valuation. These companies were dropped like hot potatoes.

For those businesses that hadn't yet reached the IPO stage and needed more venture funding, and of course those that were preparing to raise their initial rounds of investment, the future was very bleak indeed.

This change in investment appetite had some very serious implications for entrepreneurs. The business models they were following were now suspect. For example, previously some of the most exciting technology being developed included those technologies that would involve potential customers making radical changes to the way they do business. However, in the new era this was increasingly seen as too risky and expensive, and customers became more interested in technology that would result in incremental cost savings or revenue increases. This led to the slashing of capital spending plans by large companies globally, which effectively took away the potential market for the products of these early stage technology businesses – or at least delayed the eventual sales take-up by at least 18 months. This put emerging businesses into a precarious cash situation. Because of the practice of raising only enough capital to get to the next funding round, many businesses scarcely had enough cash to last a few months – a year at most. In addition, businesses that had already progressed through a number of funding rounds were left with an unwieldy shareholding structure – often containing more than five different VC funds or other institutions. As discussed earlier, the shareholder agreements in place were often extremely complex in nature and still geared toward an exit at high valuations.

In summary, this was a period of time when the world stood still for many entrepreneurs. There was also a growing realization that the future would be bleak, and that some form of return to the bubble days was unlikely, at least in the medium term.

Post-bubble: The current era

Both VC funds and investee companies emerged from the inertia of the last quarter of 2001 with a set of serious and life-threatening issues which led to the need for short-termism – or, in more dramatic terms, the need to do some firefighting. Many investors, including VC funds, angel investors, and other institutions, sought to reduce their exposure and cash outflow commitments in 2001/02. This had a knock-on effect on many investee companies who were already struggling themselves. One factor determined who failed and who lived to fight on, and that was access to cash. This became a most precious commodity post-bubble, and the response of both investors and entrepreneurs was built around strategies for managing it. This stark experience has had a profound effect on the approach of many investors to funding early-stage businesses.

Currently, the majority of VC funds show a preference for later-stage funding – that is, investing in businesses where the business model is already proven and the business has passed through cash break-even. This means that it can survive and pay its running costs on the basis of its current revenue stream. In this way, VC funds can ensure that the business already has a tried and trusted product and paying customers, and that the money they invest will go toward growing the business rather than developing the product. The potential returns are, of course, lower than investing at an earlier stage, but the risk profile is also much lower. In India, for example, over 80% of VC investment in 2003 was in profitable companies, rather than start-ups. A recent[1] survey of 190 VC companies in China revealed that 73% preferred to invest in later-stage projects.

This sets the scene for the current era of early-stage investing. VC funds now operate with a much higher-quality barrier, resulting in only the start-up or early-stage opportunities with the best potential receiving formal investments. Many of the funds take an even more cautious approach and prefer to concentrate on the later-stage funding where many of the product, implementation, and customer development risks have been successfully dealt with. Thankfully, for entrepreneurs, VC funds are not the only source of early-stage capital available. We will now take a closer look at the current availability of VC funds for early-stage businesses in Asia and the growing importance of more informal sources of capital.

FORMAL VENTURE CAPITAL

Investment by VC funds and other regulated institutions is termed *formal* venture capital. There are over 1,500 funds operating in Asia with currently some US$90 billion under management. This sounds excellent news for entrepreneurs looking to raise money for their ventures; however, despite the huge amount of money available for early-stage investing, we need to look at the figures more closely to see how much actually makes its way to early-stage entrepreneurs.

The number of VC funds in Asia has shown continuous growth over the last few years, from some 900 recorded in 1998 (see Figure 5.7). Most of the growth over this period has come from China (including Hong Kong), where the number of VC funds and companies has grown from 129 in 1998 to 420 by 2003. Other countries showing significant growth include Singapore, India, and Malaysia, where numbers have roughly doubled over the same period to 119, 81, and 44, respectively. It is interesting to note, however, that although the number of VC funds and companies has increased by 70%, the number of estimated VC professionals has only grown by 17%, to 5,162. This may be a reflection of the trend toward larger and fewer transactions. The number of investments made has fallen from a peak of 12,300 in 2000, implying that these outfits are tending to be more lean in terms of manpower.

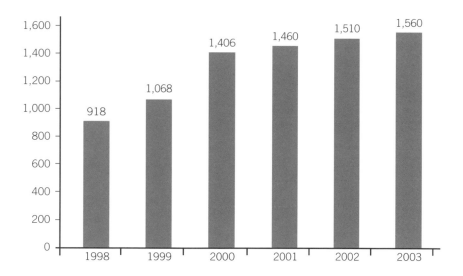

Source: Asia Venture Capital Journal statistics

Figure 5.7 Number of Venture Capital Funds and Companies in Asia

In terms of actual VC investment in Asia-Pacific over the same period, there was a steady growth from 1998 to a peak of US$12.3 billion in 2000. The burst of the tech bubble along with the world recession reversed this trend, and it took until 2003 to recover. Figure 5.8 tracks the formal investments made in Asia-Pacific between 1998 and 2003 and illustrates clearly the changes in investing sentiment over the period.

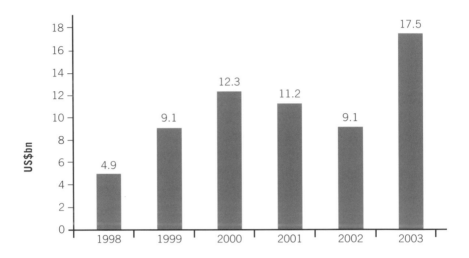

Source: Asia Venture Capital Journal statistics

Figure 5.8 Formal Investments Made in Asia-Pacific, 1998–2003

The next filter is: how much of the funds invested actually find their way to start-up or early-stage companies? Figure 5.9 compares the amount invested in Asia in this respect with that invested in the US and Europe. It also looks at investment in start-up and early-stage opportunities as a percentage of total investment. First, the amount invested in these stages in Asia is pitifully small. However, more disturbing is that investment in early-stage businesses is declining in proportion to overall VC investment. The huge increase in investment in Asia in 2003 (see Figure 5.8) is clearly not being driven by increased spending on young companies. Instead, it reflects the significant growth in investment in later-stage opportunities – management buyouts, in particular.

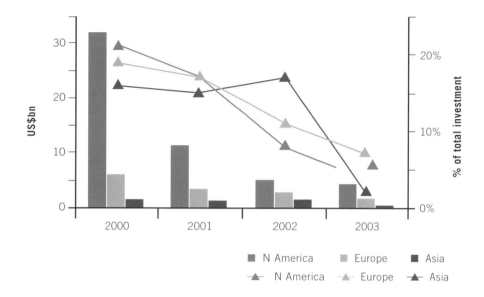

Sources: PriceWaterhouseCooopers/3i Global Private Equity Reports, 2003–04; Asia Venture Capital Journal statistics

Figure 5.9 Formal Investment in Start-up and Early-stage Businesses, 2000–03

INFORMAL VENTURE CAPITAL

Investment by individuals such as family, friends, and business angels is referred to as *informal* venture capital. For the seed phase of start-ups in Asia, the bulk of the initial funds are generally provided either by the entrepreneurs themselves or by immediate family and friends. The case study in Chapter 4 (MeritTrac) is a good example of this. We can tend to underestimate the quantity of capital from these sources, as much of it is contributed in kind. For example, in the case of MeritTrac, the founders left well-paid employment and worked for a considerable length of time on little or no wages. Again, in the rescue phase, the management team forfeited their salary for a short time to keep the business afloat. This contribution has a real value to the business and can often be underestimated when comparing this source of capital with others in terms of overall amount.

Figure 5.10 charts the prevalence rate of informal venture capital – that is, the number of adults who have invested in someone else's business during the last three years (not including listed stocks) – against the importance of informal investing in a country. The importance of the informal VC market is measured in terms of total investment as a proportion of GDP. In the United States, it is fairly normal for people to invest in this informal-type manner; however, the amount is fairly negligible in relation to the total US GDP. In Asia, we can see that the informal market is both normal and relatively more important in North Asia – China, South Korea, and Taiwan. On the other hand, India's informal investment market has been fairly insignificant both in terms of prevalence and importance.

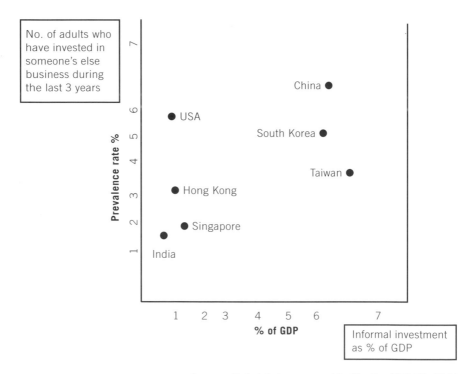

Source: Global Entrepreneurship Monitor (GEMS), 2004.

Figure 5.10 Informal Investor Prevalence Rate and Importance of Informal Investing as a Percentage of Country GDP

Looking on a global scale, the presence of informal venture capital is crucial to the provision of capital to start-up and early-stage businesses, whereas formal venture capital is provided only to businesses with very high growth potential. The *Global Entrepreneurship Monitor* (GEMS) 2004 report notes that only 37 in every 100,000 companies received formal venture capital. Moreover, less than 30% of those receiving formal venture capital were seed-stage businesses.

To illustrate the point, GEMS very usefully applies these latest statistics to Kirchhoff's Innovation Model, which is reproduced in Figure 5.11. According to these figures, informal investment funded 99.96% of all companies and provided 91.8% of the total amount of funding. Without the informal VC market, the number of new ventures would be very small indeed. Hence, it is extremely important for entrepreneurship in Asia that informal investment is both nurtured and encouraged. One way of encouraging individual investment in start-up companies is to provide tax breaks. In 2004, Singapore introduced an Enterprise Investment Initiative, which allows investors in start-ups to net off investment losses against their taxable income. This type of scheme can help to reduce the relatively high downside risk of this type of investing. However, one of the biggest impediments to developing the informal investing community is match-making. Business angels on the whole prefer to invest in a business area where they have some knowledge or experience, and therefore matching up the right investors with the right business opportunities can be a real challenge.

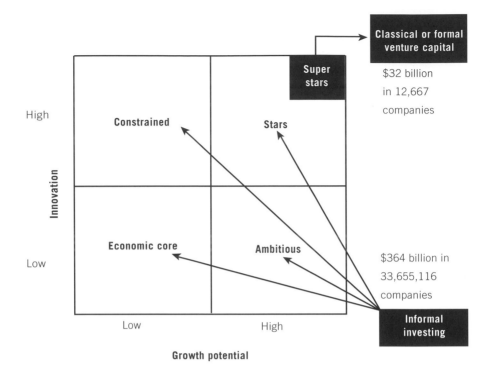

Sources: Global Entrepreneurship Monitor (GEMS), 2004; Bruce Kirchhoff, Entrepreneurship and Dynamic Capitalism: The Economics of Business Firm Formation and Growth (Prager, 1994).

Figure 5.11 Companies Classified by Innovation and Growth and Financial Support

Kirchhoff's Growth Innovation Model

This model categorizes new businesses in terms of level of innovation and growth potential. An example of a low-innovation/low-growth potential may be the setting up of a single retail outlet such as a restaurant or a "Mom & Pop" shop. This will introduce little new innovation and will also have little chance for growth beyond its current size. These are also sometimes called subsistence businesses. A low-innovation/high-growth potential business (bottom right) could be an entrepreneur planning not to set up one restaurant, but a chain of themed restaurants. A highly innovative business with low growth potential could be a business developing a very specialized type of testing equipment for use in research laboratories – that is, with a limited end-user market. The stars which have high innovative content and a high growth potential are technology businesses that have a large market opportunity – for example, a business developing software which facilitates the secure electronic transmission of original documents such as contracts or theater and cinema tickets. All these areas receive investments from informal venture capital sources; however, only those superstars that are very highly innovative and have extremely high growth potential are likely to receive funds from formal venture capital.

INVESTOR STYLES

Investor style can have a major effect on many aspects of the investment process, from the structure used, to negotiation style, and also the type of involvement post-investment. Figure 5.3 earlier in this chapter shows in a simple form that investors are structured in different ways. For example, individuals (such as business angels) have only a one-to-one relationship to consider – although, in practice, they may have their own "internal process" that may include gaining the approval of their spouse. But, in general, the process is more personal, and entrepreneurs deal directly with the decision-maker. On the other hand, a VC fund has to answer to its investors who expect certain guidelines and procedures to be followed, and this will have an effect on process, structure, and so on.

Governments in Asia have their own programs to stimulate entrepreneurship and can choose a variety of routes. One of the most popular routes, and one used extensively since around 1998 in Singapore, Malaysia, and New Zealand, is to invest into VC funds alongside private money. Most recently, Malaysia is starting to put resources into backing promising young companies. It uses local private VC funds as "outsource partners" and in 2003 provided some US$6 million in seed funding. While this may not seem much, it shows an increasing trend with more expected going forward. Some governments supplement this by also directly investing in companies – but typically alongside or matching private-based lead investors.

Understanding the make-up of the various types of investors in terms of style, motivation, process, and constraints is an important step to take before approaching potential partners and entering into negotiations with them. When acquiring potential customers, entrepreneurs are usually focused on who they target, checking first that the customer has an interest at least in the product offering. It not only saves time, but also reputation. VC funds are more impressed at the outset when a proposal is received where management have done their homework – even a small amount – beforehand.

In a similar way, entrepreneurs can be very savvy when dealing with customers and suppliers and will negotiate with real skill to win extra margins or concessions on even the smallest contracts. It is thus surprising how many of them enter into negotiations with potential investors often from a position of relative blindness. For many management teams and entrepreneurs, raising money is a new experience, but they can be surprisingly ready to negotiate on points about which they have relatively little understanding. These points of negotiation may not only determine the future running of their business, but also how the final upside is shared. Each 1% of equity, for example, can have the potential to be worth millions – but can often be negotiated away in an instant. Knowing your opponent (this may sound confrontational, but you will be on opposite sides of the negotiating table until potential investors become shareholders) is an essential prerequisite before entering into any serious discussions. To this end, we will now take a look at each of the investor types.

Founders, family, and friends

These are sometimes known as the "4Fs," with fools added to make up the fourth "F". Every start-up has some element of these, and together their importance to the generation of entrepreneurial businesses is crucial. With the exception of the founders, the amounts invested tend to be small and are motivated by a wish to support a family member or friend rather than by commercial considerations. To this extent, the "4Fs" are easy investors – they have little experience of the commercial issues to be considered when investing in a business or a requirement for due diligence. On the other hand, they are the conscience of the entrepreneur, who will want to make a good return for them for the sake of face, reputation, and personal relationships.

Business angels

Business angels are typically retired or semi-retired businessmen who, during the course of their endeavors, have become high-net-worth individuals. Their motivation as individuals can be varied, and it is worth understanding what makes them tick at a very early stage of meeting. Some are relatively passive and just want to place money in alternative investment vehicles. In Asia, these individuals often work closely with one or two advisor-boutiques who source and review deals and may also take an active involvement in the investment on their behalf – taking a success fee on entry and sometimes exit, as well as a retainer fee. Another type may have worked in, or managed, large businesses in the latter part of their career and long for a return to the excitement of being involved with a new and entrepreneurial business. A third type comes from a similar background but is very focused on the type of opportunities they look for, negotiate very hard, and are very hands-on in terms of influencing decision-making, and so on. All have their merits and disadvantages, depending on what type of partner an entrepreneur is seeking.

One of the most difficult challenges in raising angel financing is match-making – that is, matching the appropriate investment to the interested business angel. In the US and Europe, angels have tried to improve the efficiency of this process by forming angel networks. Some of these are highly organized, such as the European Business Angels Network (EBAN) or the International Angel Investment Institute (IAII). These are non-profit-making networks which have a range of activities including training for new angel investors, access to documentation, lobbying governments for changes to laws or taxation regulations which would make investing easier or more attractive, and most importantly, organizing match-making events between entrepreneurs and their members. Business angels in Asia often tend to be more anonymous and discrete – some successful Asian businessmen have been concerned that their reputation may be harmed if a start-up company fails or if they recommend such an investment to another investor or friend. However, some networks and contact-sharing are starting to develop. BANSEA (Business Angel Network South East Asia[2]) is one such organization which offers match-making and promotion events. It is encouraging to see that they are not only looking for high-growth technology businesses, but see the value in investing in attractive non-technology businesses. A recent match-making event in Bangkok included the businesses listed in Table 5.2.

Table 5.2 Types of Businesses at an Angels Match-making Event

BANSEA match-making event
Franchisor of hydraulic industrial products
Producer and distributor of preserved fruits and vegetables
Producer and distributor of wood furniture
Producer of foam from cornflour
Producer and developer of cosmetics products
Developer of e-learning solutions
Franchisor of delivery services for documents and packages

The Palo Alto, California-based IAII[3] is encouraging the formation of chapters outside the US, and has already established chapters in Hong Kong, Singapore, South Korea, and Japan. New chapters are also being formed in Bangalore, Beijing, Guangzhou, Mumbai, Shanghai, Pakistan, and Taiwan.

In Singapore, the government sponsors a network called the Dealflow Connection,[4] where entrepreneurs can match up with investors as well as understand the type of assistance available from the plethora of government assistance schemes.

Business angels have also been known to hunt in packs, and there are a number of networks existent in Asia where this is the case. In this situation, angels still invest their own money, but can also bring in other investors. This helps to spread their risk and pool their experience. However, they will still tend to make their investment decisions on an individual basis.

The main motivation for business angels is making high capital gains. Typically, they invest at an early stage of business creation when the business valuation is very low. Hopefully, over time, the business develops and may attract new investors at a higher valuation before eventually achieving a public listing or being sold to a trade buyer. At this time, the angels can sell their shares and make an attractive capital gain. As a rule of thumb, business angels look to make five to 10 times their investment. If the business already has a revenue stream at the point of investing, the expected return would be nearer the lower part of this bracket.

It is important to remember that business angels are individuals and therefore are generally constrained in two areas: the funds they have available, and the resources they can provide. Investment amounts tend to be relatively small and typically range from US$50,000 to US$200,000. This is a function of the portion of their own capital that they have decided to allocate to this "alternative" investing, but also reflects their own desire to diversify risk and create a small portfolio. In resource terms, angels are constrained, like any other individual, by there being only 24 hours in a day and competing priorities for their time. Some angels – particularly the more passive kind – get around this by sub-contracting out to small advisor boutiques or other individuals.

Pros and cons of angel investors

Process. Because angels make their own decisions, this can potentially mean that the process is quicker. Additionally, the due diligence process can be relatively short, and this will normally be carried out by the angels themselves over a few visits and meetings. However, this doesn't mean they aren't picky. As they are investing their own money, their risk profile tends to be quite low. By this, we mean they will be looking to cherry-pick projects at low entry valuations. The competition for their time and money may include a wide range of possible personal investment options – including property, for example.

Involvement post-investment. The best angels can be an asset to the business in terms of bringing their significant experience of running and building businesses to the investee company. With their own money invested, it provides a real incentive for them to help the business in any way they can, from providing advice, networking, dealing with various issues, and so on. The less desirable type is a worrier. They are extremely anxious about what is happening to their money and can take up precious management time in the process.

A difficult – and often explosive – situation can occur sometimes when a business ends up with more than one entrepreneur running it. If an angel investor sees the investment as their opportunity to realize a dream of running an entrepreneurial business, then the entrepreneur may be in for trouble.

In any event, it is well worth management teams doing their homework on any prospective angel investor before proceeding. If the need for cash means you are prepared to take all types, then at least agree ground rules at the outset concerning what the involvement will be. In this, you would include timing of updates, visits to the business, what facilities will be available to the angel, and so on.

Change in personal situation. This, unfortunately, is the key drawback of angel investors, as highlighted in the example of MeritTrac in the case study in Chapter 4. A turn for the worse in the angel investor's personal financial health led to him not being able to put in the full amount to which he had initially committed. Instead of the full US$200,000, only US$70,000 was eventually drawn down – and this was despite MeritTrac meeting all the drawdown milestones in terms of performance and developing the business. This withdrawal of committed funds nearly killed the business and led to management needing to take drastic measures to keep it afloat.

Another example may be that the angel needs to sell their shares quickly to resolve a personal issue. This could put the business in difficulty, particularly if management are not able to buy the shares and the angel is permitted to sell them to a third party. Management may be saddled with a new investor who may or may not be suitable as a partner. It is worth clarifying the process for such instances in the shareholders' agreement – and certainly there should be a stiff penalty for withdrawal of commitment without acceptable cause.

An acceptable cause might be failure of the business to meet certain milestones that were a pre-condition to drawdown.

> *... angel investors have a key and real role in providing capital and experience to businesses at seed and other early funding rounds.*

In summary, angel investors have a key and real role in providing capital and experience to businesses at seed and other early funding rounds. This is particularly true in Asia, where VC funds have mostly vacated this space since 2001 and prefer to invest when the business model has been proven, has real customers, and a growing cash flow. In some ways, this has given angels more room in which to operate – that is, they can work in a less competitive environment. In terms of non-tech-related start-ups, the lack of available funds is even more acute.

Venture capital funds

Venture capital funds are essentially companies that manage cash with the aim of making an attractive return on behalf of third-party investors. Figure 5.12 depicts a typical structure. Key parties in a VC fund are limited partners and investment managers.

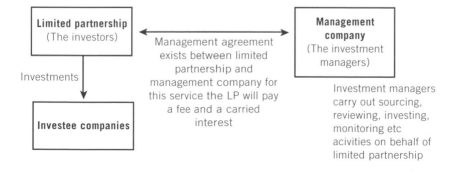

Figure 5.12 Typical VC Fund Structure

Limited partners. These are the investors in the fund and may consist of financial institutions, pension funds, individuals, governments, and so on. The limited partnership structure is used on the one hand to ensure that the fund is tax efficient, and on the other hand to limit the exposure of the investors. In this sense, the most they can lose is the amount invested.

Frequent investors in Asian VC funds are governments. For example, the Singapore and Malaysian governments have become limited partners in local funds with the key objective of stimulating the growth of VC funds and also to use private means to invest public cash. Overall, VC funds in Asia have attracted a wide range of investing institutions from Asia, the US, and Europe.

Investment managers. These are the full-time professionals who manage the fund in all respects. They are the face of the fund and handle all aspects of interface with investee companies and other third parties. Their principal tasks include sourcing and reviewing opportunities, carrying out due diligence and completing those which meet their criteria, managing the investment portfolio, and finding ways to return cash with an attractive capital gain to the limited partners.

As described above, VC funds typically invest money that has been provided by global pension funds, individuals, companies, and governments. To understand how they make their money, we need to look at this in the context of both the limited partners (the investors) and the fund or investment managers. The investors make money in one simple dimension. They commit money to a venture fund to be invested over a number of years – usually up to five. They then expect to receive more than this amount back over a longer period – usually a further five years. Their capital gain is the amount returned minus the amount invested. The return on their capital will depend not only on the amount returned but also on how long it was invested.

The fund/investment managers are rewarded in two key ways. First, they will receive a management fee that will be a percentage of the full amount committed by investors to their fund. This has been as high as 3% over the last five to 10 years in Asia, although investors have brought this down to levels nearer 2% in recent years. This fee is used to cover the overhead costs of the fund, including office expenses, travel, salaries of fund managers, and so on. There has been much debate between the major investors and VC firms about the level of this fee. If it is too high, then the fund manager can live a comfortable life on this fee alone without trying too hard.

The second method of rewarding the fund manager is designed to align the fund manager's objectives with those of the investor – that is, to maximize capital gain. The method used is called the fund carried interest. The fund carried interest or "carry" is a mechanism where the limited partners agree to give the managers a percentage of their total capital return – or, in other words, a percentage of any money that is made over and above their initial investment amount. Of course, the investors will add a hurdle rate of return that must be met before this will be triggered, but nonetheless, this can be a large amount of money. This is demonstrated in the box below.

Example: VC fund: Calculation of carried interest

Total cash invested:	$100 million
Carry:	20% of capital gain
Total cash returned:	$200 million
Capital gain:	= $200 million – $100 million
	= $100 million
Carry:	= 20% * $100 million
	= $20 million

This is a serious amount of cash and a big incentive for the fund managers to maximize gains for the investors. As mentioned above, there is also a hurdle rate of return to meet before the "carry" is authorized. This can be set in a quite a broad range, depending on the perception of the risk environment, the market rate of risk-free return, and so on. Levels of 8–12% are typical.

The main constraints of VC funds are usually fairly transparent and determined by fund size, fund life, and fund focus.

Fund size. This has an effect on two key areas. First, the size of the fund will directly impact the amount it will invest in any one business. Normally, a fund will want to invest on average 5–15% of the total fund size in any one investment. The lower limit is important, mainly for the reason of efficiency. In venture capital, the effort taken to complete and manage a small investment is typically as much as for a larger business. Completing 100 investments of $1 million over the course of three to five years would be a mammoth task – quite apart from the task of managing them all and looking for suitable exits. Some funds in Asia have actually adopted this as a strategy. In the late 1990s, several funds embarked on an approach of investing small amounts in large numbers of proposals. With the hype surrounding technology investments at the time, they believed that although many would fail there would at least be a small number that had a good chance of being stars … or perhaps the next Microsoft.

The compromise for this type of volume investing is in the area of due diligence and involvement after the investment – it is more of a fire-and-forget approach, in the hope that you may hit the jackpot. This model hasn't been a big hit for long with fund investors, who are now very much looking for VC funds who have a focused approach, global standards of due diligence, and credible post-investment track records.

Second, the size of the fund has a direct impact on the size of the management fee. If this is set at 2%, for example, then the management fee will be $2 million annually for a $100 million fund and $400,000 for a $20 million fund. The implication of this is that the size of the management fee constrains the number and quality of the executives whom the manager can hire to invest the money and manage the portfolio.

Fund life. A fund life is typically seven to 10 years. This means that the investors, or limited partners, have indicated they would like their original investment plus capital gain back within this period. This means that most of the investments need to have been made within the first three to five years – to allow a suitable time for the opportunities for exits to develop, say by a sale of the business or an IPO. For a management team raising funds, it is worth understanding where the fund is currently in its life cycle. For example, if the fund is at the beginning of its life, the investment managers will clearly be very happy that they have managed to raise the funds, and will be keen to demonstrate to their investors that they are able to complete a few interesting investments in the first year.

On the other hand, if the VC fund is nearing the end of its investing period, which is usually three to five years after the start of the fund, then it may have a more relaxed take-it-or-leave-it approach but will be particularly focused on the prospect's abilities to provide an exit within a shorter time frame.

Fund focus. A fund's limited partnership agreement will state very clearly the boundaries of the fund in terms of sector, stage of business, financial instruments to be used, and geographical limit. This is particularly important to investors where specialist knowledge of certain sectors is seen as key if the fund managers are to have a strong probability of making an attractive return. For example, biotech is seen as a specialist area – assessment, structuring, and portfolio management of biotech investments needs a strong understanding of the sector. It is usual for these biotech VC funds to contain PhDs and/or practicing doctors and consultants in their teams.

Pros and cons of VC investors

Process. This can be seen as a major drawback by entrepreneurs, who perceive the process of engaging with VC funds as long and drawn out and involving much hard work on their own part. We need to remember first that VC funds have a much larger deal flow than informal investors, and that a new business plan is competing with many other demands on their time before a decision is taken. In addition, as VC funds invest other people's money, they have an extra level of accountability over that required by individual angel investors. This means that there needs to be formal decision-making processes with appropriate documentation, along with a suitable level of due diligence that may involve industry professionals, as well as lawyers and accountants. The legal documentation required is also more thorough and will take time to complete properly.

The positive side of the process with VC funds is that generally there is more certainty of receiving funds once a decision is taken. Business angels and other informal investors are prone to short-term changes of circumstance and position, like most individuals, and therefore until the money is in the bank there is much more uncertainty.

Involvement post-investment. For entrepreneurs who enjoy being left to run the operational side of the business, but welcome assistance with strategic issues, a VC fund can be an excellent partner. They not only have much experience of being investors – that is, they generally know when to leave the entrepreneur to get on with things and when to get involved – but also have experience of developing businesses all the way to an exit, either by trade sale or IPO. Perhaps one of the biggest perceived benefits of VC funds is their network and contacts. Entrepreneurs themselves often find it difficult to get access to much-needed contacts outside their own limited sphere, and an introduction by their VC partner can be extremely valuable. Many VC funds in Asia are able to offer international reach and either have strong links with or have offices in the US and Europe. For example, Walden International invests in all situations from start-up to pre-IPO and has offices in California, Singapore, Malaysia, China, Taiwan, Hong Kong, the Philippines, Japan, and India. The box below profiles an example of a smaller fund, iGlobe Partners Pte Ltd., which operates in the similar space to Walden and has offices in Frankfurt, California, Auckland, and Singapore. In terms of technology investing, this type of international network is important both in helping the VC fund to assess the proposal and assisting the business after completion.

> **For entrepreneurs who enjoy being left to run the operational side of the business, but welcome assistance with strategic issues, a VC fund can be an excellent partner.**

Example of a VC fund: iGlobe Capital Partners

iGlobe Capital Partners [is] a fund that operates on a global basis, with a team of partners in North America, Europe, and Asia working together to help young companies become global market leaders. Our global scope provides an exceptional edge. We evaluate investment opportunities on international "best of breed" criteria. And we facilitate the worldwide expansion of portfolio companies through our substantial knowledge of the major world regions in which we operate and our far-reaching network of investors, industry experts, and other advisors. Our strategy is to invest in technology-driven companies that are led by passionate management and have globally scaleable business models. We focus on the IT arena, with particular interest in the telecommunications, storage, multimedia, semiconductor, and enterprise markets.

Source: www.iglobepartners.com.

Corporate investors

Corporate investing is prevalent in Asia and comes in two forms: corporate venture capital (CVC) and direct strategic investing. The difference between the two is related to the investor's individual objective for the investment. In its pure sense, CVC was a move by technology-based large corporates to take advantage of the potentially attractive returns from investing in young and fast-growing technology businesses. In this sense, any possible strategic benefits to the main group from the investment are secondary to the objective of financial return. Of course, their targeted sectors tend to be those where the group has experience thus ensuring that the investment has the potential to bring future strategic benefits. The investment teams are relatively independent, but are able to use the benefits of the group to assist in areas such as due diligence and contacts. CVCs active in Asia include Acer, Hitachi, Intel (profiled in the box below), LG, Legend, Motorola, Nokia, Siemens, and Sumitomo.

Example of a corporate VC: Intel

Intel officially formed a venture program in the early 1990s, as a way to help ensure our own ability to deliver products to our customers. We invested in a few companies whose products and services helped fill the gap in our own product line, capabilities, and capacity. But our plans soon grew beyond that goal. Intel had long been articulating the vision of how the industry could grow to attract new users and open up new uses for connected PCs. Now we began to back up that vision with financial commitments to innovative companies. We invested in a range of internet companies creating exciting new content and capabilities. Included are firms working to deliver more bandwidth to users and start-ups helping to bring new industries online. Intel Capital's investment criteria blend strategic focus with financial discipline, seeking companies that can succeed and have a meaningful impact on their market segment. Intel Capital typically invests in private companies alongside high-quality co-investors to help these companies grow from initial stages to successful IPOs or acquisitions. About 40% of Intel Capital's new deals in 2003 were in early-stage companies. Intel Capital continually reviews market conditions for opportunities to sell all or part of its investments. Intel Capital may decrease its investments in some companies to recoup Intel's capital for use in making new investments. It is critical that Intel Capital's decision to invest in a company satisfy a strategic goal. However, selling is done as part of prudent management of a large portfolio and strategic activities may continue with the company following a stock sale.

Source: www.intel.com/capital.

Professional CVCs such as Intel generally operate very much as conventional VC funds and are often welcomed as co-investors in opportunities which have other VC funds as investors. In the same way, they are happy to use similar investment documentation to emphasize their financial, rather than strategic, focus.

The other type of corporate investor is the pure strategic investor. This is where companies invest directly in other businesses that they believe have, or will have, a strategic value. This type of investment has been commonplace in Asia for many years. The *keiretsu* system in Japan and the *chaebol* structures in South Korea have been held together for decades by an intricate web of "strategic" investments both in terms of vertical and horizontal integration.

Many of these are customer or supplier relationships cemented by a shareholding relationship. While this kind of investment can be helpful in the short term, there can be long-term downsides in terms of flexibility once the relationship has run its course. A recent visit to an SME in the utilities sector in Southeast Asia revealed quite an interesting shareholding structure that included a Japanese equipment supplier as a large minority shareholder. When the business started up in the early 1990s, it was assisted by favorable terms from the equipment manufacturer in return for a shareholding. Today, the business needs to raise money to develop, but finds itself having to accommodate a shareholder that is slow in decision-making and long ago lost its strategic interest in the business. What is more, the business continues to be tied into buying technology that is no longer the best in the market.

Governments

As mentioned earlier in the chapter, governments can invest either directly or indirectly in businesses. When investing indirectly – that is, through a VC fund, for example – they will delegate responsibility to the fund in the same way as the fund's other investors. When investing directly, government money tends to follow or match private money, and therefore can be fairly passive. However, in the case of investors such as Singapore's Economic Development Board, the assistance and contacts they can bring can be invaluable to the investee companies.

▶▶ CONCLUSION

While the venture capital industry in Asia has grown considerably over the last few years, and has quite an immense pool of funds available for investment, not a lot of this is finding its way to early-stage businesses. One of the most frequent questions asked of VC investors concerns the proportion of proposals that are successful in getting funding. A much-used VC industry statistic states that out of 1,000 proposals, up to 100 may get first meetings, and 10 may receive offers of investment – in other words, a 1% success rate overall. Perhaps the most startling statistic of all is that some 80–90% of the proposals that are rejected are rejected in a very short space of time indeed – often as quickly as in the first five to 10 minutes. This is based on a private VC fund, which works on international benchmarks in terms of quality and due diligence and has maximizing return as the over-riding motive. Some government-influenced funds may have multiple objectives and may encourage a more aggressive approach to investing in a particular sector or business stage. MAVCAP, a government-owned VC firm in Malaysia, recorded a success rate of 8.6% in 2003 of seed companies receiving funding from a pool of 140 proposals reviewed. The lucky 10% of businesses getting a first meeting still need to be among the super stars depicted earlier in Figure 5.11. A large part of Asia's future growth will be dictated by the significant numbers of entrepreneurs operating outside this small segment, and for them it is anticipated that the main source of funding will continue for the moment to be the informal investment community.

ENDNOTES

[1] China VC Research Institute (CVCRI) Survey Report, 2004.

[2] www.bansea.org.

[3] www.angelinvestors.org.

[4] www.dealflow.org.sg.

The Check is in the Post: Managing Cash

*E*ntrepreneurial companies share a common need for cash. They may need cash with which to buy physical assets (organic growth), or perhaps to acquire other businesses (acquisitive growth). However, quite apart from needing the cash to grow the size of the business, they also need cash to sustain the increasing level of business activity this brings. This latter need for cash is better known as "working capital." The management of working capital remains a challenge for entrepreneurs worldwide – some manage it well, while others struggle to control it. Asia has its fair share of both types; however, in this chapter we look at some of the issues in Asia that may make managing cash even more challenging – these issues have a combination of many roots, including cultural, structural, and economic factors. In addition, we will look at some of the ways in which entrepreneurs in Asia are attempting to meet the cash management challenge. Finally, we will look at an area that is becoming increasingly important for ambitious and cash-hungry Asian businesses – that is, developing the role, skills, and experience of the financial officer.

INTRODUCTION

The importance of working capital often becomes apparent to entrepreneurs through bitter experience, rather than intuition. For young and growing businesses, the euphoria of getting to the stage of "sales take-off" and consistent month-on-month profitability can often deflect attention from what is happening to cash. The MeritTrac case study in Chapter 4 highlights this particular point. Entrepreneurs need to focus on ensuring that there is adequate working capital to support the growth of their businesses, because it is the existence of cash – *and not profits* – that determines short-term survivability.

Many young entrepreneurs the world over make the fatal mistake of equating cash with profitability. We have particularly seen this in Asia, where business plans submitted to investors frequently give little airtime to the cash dynamics of their business. Those that do mention cash often simply add a cash flow line to the annual profit and loss projections. Others may go as far as including a stand-alone cash projection, but again this may only be on an annual basis. As seasoned businesspeople know to their cost, the theoretical cash position at the end of the financial year can bear little relationship to the peaks and troughs of cash experienced during the year. Unfortunately, it is the unforeseen troughs in cash flow that are often the cause of business difficulties, rather than lack of profitability over the year.

Hence a growing company can be profitable but at the same time have a negative cash flow at least in the short term. Unless it plans to manage this cash flow, then the business can fail.

The divergence in the relationship between profit and cash can be present in all situations where a company is embarking on significant sales growth. If the *rate* of growth is also increasing, then the cash hole may be more pronounced.

Each business has its own cash flow dynamics, depending on its business model and the normal payment patterns in its sector. For example, a supermarket can be expected to have good cash flow as its many customers generally pay in cash or near cash – such as credit cards – but their suppliers may be paid in arrears. This creates a positive working capital profile. On the other hand, a construction business can be the opposite: its customers may pay only in stage payments related to their satisfaction with the completion of the building, whereas the suppliers of building materials may want 30 days' payment – or even cash on delivery where the reputation and standing of the construction business isn't strong. This creates a negative working capital profile, particularly if the project is a large one.

> " A growing company can be profitable but at the same time have a negative cash flow. Unless it plans to manage this cash flow, then the business can fail. "

We can see that managing the inflows and outflows of cash is a challenging task for inexperienced entrepreneurs. We might expect however that large companies with their comprehensive management systems, highly qualified chief financial officers (CFOs), and relatively stronger market positions may be able to fare somewhat better. A recent study of European corporates highlighted that even businesses operating in mature banking and settlement infrastructures struggle to manage their cash efficiently.[1] At the heart of managing cash is the ability to forecast cash flows – the repayment of a loan, for example, with excess cash isn't clever if the following week there is a large cash outflow requirement to pay creditors. The study highlighted the startling fall in predictability of cash flows over time (see Figure 6.1).

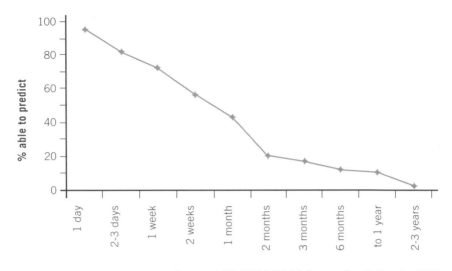

Source: ABN AMRO/BRDC Survey, Fourth Quarter 2003.

Figure 6.1 Predictability of Cash Position over Time

Account receivables and timing of payments were two of the key factors highlighted by respondents that impacted their ability to predict cash flows. This in itself isn't surprising, as getting paid and paying your own bills is the basic cash flow conundrum. However, the fact that only 72% of the corporates surveyed can predict cash balances a week ahead in a modern economy is concerning and means that large amounts of cash must be tied up in the system and are therefore not available for other uses. To take this further, only 17% of respondents were able to predict cash requirements three months ahead and, in theory, only these can take advantage of a 90-day higher interest deposit account. Most others who have less ability to predict when they need the funds will have to leave their money on easy access, lower-interest deposits and suffer a lower interest rate. This is a situation that is relevant today to large corporates in Europe, which have relatively sophisticated financial infrastructures, both internal and external, to help them develop optimal cash flow management strategies.

If we move from this sophisticated environment to the world of SMEs in Asia, then we might expect the difficulties experienced in managing cash flows to be magnified several times. The jump to

SMEs in Asia isn't achieved by a simple extrapolation based on business size or financial infrastructure. There are many issues that contribute to the higher level of complexity relating to cash management in Asia and we will review these first.

Asian entrepreneurs have grown up in a very different environment to that of their Western counterparts. Some of the characteristics of this environment are discussed below.

Combination of a relationship-based business culture and a drive for sales

It is normal in SMEs for the founder to develop and run all the customer relationships. The *face* element of dealing CEO to CEO can be all-important in developing these relationships and securing ongoing sales. Unfortunately, the tasks of credit checking, enforcement of credit terms, and general payment collection are often secondary to the central objective of increasing sales. This has led to more relaxed credit collection policies and the lengthening of accounts payable.

Infrastructure issues

Asia has essentially been – and for the most part still is – a cash and check society. India is an excellent example. The Indian banking system is quite complex, with different types of banks catering to a variety of customers spread over a large geographical area. There are some 80 commercial banks, about 200 regional rural banks, and over 350 cooperative banks. This adds up to almost 36,000 banking centers and 1,000 clearinghouses all working on a mainly paper-based system. Cash collection in this environment can be quite daunting.

> China has a do-it-yourself culture when it comes to credit. They don't want to check [financial accounts]; they want to see the person and shake hands on the deal.
>
> MING SHEN, CHINA COUNTRY MANAGER, COFACE

Regulatory issues

Cross-border trade is a way of life for thousands of SMEs in Asia. Apart from the normal cultural difficulties this may bring, entrepreneurs face a matrix of regulatory (such as currency controls) and tax considerations, depending on which country or countries they are dealing with (see Table 6.1).

Table 6.1 Relative Levels of Regulation in Asia

Regulation level	Countries
Less	Hong Kong, Japan, Singapore
Medium	Indonesia, Philippines, South Korea, Taiwan, Thailand
More	China, India, Malaysia, Pakistan, Sri Lanka, Vietnam

Large MNCs themselves find this difficult but, of course, can formulate optimum cross-border cash management strategies via their access to the best tax and legal advice, and by having sufficient critical mass to establish pools of cash or a network of non-resident bank accounts run from a central and less-regulated country such as Hong Kong or Singapore. Unfortunately, SMEs have to transact business the hard way and this can result in valuable cash being tied up for prolonged periods of time.

Legal protection

Many of us have heard stories in Asia where a customer has defaulted on a payment and has confidently challenged the creditor to take them to court. After a long and frustrating dialogue the debtor cheekily offers a derisory settlement – knowing that the business has a limited ability to enforce payment. The ability to enforce a contract is crucial for businesses to be able to interact with one another – particularly between countries. Asia hasn't had a strong reputation in this area. In countries within Asia, there are informal methods of sorting out contract issues in a fair way. These can be very efficient. For example, in Japan there has been a fairly widespread code of honor between owners of businesses that has historically been relied upon in these situations. This is fine where the business environment is such that those entering into a contract know that the counter-party will have the means to resolve an issue should one arise sometime in the future. However, the Asian crises and recent recession have weakened this area of comfort, in that businesses have defaulted on contracts and, although they may have the will to honor their commitments, may have lost the means to do it. The implication of this is not only that those outside the 'honor' systems, such as foreign businesses, but also more and more those previously within them now need to rely on the legal system to enforce contracts and resolve non-payment issues. There is, of course, a disparity in terms of efficiency, transparency, speed, and cost of enforcing contracts through the courts across countries. The World Bank's *Doing Business 2005* report contains for the first time an indication of the ability to enforce contracts across countries. It measures three key areas: the number of procedures involved, the time in days it takes until the payment is enforced, and the associated cost in terms of the overall debt itself. Table 6.2 shows the findings of the report in respect of some Asian countries. OECD average and US figures are included as reference points.

Table 6.2 Ability to Enforce Contracts

	Number of procedures	Time (days)	Cost (% of debt)
Cambodia	31	401	121.3
China	25	241	25.5
Hong Kong	16	211	12.9
India	40	425	43.1
Indonesia	34	570	126.5
Japan	16	60	8.6
Republic of Korea	29	75	5.4
Malaysia	31	300	20.2
OECD average	19	229	10.8
Pakistan	46	395	35.2
Philippines	25	380	50.7
Singapore	23	69	9.0
Sri Lanka	17	440	21.3
Taiwan	22	210	7.7
Thailand	26	390	13.4
United States	17	250	7.5
Vietnam	37	404	30.1

Source: World Bank, Doing Business 2005.

We can see from this table that Hong Kong, Japan, South Korea, Singapore, and Taiwan provide a very acceptable environment in terms of being able to enforce contracts. The cost in terms of fees – including court fees, attorney fees, assessors' fees, and so on – can be excessive in some countries and a real deterrent to entering an enforcement process. In the case of Indonesia and Cambodia, you may end up spending more than the amount of the debt you are owed if you try to recover it. Even at lower cost levels, the fees involved may be seen as prohibitive. The potential cost of claiming may also be seen as a basis of a discount that a business is willing to give to a debtor to settle out of court. Overall, with obvious exceptions, Asia as a region has a poor track record in contract enforcement and this ability in terms of complexity, cost, and time needs to be improved to build the confidence needed to facilitate more open trade.

Plenty of collateral for banks to lend against

In general, SMEs' idea of cash management is to ask their bank for some extra facility to tide them over for a few days. This mentality has not traditionally been challenged by the banks. The key comfort for banks has been the ever-increasing collateral provided by hitherto upwardly mobile land and property values and ever-increasing accounts payable. In addition, lending to SMEs provides attractive margins relative to the very competitive area of servicing large corporates.

Boom mentality

Entrepreneurs as a group can tend to drive sales at the expense of sensible cash and credit management, but many believe that Asia breeds a particularly aggressive type of entrepreneur in this respect.

Lack of resources

The smallest department in many Asian SMEs is often the finance and credit collection department. This is a function both of the keenness of the founder to keep his business lean in terms of the "non-productive" employees and of the lack of importance generally attached to this function. The other implication of this is that SMEs don't really have enough managers of the right level and standing to deal with institutions such as banks when the business hits cash problems.

> " Asia seems to be a special case. The boom mentality encourages them to stimulate sales and allow terms to slip, when times are good. But companies in sectors hit by a temporary downturn get caught up in a competitive trap, spinning new sales to survive. "
>
> MICHAEL BRAME,
> REL CONSULTANCY, *CFO ASIA*,
> MARCH 2004

General credit risk in Asia

Asia has typically been seen as a questionable credit risk. Its reputation for poor corporate governance, lack of transparency and information, and unstable politics and economic growth has all served to increase the risk of not being paid. Of course, the risk is higher for SMEs given their size and relative lack of resources to pursue difficult clients. The diversity of culture, politics, economies, and regulatory environments in Asia does, however, show itself in the degree of this risk across countries. International credit agencies apply a methodology to produce real-time credit ratings for countries across the world for their clients. These are calculated on the basis of several indicators, including political factors, the risk of currency issues, the ability of a country to meet its commitments abroad, the risk of fluctuations in currency – in particular, the likelihood of sudden devaluations due to heavy capital flows, the robustness of the banking sector, economic cyclical risks, and the payment trends for transactions. The ratings of most Asian countries dipped during the recent recession/Middle East war/SARS crisis but have recovered during the course of 2003 and 2004. These credit ratings are continually updated. Table 6.3 shows the seven different rating levels and their definitions, together with the current (January 2005) rating applied to Asian countries.

Table 6.3 Coface Credit Ratings and Current Asian Ratings, as at January 2005

Rating	Description	Countries (Jan 2005)
A1	The steady political and economic environment has positive effects on an already good payment record of companies. Very weak default probability.	Japan, Hong Kong Singapore, Taiwan
A2	Default probability is still weak even in the case when one country's political and economic environment, or the payment record of companies is not as good as in A1-rated countries.	Malaysia, Thailand South Korea
A3	Adverse political or economic circumstances may lead to a worsening payment record that is already lower than the previous categories, although the probability of a payment default is still low.	China, India
A4	An already patchy payment record could be further worsened by a deteriorating political and economic environment. Nevertheless, the probability of a default is still acceptable.	Philippines (watch listed for possible move to B)

Table 6.3 (cont'd)

B	An unsteady polical and economic environment is likely to affect further an already poor payment record.	Indonesia, Vietnam, Sri Lanka, PNG
C	A very unsteady political and economic environment could deteriorate an already bad payment record.	Pakistan
D	The high risk profile of a country's economic and political environment will further worsen a generally very bad payment record.	Cambodia, Myanmar, North Korea

Source: www.cofacerating.com

The combination in Asia of the particular set of characteristics discussed above suggests that managing cash in Asia is going to be more difficult with the implication that a lot of cash will be tied up in non-productive activities. An annual survey by CFO Asia/REL, which reviews over 1,000 listed companies in Asia-Pacific, looks at this specifically. The figures for 2004 reveal the following, rather concerning, developments over the 2003 data:

- Days' working capital has ballooned from 42 days to 83 days on average. This means that it now takes Asian companies twice as long to convert their working capital to cash than it did 12 months previously.
- The amount of "opportunity money" doubled from US$23 billion to US$46 billion. Opportunity money is calculated as the extra cash a company would have available if it managed its working capital at a benchmark rate compared to an average for its peer group and its market.

These are quite startling figures, which indicate that vast amounts of money are currently tied up in the working capital process – the US$46 billion would require annual servicing of almost US$1 billion at an interest rate of only 2%. This represents profit lost to the businesses surveyed every year. Looking forward, there may be more serious implications, however, as Asian businesses expand to meet the high expected growth in their markets. At current cash-hungry working capital levels, the need for cash to facilitate future growth will make this a key and potentially lethal bottleneck going forward. Again, this survey related to Asian corporates, which we can expect are relatively more sophisticated in terms of cash management than SMEs. It isn't surprising, therefore, that our survey of Asian entrepreneurs and those connected with advising them highlighted *managing cash* as the most significant issue facing entrepreneurs in Asia at the present time.

Apart, then, from the specific Asian characteristics relating to cash management already discussed, there are new pressures that are forcing Asian entrepreneurs to focus on this area.

Asian crisis in 1997 followed by recession in 2001–03

The effect of these key events, accentuated by the impact of SARS in 2003, has been to change the general credit environment in which Asian businesses now operate. Perhaps the biggest wake-up call has been in the area of the traditional cosy business-to-business relationships of the past. These were relationships where payment collection took second place to preserving good relationships at all costs between the company owners. The realization by these same business owners that, in times of crisis or recession, healthy cash balances can be the difference between survival and failure has been a hard lesson for many. The fall in property values at this time has accentuated the point, as companies in cash crises have found that their traditional source of spare cash – the banks – were not only unwilling to lend against a reducing collateral position, but were actively trying to reduce existing facilities.

High growth rates

Looking at Asia as a whole, forecasters are telling us that growth rates are on the increase and that the slowdown that characterized the last few years is over. This growth is being spearheaded by the Indian and Chinese economies – where growth rates of some 8% or more are anticipated. Within this composite growth rate, the growth experienced by the SME sector is much higher.

The macro trends operating within this large picture include, for example, the transfer of manufacturing operations to Asia. In the past, this was driven by the transfer of relatively simple yet highly labor-intensive operations to low-cost areas. The current phase of growth continues to include this, but is also characterized by the movement of production to Asia to support the growing consumer demand *in* Asia for the end-product. This means that there are opportunities for businesses to carry out increasingly complicated and relatively less labor-intensive operations in Asia.

In summary, the growth rates forecast in Asia for the next decade or so are the sum of all the growth rates of the SMEs, which themselves make up over 90% of businesses in the region and contribute over 50% of output.[2] Because of their relatively small size, these SMEs will be growing faster than the composite rate and so the need for them to source and manage working capital will be crucial.

Move to open book accounting from letters of credit

There has been a trend over recent years to open book, unsecured-type transactions. In particular, large foreign companies don't want to have the extra cost of guarantees such as letters of credit (LCs) when dealing with Asian businesses. Instead, they are insisting on normal open account terms. This is having quite an effect on Asian SMEs of all sizes. LCs have traditionally been used as a form of security in Asia against which businesses can borrow money, rather than to cover the concern that a foreign customer might not pay. As soon as an LC has been received, an SME can go to the bank and use it as collateral to raise cash. The effect of moving to open book accounting has been that Asian SMEs now have to wait 60–90 days (depending on the payment terms) before they get their cash.

SOME SOLUTIONS TO WORKING CAPITAL ISSUES

Bank facilities

The commercial banks remain the first choice of entrepreneurs in terms of finding working capital solutions. This is fine for businesses that have room for growth under the umbrella of the collateral available to the banks. However, many businesses have already used this to fund capital assets, and banks will be reluctant to provide further facilities unless, for example, the business has healthy credit accounts, the owner has a healthy *private* account over which they can take some guarantee, the business has a further injection of equity, or perhaps the cash flows are stable and from a reliable customer. The reduction in the value of land and property in Asia over the last few years – and hence the reduction of security available to banks – has made it more difficult for businesses to access cash for working capital, and hence we have seen an increase in the use of products such as factoring.

Factoring

The use of factoring companies to finance working capital is starting to become more popular in Asia. Figure 6.2 shows the explosive growth of factoring, particularly in India and China, since 1998. This growth is expected to continue.

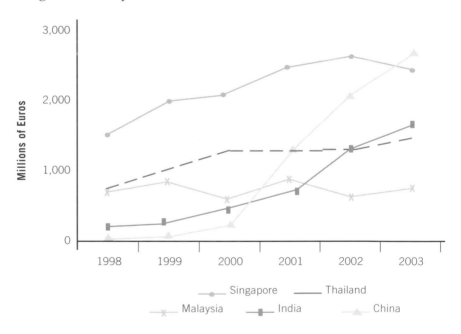

Source: Factors Chain International – a global network of factoring companies (www.factors-chain.com).

Figure 6.2 Factoring Growth in Asia, 1998–2003

Factoring is a process that uses the receivables, rather than real estate or other physical assets, as collateral. The business "sells" its customer invoices to the factoring company, which pays some 70–90% of the value of the invoices immediately in cash. The amount advanced typically depends on the level of risk in terms of potential default by the customers. The factoring company then releases the balance of the value once the customers have paid the bills. For this service, the factoring company will charge an interest and/or service fee to the business. This can release significant amounts of previously tied-up cash. This is no substitute for good customer credit management and doesn't solve the problem of payment default. Where it does help, though, is that with a factoring arrangement a business now has a large and

> "Our office in Amsterdam is overwhelmed with the number of inquiries from financial institutions wishing to diversify into factoring. Among them are some of the finest names in worldwide banking, although the interest seems to be the greatest from the side of the two super markets in Asia, China and India. It will take several more years for those countries to develop a sophisticated level of factoring expertise, but the movement is there."

JEROEN KOHNSTAMM,
SECRETARY GENERAL,
FACTORS CHAIN INTERNATIONAL, APRIL 2004

professional institution chasing the bad debts. It is a great system for a growing business that has large and relatively blue-chip customers – that is, customers with little payment risk but who may demand long payment terms. On the downside, there has been a general impression in Asia that factoring is a last resort method of sorting out cash issues – so a company "selling" its debtor book must be in some trouble – and it can bring a perceived loss of face. However, as the need to release cash tied up in working capital is becoming more widespread, this method of financing is becoming more accepted. The case study below illustrates how Kenmark Industrial Co. used factoring to fund its expansion into a new market.

Kenmark's expansion into Australia

Based in Taiwan, Kenmark Industrial Co., Ltd. is an international trading company specializing in the sale of hardware, tools, home furnishings, gardening accessories, electrical and electronic products, and general merchandise. The company is also a manufacturer of ready-to-assemble products, such as computer workstations, audiovisual and CD stereo cabinets, television cabinets, and game stations. Kenmark was a small-sized trading company when established in 1978, but now has production facilities based in Malaysia and marketing subsidiaries in Hong Kong, Malaysia, Singapore, Japan, Europe, New Zealand, Australia, the United States, and Canada.In 1992, Kenmark planned to take a big step by penetrating the home furnishings, gardening, and electronics markets in Australia. Coles Myer, the largest retailer in Australia, was very satisfied with Kenmark's quality products but required Kenmark to provide the logistics and after-sales service locally. "It was a great business opportunity, but also a big challenge to us," James Hwang, the chairman of Kenmark, recalls. "I needed to establish a subsidiary in Australia to fulfil my buyers' inventory requirements, distribution, and after-sales service. However, I also had to consider other issues before undertaking this expansion, such as how to obtain funding support, relieve the burden of debt collection, and manage the potential credit risks raised by trading on open account terms. In order to solve these problems, we contacted several Taiwanese banks and financial institutions for a solution," says Mr. Hwang. "We knew what we needed, but it was very difficult at that time to find a partner to fully satisfy our needs." Fortunately, after evaluating Kenmark's business model, Chailease Credit Services Co., Ltd., located in Taiwan, and Scottish Pacific Business Finance Pty. Ltd., in Australia, jointly provided a back-to-back factoring program to match Kenmark's needs. Under this program, Chailease arranged immediate funding on a with-recourse basis against Kenmark Taiwan's export sales to its subsidiary company in Australia. At the same time, Scottish Pacific provided the collection and risk coverage services of the subsidiary's local Australian sales. Kenmark is also now utilizing Chailease's export factoring service, which provides funding, credit protection, and collection of foreign invoices, for Kenmark's sales to Asia and Europe. By being able to offer open account terms at the request of its foreign buyers, Kenmark's Australian sales volume, which was A$2 million at the beginning of 1992, increased to A$20 million in 2002. According to Mr. Hwang, "The factoring service strengthened our working capital, helped us collect foreign accounts receivable, and freed us from the worry of any credit risk of approved buyers." Mr. Hwang concludes, "We're fully confident about the future, as we not only have excellent products and services, but the factoring program is also helping us to continually focus on improvement of sales and service quality, which will enable us to move ahead of our competitors."

Source: www.factors-chain.com

Countertrade

This is otherwise known as barter, and has been a method used by some businesses to open up new markets in circumstances where there are potential payment issues, poor credit records, or where the general legal and regulatory environment isn't conducive to open trading. The traditional idea of barter involves bilateral exchange of goods or services and has been used by MNCs as a means to open up developing markets. For example, General Motors has traded locomotives for tea in Sri Lanka, then sold the tea for cash to English tea dealers; and Coca-Cola has traded for everything from Korean toothpick frills to Bulgarian forklifts in order to penetrate foreign markets.[3] However, simple bilateral barter clearly has its limitations, particularly if you are an SME without the trading reach of MNCs such as these. To make it easier, barter or online countertrading exchanges have developed to facilitate this type of trade. Businesses wishing to participate may join as a member and then "buy" and "sell" a multitude of items using the exchange's "currency." Examples of exchanges in Asia include www.asiabarterzone.com, which focuses on Malaysia and uses Trade Ringgit Malaysia (TRM) as its cash substitute (equivalent to 1 cash Malaysian ringgit). Another is www.BarterAsia.com, based in Hong Kong, which supplies trade credits. Countertrade is growing in popularity as an effective method of keeping valuable cash resources out of the trading cycle. The International Monetary Fund (IMF) estimates that some 8% of total world trade is now carried out on a non-cash basis. The following box is a very useful illustration from BarterAsia's website, which describes a typical countertrade transaction.

BarterAsia.com

This illustration focuses on how an advertising agency could barter away their services in return for a variety of other goods and services. Alternatively, the advertising agency could be replaced with any other company that may be involved in, but not limited to, travel, media, technologies, food and beverages, textiles, and financial services. The possibilities are endless.

1. Our advertising agency member would provide a total of $150,000 worth of services to our hotel member.
2. BarterAsia would issue the ad agency with $150,000 worth of trade credits.
3. The advertising agency has the freedom to spend their trade credits with any one or more of our barter exchange members.
4. Rather than having to take the hotel's services as their entire compensation, the ad agency can spend $80,000 in trade credits to purchase computers from our computer company, and spend $70,000 in trade credits on our legal firm member to assist them in drafting legal documents.
5. The legal firm could then use their $70,000 in trade credits to purchase hotel rooms from our hotel member.
6. The computer company has the flexibility to use their $80,000 in trade credits in any one of the following ways:
   – Purchase services from the hotel.
   – Choose to save these credits for future use.
   – Spend them immediately with another member or members for other products or services.

Raising equity capital

Some businesses turn to using equity to fund working capital. However, it is generally a measure of last resort. We haven't met many entrepreneurs who would choose to use equity to finance working capital requirements if there are other less expensive options available. Indeed, from a financial planning perspective, using equity to fund this isn't a good "match." Bank overdrafts or factoring are appropriate ways of funding working capital, whereas equity should be used for higher-risk and higher-return projects such as rapid expansion situations or acquisitions. If we look at this from the point of view of potential investors, it is unlikely they will be attracted by a business that cannot manage its working capital or cannot raise standard working capital finance. They will see the need for cash as a symptom, rather than the cause, of the problem. The root cause is likely to be more serious and can involve management ability or sector issues, neither of which make an attractive investment proposition. We will be looking more closely at raising private and public equity for expansion in later chapters.

Credit insurance and credit histories

Businesses are increasingly using trade insurance as a means of cover for non-payment. According to Coface, the international credit insurer, Chinese authorities aim to increase the level of trade covered by credit insurance from less than 1% currently to 10% over the next 10 years. This compares with the current percentage of trade covered by trade insurance in Europe, which is almost 25%. Coface, along with other credit insurers, is expanding rapidly in Asia and together they are increasing the number of businesses for which ratings are maintained. Ordering financial and credit histories of clients costs money and, despite the overall improvement in credit information on businesses in Asia, the coverage is still thin. D&B, a global provider of company credit information (www.dnb.com), have expanded their China database from 40,000 businesses in 1999 to over 500,000 in 2004. Although this is a significant undertaking, the importance of credit information is understood by many Asian governments and there is a concerted effort to support the development of robust credit histories. This will not only facilitate cheaper loans and insurance for SMEs, but will also increase the confidence of potential trading partners.

IMPROVING WORKING CAPITAL MANAGEMENT

It is important to remember that there are two ways of managing cash flow. The first is to increase the amount of cash available to service expansion – by taking out bank loans or factoring, for example. This, of course, has a price in the interest and servicing charges paid. The second is to improve the efficiency of using the existing cash in the business. This is more cost effective and can be achieved by a variety of methods, such as implementing a customer credit system, or increasing the cost of withholding payment by charging interest on overdue accounts or, conversely, by providing a discount for those who can pay early. Given the natural drive in Asia toward increasing sales, linking sales commission to customer payments rather than orders has been adopted successfully by some businesses as a means of changing the culture.

On a practical note, SMEs should take advantage of reviewing credit histories of potential customers, which, although expensive, can help to assess potential credit risks. A company with a good history will be reluctant to spoil its credit record and is likely to be a good paying customer. On the other hand, those without credit histories can be given special care initially until a payment track record is established. It is possible for SMEs to run their own simple credit checks by looking for newspaper reports, or speaking to other suppliers – a potential customer with a happy supplier base should be able to introduce them to one or two non-competing suppliers as referees. Remember, the customer may be switching business because it is on credit hold with its other suppliers. After a customer has been accepted, it is important to monitor the account on an ongoing basis and to develop a clear picture of a customer's inventory ordering and payment patterns. It may be best to start a customer with small quantities and then only release further quantities when payment is made. In this way, a customer can create a track record with the supplier. It is worth being aware of the market conditions facing large customers so that a supplier can be aware in advance of any potential issues likely to affect payments or ordering.

One of the key principles of credit risk monitoring is that customers shouldn't be treated as a homogenous group but will have different risk profiles that will also change over time – these should be monitored and the relationship changed as necessary. Essentially, any business that allows customers to pay at a later date is in the business of providing credit facilities and should develop the appropriate skills and processes to carry out the function effectively.

The following examples show how two businesses in China are implementing their own credit control systems.

Nanfou Batteries, China

Nanfou Batteries in Fujian province has a list of factors to assess the credit risk of potential and existing customers, and assigns a score for each, with 10 being the highest. They are then weighted on a scale of 100%. "[For example] If last year's sales were above 10 million renminbi (US$1.2 million), the company gets 10 marks, or 8 marks for sales between 5 million and 10 million renminbi," says Huang Gongwei, head of the credit department. "New clients are rated similar to old clients, but we eliminate certain considerations such as record of cancelled payments and instead adjust the weighting on each factor," he says. Clients are then categorized as good, normal, restricted, and "clean-up" for delinquents that are making good. However, Nanfou still uses "subjective factors" in its credit rating system. "Subject factors occupy 20% of our credit consideration, including the opinion of our frontline sales staff regarding the clients, whether they are very good, good, ordinary, bad, or very bad," says Huang.

Source: CFO Asia, July 2002

Norin Optech, China

Norin Optech, a two-year-old, Guangzhou-based manufacturer of optical equipment, uses software provided by D&B, called Risk Assessment Manager (RAM). "We assess the creditworthiness of our clients through internal and external outsourced collection of information, setting up proper client files, and frequently updating them," says Cheng Jingjing of the operations management department, which has the final say on granting of credit. This includes financial information, as well as transaction history and payment records, among others. The end-result is a credit score — a departure from its earlier "overly subjective decision-making habits" — which then guides Norin on setting the length of credit to grant. Norin has also sought the help of external consultants to help it on handling bad debts.

Source: CFO Asia, July 2002

The two firms discussed above are good examples of businesses that are starting to recognize the importance of putting resources and systems into their credit management strategy. The danger is always that subjectivity can creep in and be the final arbiter – in Nanfou's case the 20% subjectivity factor needs to be closely watched, and in the example of Norin, it may not be ideal to leave the final decision on credit to the operations department rather than the finance department.

IMPROVING FINANCIAL TECHNOLOGY

More and more commercial banks are providing e-commerce solutions for Asian businesses. This is providing the opportunity to reduce the lag effect of the cash and check payment system, which still predominates, and to release more cash into productive activities as well as provide more accurate forecasting of cash flow. Bankers are finding the going tough, though, as this isn't necessarily seen as a benefit by entrepreneurs, for a number of reasons. First, many entrepreneurs prefer to control the payment of cash directly by signing checks rather than to delegate to an employee who is trained to use the electronic payment system. Second, a check can take some four to five days – or sometimes longer – before it is debited from your account. From a cash flow viewpoint, this is much more preferable than one-click immediate payments over the internet. Furthermore, checks are seen as a cash control method, and the internal "system" for approving and signing them can provide a matrix of effective excuses for why a payment hasn't yet been made. It may be a long time before Asia's paper systems of trade – steeped in customs such as needing a signature or government official's chop – can be electronically reengineered. In the end, the whole system can only operate as fast as the slowest document.

WANTED: QUALIFIED CFO…

One of the areas that is receiving growing attention in Asia is the quality of chief financial officers. CFOs in Asia have been better known as finance managers or, for example in Japan, they may have a title such as "general manager, administration department." Their main role has been to collate the financial information required, to check it, and then present it to the CEO or president as a report. They will also coordinate reports required by outside institutions such as banks or tax and regulatory authorities. Figure 6.3 illustrates this role. Note that the information flow is typically one way, with an emphasis on ensuring accuracy. A good finance manager is often seen as one who can produce accurate and timely work. The role has typically been a back-office one where skills such as an ability to communicate or negotiate either inside or outside the company have been seen as secondary to those of numeracy and attention to detail. All this can be accentuated in an SME, where the founder typically likes to control all the pursestrings and make decisions unilaterally concerning financial issues, particularly if the founder is a majority owner of the business.

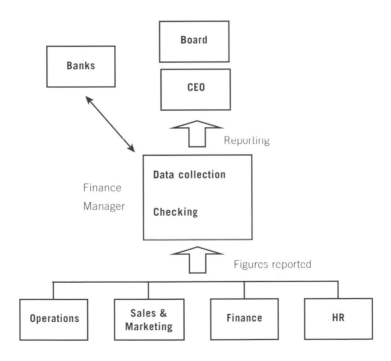

Figure 6.3 Traditional Finance Manager in Asia

This system has generally worked while a business has been relatively small and the main external financial relationship has been with the local bank. In the past, due to the rising property market, banks have been comfortable funding expansion, and even some of the larger SMEs have been able to continue with this type of reporting. Those who are involved with meeting management teams in the region will have noted that a full-blooded CFO is the exception rather than the norm.

How to spot a finance manager…

There are a number of indications that a business has a finance manager type, rather than a CFO. Some of them are outlined below:

- No board seat – founders don't normally like to involve their finance managers in board matters.
- At meetings with outside financial institutions, a traditional finance manager may or may not be present. If present, they are likely to be silent unless asked a specific question by their CEO. They are unlikely to attend a meeting by themselves unless it is a "process" or information-type meeting.
- They have little delegated authority.
- They are process- and rule-driven.

" In China, the finance and accounting departments of most companies are still at the traditional management level. The accounting department deals with data and focuses mainly on the accuracy of the data…. what they lack is the further analysis of the data, which means managers do not have a solid basis for making key business decisions. "

WANG BO, VICE PRESIDENT,
ACCENTURE CHINA,
CHINA BUSINESS WEEKLY,
JUNE 6, 2004

- They are reactive rather than proactive.
- They are very well organized, but will tend work at one speed.
- They thrive on the status quo and are uncomfortable with change.
- They may have little knowledge of or interaction with the operations side of the business.
- They are unlikely to venture opinions on strategic issues.

Of course, everyone is different, and not all finance managers will fit into this cameo, but some characteristics may be familiar. In many respects, the type of finance managers found in Asia is a reflection of the size of business and the ambition of the entrepreneur. Of course, smaller businesses cannot afford to hire a well-qualified and experienced finance manager, nor can a finance manager develop skills in an environment where those skills are not valued. Despite this, the relative lack of both experience and skills of finance managers in Asia has been the subject of growing debate and this has been driven by a number of factors, including the following.

Increasing demands for analysis from lending institutions

In the past, banks were largely content with the ability to take charge over property and land in return for providing loans and cash facilities. These fixed assets had a long track record of steady appreciation in values, and as long as the loan was covered then the bank had rights to an attractive asset with a ready market cash value in the event of default. With the end of this upward trend in property and land values, and the high level of default after the Asian crisis and in the recent recession, lending institutions have become more interested in the real ability of businesses to meet interest payments and capital repayment schedules. This has called for a higher level of financial information from business – detailed analysis both in terms of profit and loss, and cash flows, for example. In most cases, this type of work can be an iterative process involving several scenarios and analysis and may be beyond the capabilities of many financial managers.

Growing variety of financial instruments available

The previous comfortable relationship with one bank has been replaced not only with other banking solutions (both with local and international banks), but also with other types of financing options, including leasing, factoring, and equity solutions such as venture capital. These bring a new dimension to the job of the financial manager, whose CEO now expects them to look for optimal funding solutions, to liaise with different financial providers, and to propose various options to the board. Although SMEs in Asia are becoming more aware of the different banking and financial products available, there is still a concern that finance managers are not so sophisticated in terms of matching credit facilities to the funding need, both in terms of risk and term.

The growing need for equity financing

The rapid growth being experienced by some SMEs has introduced the necessity for equity financing. This may be in the form of a public listing, or raising private equity or venture capital. This can be a significant step up for finance managers, who now may need to handle meetings and negotiations with sophisticated financial advisors and investors and provide detailed forecast financials, together with assumptions and commentary. The introduction of outside professional shareholders can often prove a catalyst for professionalizing the business. In the case of management, for example, investors are looking for a well-balanced management team, and the typical case of a strong entrepreneur supported by a subservient second tier – including the finance manager – can be seen as a weakness. In particular, investors will be looking for a CFO who can demonstrate strong knowledge of the business and its key issues, and who is prepared to raise issues confidently and challenge the CEO where necessary.

Growing emphasis on cash management

The lessons from the Asian crises and recent recession have increased the importance of developing strong cash management techniques and strategies. This calls for fairly aggressive and proactive involvement by the finance department, which in turn requires a strong leader. Finance managers are not naturally motivational leaders and often find it hard to implement and drive this type of internal and external program.

Increasing trend toward corporate governance and focus on shareholder value

The drive to improve the level of corporate governance and transparency in the region is putting new pressures on finance managers. Only a few years ago, it was possible for SMEs to list in Asia with few extra duties in terms of reporting. However, more recently there has been much more focus on transparency and good governance – for example, the need for quarterly or six-monthly reporting, and to support larger board structures that now contain independent directors. In addition, with steady stock-market appreciation now a phenomenon of the past, investors are taking more interest in relative performance of businesses. The knock-on effect of this is that the finance manager not only needs to collate and report historical figures, but also needs to understand the drivers of performance and interact with the rest of the business to improve them.

Characteristics of CFOs

This growing need for more skills and more experience is providing a growing demand for well-qualified CFOs. The new characteristics of the CFO include:

- numeracy, attention to detail, standard technical skills;
- strong analytical and problem-solving skills;
- intimate knowledge of the key drivers of the business;

- strong relationships with other key departments within the business;
- drive for continuous improvement of the business and systems;
- confidence to challenge peers and the CEO where required;
- strong relationships with a variety of financial institutions;
- potential to be a director; and
- ability to lead financial negotiations and lead/support due diligence procedures (for example, for acquisition, listing, private equity situations).

This growing CFO role is illustrated in Figure 6.4. (The increasing complexity over Figure 6.3 is evident.) Key differences to highlight are the two-way relationships and iterative information flows, an increasing and more complex set of tasks, and more relationships both internally and externally. It's not surprising that an individual fulfilling the role of financial manager is unlikely to slot into the demands of the new role. This may be because of lack of training or experience, but could also be due to their personal characteristics such as unwillingness to change, dislike of ambiguity in their work, or general lack of ambition to broaden their work. In reality, those financial managers who have the ability to meet the challenge will drive the role change themselves. For other businesses a catalyst is required, such as a public listing or the introduction of a new institutional shareholder. Both of these are likely to demand the appointment of a suitable CFO as a prerequisite.

There are many good CFOs in Asia, many of whom have either trained and worked abroad or perhaps have developed their experience and skills working for MNCs. Having said this, the overall supply remains limited. It is anticipated that demand for good CFOs will continue to exceed supply for some time, and that while there are plenty of young candidates with future CFO potential, they will be reluctant to develop their career paths in SMEs until entrepreneurs value their input by giving them the appropriate remuneration package and responsibility. Entrepreneurs who are only willing to pay for the cost of a traditional finance manager will continue to get exactly what they pay for.

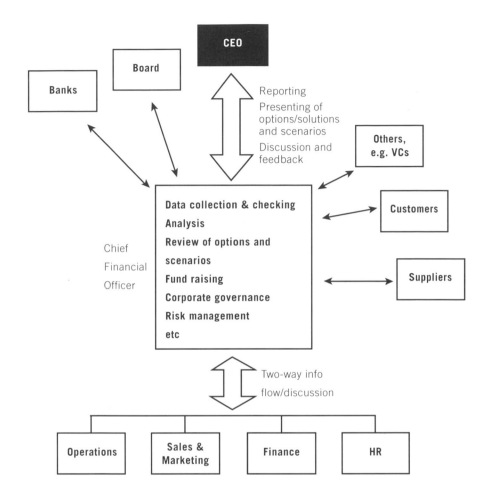

Figure 6.4 Moving to the CFO Role

▶▶ CONCLUSION

The effective management of cash is a critical issue for all growing businesses the world over. For growing Asian businesses, traditional business practices together with the complexities of cross-border trade make the challenge of managing their cash flows even greater. Already we are seeing an increasing acceptance of new methods that help to ease cash flow, including the adoption of solutions such as factoring together with the introduction of better internal processes such as customer credit controls. However, for many entrepreneurs who aim to be part of Asia's ongoing growth story in Asia, the singular drive for sales will continue to eclipse a growing cash management issue within their businesses. It is unusual for entrepreneurs themselves to have the background and experience to keep up with and implement new cash management practices, but the good ones will recognize their shortcomings early and ensure that they either recruit well-qualified CFOs, or develop and empower their existing financial managers to carry out this increasingly important function.

ENDNOTES

[1] ABN AMRO/BRDC Survey, Fourth Quarter 2003.

[2] Asia Pacific Economic Cooperation (APEC) statistics. (APEC is the premier forum for facilitating economic growth, cooperation, trade, and investment in the Asia-Pacific region.)

[3] www.BarterAsia.com.

Government and Entrepreneurship

*I*n this chapter we take a look at what the governments of the Asia-Pacific region are doing to foster a better climate for entrepreneurship in their respective countries. All countries have launched some form of activity designed to do this, but there emerges a wide gap between best practice, which ranks among the very best in the world, and the timid efforts of the laggards.

We focus especially on two of the parameters that appear to encourage entrepreneurial activity, as identified by the GEM report we looked at in Chapter 1 – having entrepreneurs in your close environment, and belief that you have the skills – and also on the level of official and administrative burden.

We close the chapter with a look at how the various government efforts have been perceived by entrepreneurs, and we make the surprising discovery that the most active government is by no means the most favorably perceived. We offer an explanation as to why this might be so.

GOVERNMENT EFFORTS TO ENCOURAGE ENTREPRENEURSHIP

There was a growing realization through the 1980s and 1990s that job creation didn't come from large multinational companies, but rather from the birth and growth of entrepreneurial firms. For example, the 1998 study of European high-growth companies referred to in Chapter 1 found that over the prior five-year period, the 500 companies included in the report had created 200,000 jobs, while Europe's 500 largest companies had eliminated over 600,000.[1]

This, however, was by no means a new phenomenon; already in the 1940s, the Austrian economist Joseph Schumpeter used his famous phrase "creative destruction,"[2] referring to the process of "churn" whereby new firms are created to exploit new products or processes, replacing outdated existing ones. And nearly 200 years before Schumpeter, Richard Cantillon, generally considered to have been the first person to use the word "entrepreneur" in its present-day usage, wrote: "The entrepreneur is the principal agent of economic growth and renewal."[3]

However, it wasn't until the last 20 years of the 20th century that governments started to take an interest in how central policy could encourage and foment new firm creation. Although the whole process got a sharp injection of energy with the development of the "technical/knowledge" revolution and the dot.com phenomenon, during which for a while the world's youth wanted to drop whatever it was doing in order to launch a dot.com company, while the world's venture capitalists were falling over each other to fund them, the trend was already established well before.

And in most of Asia, the challenge wasn't to develop an entrepreneurship culture from scratch, but to restart an activity that had fallen somewhat by the wayside.

Singapore appears to have been the first country in the region to realize the economic potential of its smaller companies. In 1985, Singapore's economy declined by 1.7%, the first time since independence that the economy had a negative GDP growth.

A survey conducted by the Ministry of Trade and Industry indicated that in 1985 the profitability of foreign manufacturing companies dropped by 70% while the decline in profitability for Singaporean-owned SMEs was only 35%. It was then that the Government realised the significant role which small manufacturing enterprises can play in Singapore's future economic growth. The Economic Sub-Committee on "Entrepreneurship Development" advised the Government that SMEs could be the catalyst for Singapore's social and technological changes as these Singaporean-owned SMEs identify and establish themselves in new market niches.[4]

This led to the development of the first Singapore SME Master Plan (1989).

But Singapore has gone much further than this. It is one of the few places in the world to have named a minister with special responsibility for entrepreneurship.[5] This was done in March 2003, and the period since then has seen the introduction of a wide range of measures designed to help entrepreneurs launch new companies. These have ranged from financing schemes, through specially organized networking events to encourage mutual help and support, streamlined company registration procedures, a new look at bankruptcy laws, and a special work permit to smooth the path for would-be entrepreneurs from outside Singapore (see below).

The whole effort has been given further impetus by the creation of the Action Community for Entrepreneurship (ACE), and a glance at their website (www.ace.org.sg) will be sufficient to give a complete idea of the scope of what has been undertaken.

Elsewhere in the region, as early as 1995 Malaysia created a Ministry of Entrepreneur Development;[6] while in 1996, Australia created a Small Business Deregulation Taskforce which undertook a national survey of the paperwork burden on small businesses in order to identify and recommend areas for improvement. In the same year, South Korea created its Small and Medium Business Administration in order to provide SMEs with practical support.

China, of course, constitutes a special case, as over the last 25 years it has gradually been *developing* a private business sector, as distinct from encouraging and easing the path for an already existing one. To quote a recent study on the subject:[7]

> Over the past ten years private firms have marched from the fringes of the Chinese economy to take center stage. Accompanying this march has been the institutional evolution of Chinese private firms... Since the mid-1990s, economic, legal, and political initiatives have allowed private firms to clarify their ownership structures and attain a certain degree of organizational clarity vis-à-vis their social and political environments.

Figure 7.1 shows just how dramatic and rapid the change has been in China over the past 20 years.

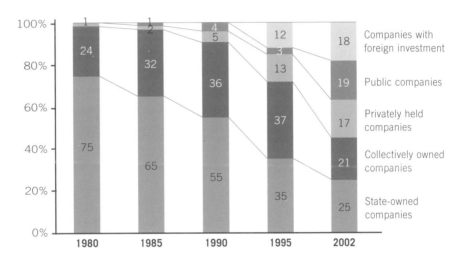

Source: China Industry Economy Yearbook, 2001

Figure 7.1 The Evolution of Company Ownership in China, 1980–2002

In addition to the initiatives and activity undertaken by the region's governments in their own countries, there has even been one case of a country's government launching initiatives in other countries. Such is the case of India, which in November 2004 launched the Lao-India Entrepreneurship Development Centre in Vientiane.

At the opening ceremony, the Indian External Affairs Minister, K. Natwar Singh, emphasized the need to build a strong entrepreneurial cadre in this era of globalization, and said that he expected the center to contribute toward SMEs and creating new employment opportunities. The rationale for establishing the center grew out of India's commitment to the Initiative for ASEAN Integration, designed to help the four latest partners of the grouping, and indeed, three more such centers are planned for Cambodia, Myanmar, and Vietnam for early 2005 with a reported total cost of US$4.6 million.[8]

Thus it is that various Asia-Pacific countries have put in place a variety of measures designed to make launching and running a new company a less arduous task than it has been hitherto. The following summary looks at what has been done along the parameters that appear to encourage entrepreneurial activity, as identified by the GEM report (see Chapter 1).

> " ... over the last 25 years [China] has gradually been *developing* a private business sector, as distinct from encouraging and easing the path for an already existing one. "

Having entrepreneurs in your close environment

Of course, any policy that encourages the emergence of a greater number of entrepreneurs will, over time, produce a more entrepreneurial environment. As we observed in Chapter 1, you are more likely to become an entrepreneur if someone in your environment, including both family and community, is or has been one. However, the length of time necessary to achieve this can probably be measured in generations rather than years.

Recognizing this, Singapore is actively trying to accelerate the process by attracting would-be entrepreneurs from overseas to go there to set up their business. The specific measure that makes this an easier process than before is the EntrePass scheme, which gets around the difficulty for entrepreneurs posed by normal residence requirements (university/college inscription certificate or a job contract) by granting a two-year residence/work permit on the strength of a business plan, presented to an approval committee.

> **Singapore is actively trying to accelerate the process by attracting would-be entrepreneurs from overseas to go there to set up their business.**

During the first six months of operation, this scheme had attracted over 800 applicants, of which around 30% were approved.

One measure of success in this area is if a country has any "icon" entrepreneurs with almost the status of folk heroes, such as Bill Gates in the United States or Sir Richard Branson in the UK. India certainly has one in the person of Narayana Murthy (see box), co-founder of Infosys (now a billion-dollar company), and universally revered in his country, to the extent that some people tip him as a future president of the republic, something that can't be said of Bill Gates!

Singapore's Sim Wong Hoo is also widely admired in his country but cannot yet be said to have achieved true icon status. There is, however, a new generation of young entrepreneurs with which the younger generation more readily identify, such as Elim Chew of 77th Street, a young people's fashion business.

Malaysia is still not quite sure what to make of Tony Fernandes of Air Asia, as the country has never before seen this sort of flamboyant entrepreneur, very much in the mold of (and in the same industry as) Stelios Haji-Ioannou of EasyJet fame in the UK.

Narayana Murthy:
An Asian icon of entrepreneurship

Narayana Murthy is undoubtedly one of the most famous persons in the IT world. He is known not just for building the biggest IT empire in India, but also as an icon for the new generation of Indian entrepreneurs who are bringing India on to the world's IT map and providing jobs to thousands.

He was born in August 1946 in Karnataka, India, and obtained his Bachelor of

Electrical Engineering from the University of Mysore in 1967 and his Master of Technology from the Indian Institute of Technology, Kanpur, in 1969.

In 1981, with just US$250, Murthy together with six other software professionals founded Infosys, which has since become a world leader in consulting and information technology services. In March 1999, the company became the first India-registered company to be listed on an American stock exchange (Nasdaq), and sales that year reached just over US$120 million. Revenue had grown to over US$1 billion in 2003, and market capitalization as of March 2004 stood at US$12 billion, four times greater than when the company listed on the Nasdaq. Currently employing around 25,000 people worldwide, Infosys is widely acknowledged as a highly respected, dynamic, and innovative company. Today, Murthy is chairman of the board and chief mentor officer.

He has received many honors and awards, including Businessman of the Year for 1999 by *Business India*, and in June 2000 he was featured in *Asiaweek*'s Power 50, a list of Asia's most powerful people. *Business Week* chose him as one of their "stars of Asia" for three successive years (1998–2000), and he was named Asia's Businessmen of the Year for 2003 by *Fortune*. He is a member of the Prime Minister's Council on Trade and Industry, and a director on the board of the Reserve Bank of India (RBI).

Narayana Murthy has been a famous man for a long time now, not just for the enormous success of his business, but more for the breadth and scope of dreams and experiences he has created for all of India, and for providing a living example that all actual or aspiring entrepreneurs would like to follow.

In this area, China is once again different. Entrepreneurs there first started to become prominent in the public's consciousness when *Forbes* magazine first started to publish their now-famous list of the country's 50 richest entrepreneurs.

When China's "rich list" was first published in 1999 by *Forbes*, an American magazine, Rupert Hoogewerf, the journalist who compiled it, was threatened by some of the people he wanted to include. Nowadays, businessmen complain when they are omitted. "It is becoming an honour to be on the list. It gives kudos with local governments and recognition overseas," says Mr Hoogewerf. Indeed, rich lists have turned into a small business in their own right. Mr Hoogewerf has taken his contact book to *Chinamoney*, part of Britain's *Euromoney*, and *Forbes* is working on a rival tally.

The entry bar has gone up steeply in recent years. In 1999, all a candidate needed to make the list was $6m. By last year, the figure had risen to $110m. On average, the latest crop of China's rich are 44 years old and worth $230m. Their combined wealth of $23 billion is equivalent to 1.6% of GDP. Startlingly, a quarter are members of the Communist Party.[9]

Belief that you have the skills

The topic of entrepreneurship education is one that not only involves governments; many private initiatives exist, ranging from the fragmented and small-scale entrepreneurship workshop activities of individual entrepreneurship clubs or networking groups, through to projects on a national scale, such as that undertaken by the Wadhwani Foundation in India.

In its own words, "The Wadhwani Foundation funds not-for-profit efforts that inspire, educate and support new entrepreneurs, and create environments where they can succeed."[10] Founded by serial entrepreneur Romesh Wadhwani, the Foundation funds a variety of entrepreneurship education-related projects, of which the principal one, the National Entrepreneurship Network (NEN), brings together five prestigious Indian higher education institutions[11] in a collaboration to perform research and develop and deliver world-class education, skill-building programs, networking activities, and company-starting assistance to new, high-growth entrepreneurs.

NEN was launched in 2003 through an India-wide selection process to select the founding partner institutions to anchor this network. The goal is to launch 2,500 entrepreneurs who will create a minimum of 500,000 jobs by 2014. This will create as much value for the Indian economy over the next 10 years as the IT industry has over the past 15.

Another excellent example is to be found in New Zealand, where the Enterprise New Zealand Trust's (ENZT) Young Enterprise Scheme (YES) has been in existence since the early 1980s. It now has government support through the Ministry of Commerce but is also heavily dependent on support from the business world. The stated objective of ENZT is: "To promote enterprise education, economic literacy and business understanding, and the development of a 'can do' attitude in cooperation with New Zealand businesses. We have to change our education system to produce job creators rather than just job seekers."

> " New Zealand has one of the highest levels of entrepreneurial activity in the region. "

YES is a program that gives secondary school students the opportunity to start their own businesses during the course of the school year and within the school environment (that is, it is a "real-life" experience, not a simulation). Participants form a company (including fulfilling roles as company directors), and develop a product or service which they then market and sell – liquidating the company at the end of the school year.

The effectiveness of this scheme can be gauged from a piece of research done in 2003 by Kate Lewis of Massey University,[12] which serves as a direct link between the results of the program and the findings of the GEM report (see box). It is certainly true that New Zealand has one of the highest levels of entrepreneurial activity in the region (see Chapter 1).

Young Enterprise encourages entrepreneurship

Young Enterprisers gain many benefits by participating in the Young Enterprise Scheme. This is the finding of an independent research report undertaken by the New Zealand Centre for SME Research, and released by Enterprise New Zealand Trust (ENZT). The report established that the benefits of YES, which is an experiential, enterprise education activity, range from issues of personal development to the accumulation of a portfolio of "enterprising" skills.

The research found that YES influences the career intentions and employability of participants. Fifty-one percent of the students surveyed described it as "very likely" or "likely" that they would run their own business at some stage in the future. The average suggested start-up age was 28. Seventy-three percent believed their YES participation had enhanced their employability.

"No other programme or curriculum at senior secondary level influences students to become entrepreneurs," said Ken Baker, the Trust's executive director. "These students personally benefit from a unique experience. They are likely to make an important contribution to the economic well-being of New Zealanders. It is our hope that ENZT can begin to track past Young Enterprisers to see if this result holds over time."

YES students strongly believe in the scheme's advantages. Eighty-eight percent of the students surveyed thought that it was important that students are encouraged to be enterprising – and 63% of the students surveyed thought participating in the YES taught them how to be more enterprising. This impact of YES participation appears amplified for those students who are exposed to enterprising role models through their own family or friends. Eighty-three percent of the students surveyed knew somebody who ran their own business. (For 52% it was a parent.) Sixty-three percent of those who had a self-employed parent described it as "very likely" or "likely" that they would run their own business in the future.

Source: ENZT media release

Level of official and administrative burden

This is perhaps the area where it should be easiest for governments to make improvements, given that all of the administrative requirements placed on a firm ultimately stem from one or other government department, and in many cases still today involve repeating the same information on a variety of different forms.

For example, as is clear from Table 1.2 in Chapter 1, at the time the figures were compiled (early 2003), in Australia it took just two days and two procedures to register a new company. At the other end of the scale, achieving the same result in Indonesia took nearly six times as many procedures and a staggering 84 times as many days.

In view of this, it comes as no surprise that Australian government agencies are required to prepare regulation impact statements, which include an assessment of the impact of each option on small business compliance costs and the paperwork burden.

But other countries have also been actively seeking to reduce the level of administrative hassle new companies have to face.

Vietnam passed a law in 2000 making it easier to set up small businesses. The result was the creation of over 50,000 new companies by the end of 2002.[13]

Even Japan seems to be waking up to the idea that encouraging a greater degree of entrepreneurship in their country, one of the least entrepreneurial in the world, might be a productive idea (see box).

Encouraging entrepreneurship in Japan

Deflation is a wonderful thing. A mere 50 yen will now buy you a hamburger in Tokyo. And a single yen – less than an American cent – can get you an entrepreneur.

A new law, sponsored by the Ministry of Economy, Trade and Industry (METI), makes it possible to found a business in Japan with capital of just one yen (excluding registration taxes of around ¥250,000 (US$2,100)). In an effort to reinvigorate their catatonic economy, the bureaucrats are exempting start-ups from old rules that required big joint-stock companies to have at least ¥10 million of capital, and even small limited-liability firms ¥3 million. The exemption lasts for five years.

Japan has always been better known for improving on other people's ideas than coming up with its own. But its government seems, at last, to have grasped the connection between Japan's miserable showing in international entrepreneurial rankings and its economic malaise (though a very high proportion of entrepreneurs can sometimes be a sign of structural problems for bigger companies, as in Thailand). With many Japanese firms being outgunned by South Korean and Chinese rivals, both on cost and increasingly on quality, the government is emphasizing innovation and flexibility.

Some entrepreneurs are rising to the challenge – thanks in part to higher unemployment and longer living. Several new entrepreneurs are over Japan's traditional retirement age. One entrepreneur has begun a pet-cloning business to cater to a growing number of Japanese women who are fonder of their cat or dog than their man. A 61-year-old former golf-course manager is embarking on a second career to develop a better turf on which to play his favorite sport. Others are trying their luck as computer programmers, consultants, and travel agents. There is even the odd aspiring used-car salesman.

Yet between February 1, 2003, when the new law came into force, and June 6, there were only 3,099 applications to start a new company. This annual rate of less than 10,000 falls far short of the ministry's goal of doubling the number of company formations to 360,000 a year by 2006.

Cutting the minimum capital requirement is a small positive step. But Japan is littered with barriers to risk-taking and innovation, from an archaic education system that fosters rote learning to bureaucratic impediments such as restrictions on firing workers. Japan's social system is based on acceding to group wishes and not displaying too much individuality. So it takes a brave Japanese to go and found a business. Alas, it may take more than bureaucratic fiat to transform Japan into a hotbed of entrepreneurial activity.

Following a simplification of business registration procedures in February 2003, nearly 15,000 new companies have been established. Also, in July 2003, the Japanese METI helped to establish a new Internet-based service named Dream Gate, which has been helping young Japanese people to "chase the dream" of entrepreneurship. Using a popular celebrity wrestler in Japan, Bob Sapp, a native of Colorado, as a spokesperson, this site has been receiving a lot of traffic, and almost a quarter of a million people have registered to use this service.

Various governments have created websites providing a wealth of information about how to go about creating and managing a new business in their respective countries – for instance:

- **Australia**: www.business.gov.au/Business+Entry+Point
- **Hong Kong**: www.esdlife.com/app/app8003/g.htm
- **Malaysia**:
  www.gov.my/MyGov/BizSpace/Biz%20Life%20Cycle/
- **New Zealand**:
  www.biz.org.nz/public/home.aspx?sectionid=53
- **Pakistan**: www.smeda.org.pk
- **Singapore**: www.ace.org.sg

However, the country that has been most actively seeking to minimize administrative burden and make itself business-friendly is, without doubt, Singapore. Mention has already been made of the Action Community for Entrepreneurship, but pro-entrepreneurship initiatives are by no means limited to this umbrella organization; they can be found permeating all parts of government. Two striking examples will help to prove the point:

- The "cut red tape" website is dedicated to streamlining government procedures by calling for suggestions from the general public, businesspeople, and so on (www.cutredtape.gov.sg).
- The mission of the Pro-Enterprise Panel (PEP) of the Ministry of Trade and Industry is to ensure that government regulations and rules remain relevant and supportive of a pro-business environment. For example, a recent feedback led to a liberalization of the rules on the use of HDB (Singapore Housing Development Board) flats to allow entrepreneurs to operate from home, thus effectively lowering the barrier to entry by young entrepreneurs. One of the authors has recently been personally involved in another case in which an appeal to the PEP produced an immediate relaxation in a bureaucratic hard line being adopted by a government agency toward a start-up company.

Singapore has even introduced an award scheme to recognize the government agencies perceived as most enterprise-friendly by a panel of SME CEOs.

ENTREPRENEURS' PERCEPTION OF GOVERNMENT EFFORTS

One of the areas we explored in the online survey we referred to in Chapter 2 was the perception of government efforts to encourage entrepreneurship by those actively engaged in this area. We found a very mixed picture, as can be seen in Table 7.1.

Table 7.1 Perception of Government Efforts to Encourage Entrepreneurship

Country	% replying that their government is making special efforts	Evaluation of government efforts		
		Ineffectual or not very effective (%)	OK (%)	Good or Excellent (%)
Australia	20			100
China	75			100
Hong Kong	75	50	17	33
India	86	33	34	33
Indonesia	0			
Malaysia	100		33	67
New Zealand	100	33		67
Pakistan	50	100		
Singapore	89	24	38	38
South Korea	100	67		33
Thailand	50			100

Various comments can be made with regard to these figures:

- Only three countries – Australia, China, and Thailand – get a 100% positive rating.
- Pakistan gets a totally negative rating, while none of our respondents in Indonesia was aware of any specific government efforts to encourage entrepreneurship in that country.
- South Korean efforts get a mostly negative rating, while opinions in Hong Kong are divided.
- In all cases, those who responded that the government of their country wasn't making any special efforts to encourage entrepreneurship also stated that, in their opinion, such efforts ought to be made.

Singapore is an interesting case given that it was the first country in the region to realize the potential of SMEs, and to develop measures nearly 20 years ago to help small businesses. It is difficult to pinpoint why there should still be entrepreneurs who are unaware of government efforts, while quite a lot of them who consider the efforts that have been made as ineffectual.

This may have something to do with the fact that the measures in favor of small businesses have still been administered by bureaucrats, steeped in the ways of the administration. As recently as 1999, perhaps Singapore's most famous entrepreneur, Sim Wong Hoo of Creative Technologies, felt moved to write his now famous "NUTS" piece.

NUTS stands for "No U-turn Syndrome," which Sim sums up as follows:

> NUTS is when you want to do something and you seek approval of a higher authority. When there is no rule saying that you can do such a thing, then the standard answer is NO ...
>
> In the US, when there is no sign on the road, it means that you can make a U-turn. When the authorities do not want people to make U-turns, they will put up signs to tell you not to make U-turns. In Singapore, it is the reverse. When there is no sign on the road, you are not allowed to make U-turns. When the authorities allow you to make U-turns, then they will put up signs to give you that right.
>
> The two different systems serve the same purpose – to better manage the traffic. They may look quite similar, just coming from different directions, but the social repercussion is significant.[14]

It is much to the Singapore government's credit that this message appears to have been received and understood. In the Prime Minister's speech on National Day (August 9) 2003, he said that henceforth the default answer would be "yes" rather than "no."

As one of our entrepreneur acquaintances never tires of saying, the best thing governments can do to help entrepreneurs may simply be to keep out of the way.

▶▶ CONCLUSION

Some remarks that Dr Erik Pages, research director of the Washington, DC-based National Commission on Entrepreneurship made in his introduction to the report of a workshop held in 2002[15] will serve perfectly as the conclusion to this chapter on government support of entrepreneurship:

> The scope of government policies designed to help SMEs in Asia is truly breathtaking. Every workshop participant could point to a host of support services that could be accessed by budding entrepreneurs. This plethora of support services led one participant to quip that Asia's governments may be providing too much support to entrepreneurs.
>
> While a rich tapestry of SME support programs is already in place, the challenge ahead is not about new programs. It is about a new mindset. Can the region's governments create a system that, in the words of one participant, "balances maximum support and minimum interference" for local entrepreneurs? A successful entrepreneurship strategy will require that the region's governments accept a less proactive role in terms of managing economic development. The region must evolve from the old developmentalist state model to embrace an entrepreneurial state model. This shift will pose a significant challenge for both entrepreneurs and policy makers. The state can no longer create market opportunities or provide preferential access to them. At the same time, entrepreneurs must look to global markets for new business, financing and strategic partnerships. A more open and competitive system will likely emerge.

ENDNOTES

[1] Juan Roure, Towards a European Model of Entrepreneurial Growth: Lessons from Europe's 500 Most Dynamic Entrepreneurs and Their Companies (IESE Barcelona), unpublished.

[2] Capitalism, Socialism and Democracy (1942). The phrase was actually coined by Werner Sombart, a German economist of the generation preceding Schumpeter's.

[3] Essai sur la nature de Commerce en Général (1755).

[4] Ben Chan, "Vibrant Entrepreneurial Spirit in International Markets – New Possibilities for Singaporean-owned Small and Medium Enterprises," USASBE Annual National Conference 1997, Entrepreneurship: The Engine of Global Economic Development.

[5] We know of only two other countries – Croatia and Russia – to have included the word "entrepreneurship" in a ministerial title. Malaysia uses the word "entrepreneurial." The European Union has a Commissioner for Enterprise, which is largely concerned with entrepreneurship.

[6] Now known as the Ministry of Entrepreneurial and Co-operative Development.

[7] Christopher A. McNally, Hong Guo, and Guangwei Hu, "Entrepreneurship in a Transitioning Economy: Political Guanxi Networks in China's Private Sector," unpublished working paper, May 2004.

[8] The Hindu, November 28, 2004.

[9] The Economist, March 20, 2004, special section, p. 16.

[10] www.wadhwani-foundation.org.

[11] Birla Institute of Technology and Science, Pilani; Indian Institute of Technology, Bombay; Indian Institute of Management, Ahmedabad; Institute of Bioinformatics and Applied Biotechnology, Bangalore; and S. P. Jain Institute of Management and Research, Mumbai.

[12] In the context of the 16th Annual Conference of Small Enterprise Association of Australia and New Zealand, September 28 – October 1, 2003.

[13] The Economist, May 8, 2004, p. 27.

[14] Sim Wong Hoo, Chaotic Thoughts from the Old Millennium (Creative O Pte Ltd., 1999).

[15] In July 2002, the Mansfield Foundation launched a project aimed at developing a broad picture of the state of entrepreneurship in Asia, as well as the policies that help or hinder new business creation from one country to another. The project began as a three-day workshop meeting in Hong Kong of nine entrepreneurship experts representing nine economies in Asia: Hong Kong, South Korea, Singapore, China, Malaysia, Japan, Taiwan, Vietnam, and Thailand. During the workshop sessions, participants provided overviews of entrepreneurial activity in their respective economies, including the rate of business start-ups, cultural and demographic factors, the business environment, and the role of government policies in fostering or hampering new business development.

The workshop report can be found at www.mansfieldfdn.org/programs/entrepreneurship.htm.

SECTION III

Growing Pains

*I*t is easy to assume that getting a business off the ground is the hard part. However, many businesses run into problems at the point after they have been successfully launched when the company enters into a growth phase.

In this section, we look at the issues that confront the entrepreneur in the growth phase, and which in many cases he didn't even suspect existed during the planning and financing stages of his venture.

Chapter 8 looks at the changing relative importance of issues such as organization structure and governance, Chapter 9 focuses on financing the growth phase, while Chapter 10 considers the implications and issues involved when a company goes international. Chapter 11, which ends this section, covers the topic of IPOs.

Managing Growth

*D*uring the growth phases of a venture's life, the entrepreneur's ability to act and be totally involved in absolutely everything that is going on diminishes, while factors such as structure and systems, people development, organizational culture, and governance assume a steadily increasing role.

The growth phase will also typically involve seeking partnerships and alliances, and taking the company international.

In this chapter we present a schematic seven-phase venture growth model, and we consider the various factors and issues that comprise it – with the exception of internationalization, to which we have devoted a separate chapter (see Chapter 10).

THE SEVEN PHASES OF NEW VENTURE GROWTH

As all entrepreneurs know, the first stages of a new venture launch are somewhat akin to white-water canoeing. You launch your carefully crafted business plan out on to the waters of reality like a kayak, and before you know it all hell has broken loose. Rocks (for instance, slower-than-anticipated sales growth) and boulders (for instance, longer-than-anticipated product development costs and lead times) emerge with frightening suddenness out of the spray, and all your energy and waking hours are devoted to keeping your fragile craft from being smashed to pieces on them by the raging current that is remorselessly carrying you along.

Then, if you navigate the rapids successfully, you reach a calmer period. The brute fight for survival is behind you and you no longer have sleepless nights wondering how you are going to pay salaries this month. True, the river still holds dangers, but you are past the initial life-threatening stretch.

You are now faced with a choice: either you opt to hold your business at the level it has reached, or you decide to go for growth. If you decide on the latter course of action, then you will find yourself faced with issues you didn't even suspect existed when you were first trying to get your venture launched. As your company grows, factors that were less important, or quite simply not even considered, at the very beginning progressively assume a much greater importance, while at the same time your ability to act unilaterally in "shoot from the hip" mode is steadily reduced. This process is presented in schematic form in Figure 8.1, which graphically shows how the relative importance of the various sustainable growth factors changes over time.[1]

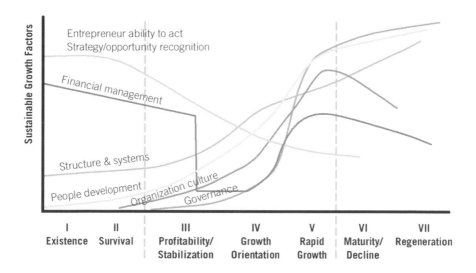

Figure 8.1 The Seven Phases of New Venture Development

We should stress that this model looks at the *relative* importance of the various factors. For instance, financial management is always very important for a new venture; however, whereas it is crucially important in the early stages during which the venture has to manage its cash resources extremely carefully, it becomes relatively less of a crucial issue as soon as the venture reaches profitability and a stable financial position is achieved. Its relative importance then increases again during a phase of rapid growth, as such growth will again put pressure on the venture's financial resources.

In the following pages we take a closer look at the factors mentioned in the model.

Structure

A new company is generally launched by a very small number of people, sometimes as few as the two or three partners of the founding team. Relationships are tight-knit and informal, with no rigid reporting lines, even though one member of the team may be the lead entrepreneur acting as CEO. In many cases, everyone shares the same office.

As the headcount grows in the early stages, this informal arrangement generally expands to include the new hires in the same loose configuration. In most cases, even if an assistant or secretary is hired, he or she will more often than not collaborate with the whole team, rather than with any one member of it. The CEO will know everyone, and in turn everyone will have unobstructed access to him or her.

This sort of arrangement works very well up to a certain size, beyond which various phenomena start to come into play:

- The CEO's own span of control will be increasingly stretched, and he or she will not be able, nor should an attempt be made, to be actively involved in absolutely everything, or even to know every one of the employees.
- This will lead to the emergence of a traditional sort of "layered" organization structure with its associated hierarchies, in place of the initial hierarchy-free circular structure with everyone grouped around and reporting directly to the CEO.
- Some of the initial team will either not like the changes they see happening in the company, or may not have the skill set appropriate for the company's changing needs as it grows. For instance, it is typically difficult for someone who has had a direct reporting line and access to the CEO to have to switch to reporting to someone else, the more so if that someone else is somebody new in the company who wasn't part of the pioneer phase.
- The commitment and dedication of the new people aren't the same as those of the pioneer team. There is nothing intrinsically bad about this; it simply reflects the fact that employee number 100 won't feel the same about the company as employee number 10 did, basically because the company will have changed from the "all hands on deck" wild kayak ride of the initial phases, to a much more stable and orderly place. This will attract a different kind of person.

Exactly when these phenomena start to kick in isn't something that can be precisely measured, but the further the headcount advances beyond, say, 20 people, the more the pressures will build.

All of this produces a time of turmoil for the growing venture as it transitions from the new venture struggling for its very existence into a more mature organization. It is generally accompanied by higher than usual staff turnover, as new people arrive and some of the original team either leave or are fired.

Team building and people development

It is also a time during which the CEO needs to be devoting a lot of effort to building the optimal team to carry the company forward, and this team-building activity will also evolve over time.

In the initial stages, the venture has no time to train new hires. Its search for immediate results naturally leads it to look for suitably qualified talent, often from competitors, and such talent tends to be attracted by "creative" remuneration packages, often including equity or stock options. As the venture matures, so the focus on immediate results evolves into looking ahead to future desired results. In approaching this task, the CEO must consider what roles will be needed down the road and when; and who, if anybody,

> ...it is often acknowledged by CEOs of all sizes of companies that people management and team building are absolutely critical to the success of a venture.

within the current organization has the potential to be developed in order to be able to fill them.

Over time all this occupies an increasing amount of the CEO's time and energy. Thus Jack Welch, the former CEO of General Electric, had this to say:

If we don't get the people thing right, we lose; it is the most important thing in all businesses.

We can put this into a specifically Asian context by looking at the 2004 survey of the Technology Fast 500 Asia Pacific winning CEOs, carried out by Deloitte Touche Tohmatsu.[2] As can be seen in Figure 8.2, developing leaders and delegating responsibility was the main personal challenge identified by this group of CEOs, coming higher even than achieving and sustaining profitability – a clear example of the changing relative importance of these issues in growing companies illustrated in Figure 8.1.

Source: The Technology Fast 500 Asia Pacific Winning CEOs Survey, 2004

Figure 8.2 Main Personal Challenges of Technology Fast 500 Asia Pacific CEOs, 2004

A key aspect of people development concerns the founder/CEO himself. It is generally accepted that the mix of talents, energy, and drive needed at the start-up phase are not the same as those needed when a company moves down the growth curve. If this fact is recognized, then it can be planned for, and indeed, some particularly insightful company founders choose to bring into their company a new CEO in their place when the company reaches a certain developmental point. This releases them either to assume another role within the company, or even to leave in order to become involved in another start-up (the serial entrepreneur phenomenon).

However, in many cases, founder/CEOs don't have this insight, and this produces situations which can lead to the company's downfall (or, at the very least, non-optimal performance); or even, in cases where the company is venture capital funded, to the removal of the founder/CEO by the VC. This isn't as brutal as it sounds; both of the authors of this book have personal knowledge and experience of companies that have been saved by action of this sort, thus providing the CEOs involved (as well as the VCs themselves and other equity holders) with a return on their equity they would otherwise not have had.

> " It is generally accepted that the mix of talents, energy, and drive needed at the start-up phase are not the same as those needed when a company moves down the growth curve. "

Organization culture

This is an aspect of new venture development that is frequently not explicitly addressed in the start-up phase. Organizational cultures tend to develop around the persona of the founder/CEO, very few of whom stop to give any sort of conscious consideration to what sort of a company they want theirs to be. And indeed, at the very beginning, as there are typically very few employees, and those that are there tend to know and trust each other, the question of company values can be implicitly understood rather than explicitly stated.

And yet, this has multiple repercussions that become more and more important as the company grows. The new recruit into most large companies will generally be given a copy of his or her new employer's declaration of principles, setting out what kind of a company it strives to be. But companies aren't born with such a declaration. Someone, at some point, has to enunciate what particular values are espoused by a company, and in new ventures the only person who can do this is the founder/CEO. A glance at Figure 8.2 will show that engaging employees in the company's vision was judged to be the main personal challenge by nearly 20% of this group of CEOs.

Such a statement of values can include anything from how customers are to be treated, through to what constitutes acceptable behavior by employees during work hours. Crucially, it also includes issues of an ethical nature, such as the degree of hospitality that can legitimately be accepted from a supplier.

Having said that, organizational culture also has an element that tends to be "unspoken" in that it has to do with what kind of a work atmosphere prevails. This was something that was made much of during the dot.com boom, as new start-ups vied to outdo each other in "creative" cultures, many involving pool tables and pizza at two in the morning.

Steve Simpson, who heads Keystone Management Services, a company based in Perth, Western Australia, describes the potential impact of these unspoken elements thus:

For a long time, the term "organisational culture" has been used to describe the unique group characteristics that exist when people are brought together to work. But what really drives an organisation's culture are the tacitly accepted ground rules which everyone knows.

The problem is that the term "organisational culture" has always had a theoretical orientation. The various explanations of the term have lacked a practical orientation, and have on many occasions contributed to a sense of impotence among managers. (...)

In creating a management awareness of organisational culture, many academics have created a monster. Management have been aware of a counter-productive culture, but at the same time have felt powerless to tackle it. This powerlessness has manifested itself in many forms. Many businesses have created impressive documents that make proclamations about the importance of customers, staff, and the organisational commitment to these as the key priorities. Meanwhile, practice "on the ground" often works counter to these commitments.

As a result, the workforce culture is further entrenched in its negative orientation, as what staff read in corporate literature is known not to reflect reality. Cynicism builds, and the gap between rhetoric and reality widens.

By bringing a firm's "unwritten ground rules" to the surface, and through focussing on the creation of positive ones, the concept of corporate culture is finally able to be managed.[3]

Governance structures

Many new ventures don't give any thought to governance issues until they really have to do so – for instance, ahead of an IPO, for which a fully functioning board of directors is a must. And even in this circumstance, it is surprising how many companies just "go through the motions" by appointing family members to their boards, rather than go out and look for people who could really add value by their presence.

But what exactly is understood by corporate governance? In November 2000, the Singapore government's corporate government committee defined it thus:

> ...the processes and structure by which the business and affairs of the company are directed and managed in order to enhance long term shareholder value through enhancing corporate performance and accountability, whilst taking into account the interests of other stakeholders. Good corporate governance therefore embodies both enterprise and accountability.

The principles of good governance could be said to consist of transparency, accountability, fairness, integrity, and independence. This translates into the key functions of a board of directors, which can be summed up as follows:

- *strategy*: determining strategic direction;
- *resources*: ensuring that the business has the right resources to enable it to carry out its strategy;
- *shareholder value*: maximizing value growth for the benefit of all shareholders; and
- *legal and regulatory framework*: keeping the business honest.

One issue that is particularly sensitive in governance issues is the role of the chairman of the board of directors, and in particular, the question of whether this role should be assumed by the company's CEO. Practice around the world is radically uneven. For instance, in the United Kingdom about 95% of all FTSE 350 companies adhere to the principle that different people should hold each of these roles. In the United States, by contrast, nearly 80% of S&P 500 companies combine them – a proportion that has barely changed in the past 15 years.[4] One reason advanced as to why this discrepancy exists between the two countries is that the role of chairman carries with it a lot more prestige in the UK than it does in the US.

As far as practice in Asia is concerned, we only have figures for two countries – Australia, where in 2000 there was 90% separation; and Singapore, where in 2003 the figure was 55%.

However, despite this there is a growing body of opinion that holds that the two roles are different and potentially conflicting, and that their separation constitutes an indispensable component of board independence.

> The CEO runs the company; the chairman runs the board, one of whose functions is to monitor the CEO properly.[5]

We rather like the idea of thinking of the chairman as CGO – chief governance officer.

Of course, the whole topic of corporate transparency in Asia has been of increasing concern over recent years, a development greatly fueled by the financial crisis that hit the region in 1997.

> The crisis fundamentally changed the view of how you are successful in Asia. Prior to the crisis, the view was that opacity, family control and fast decision-taking were part of the Asian miracle. The myth of the family businesses being utterly brilliant was shot down. That's a good thing. People now realize that transparency, controls and rules are more useful in the long run than some mythical combination of family and opacity.[6]

Progress toward reform has been made, but in the view of many commentators, much still remains to be done (see box), for the reality is that Asia still lags the US and Europe in the development of a solid corporate governance culture.

In a recent global study by Governance Metrics International (GMI),[7] a US governance research agency, of the 26 companies that received scores of 10, GMI's highest rating, only one, an Australian company, came from the Asia-Pacific region. At the other end of the scale, of the 25 companies that received GMI's lowest overall global rating of 1, 15 were located in Asia-Pacific – 13 in Japan, and one each in New Zealand and Hong Kong. On a national level, out of the 23 countries surveyed, US companies had the highest overall average rating of 7.23, followed by Canada (7.19), United Kingdom (7.12), and Australia (6.73). Other Asia-Pacific countries ranked were New Zealand (9th), Singapore (14th), and Hong Kong (18th). Japan was next to last.

> " …Asia still lags the US and Europe in the development of a solid corporate governance culture. "

Weak rules hinder corporate governance reform in Asia

Asian regulators have made many advances, mainly by matching their accounting and auditing standards to international norms. And all but a few have strengthened securities laws, mandating, for example, the disclosure of ownership for stakes above 5%, prompt reporting of share transactions by directors and controlling shareholders, and continuous disclosure of material transactions (including significant connected transactions). Yet the list of continuing areas of weakness is long.

While four countries (Singapore, Malaysia, Indonesia, and Thailand) have moved to a two-month deadline for reporting annual results, others have not. Some, most notably Hong Kong, South Korea, and Taiwan, have not even shortened their annual-reporting deadlines in recent years.

Only South Korea has been bold enough to pass a law allowing fully-fledged class actions for securities violations. Two other countries (China and Taiwan) allow a variation on this theme, and Thailand has a bill under consideration.

Meanwhile, only two markets (Hong Kong and Taiwan) have brought in rules requiring the main resolutions at annual general meetings to be subject to a vote by poll, rather than a show of hands. No market as yet mandates poll voting for all resolutions.

Although all 10 of Asia's largest markets have a national code of best practice based largely on international corporate governance standards, only India, Malaysia, the Philippines, and Taiwan include a truly robust definition of independent director. Definitions elsewhere contain loopholes that allow people quite closely connected with either management or the controlling shareholder to become so-called independent directors. And only a few markets have adopted mandatory disclosure of director remuneration by name (as opposed to in aggregate).

Regulators have also shown a degree of ambivalence toward independent board committees. Only the audit committee has become mandatory in all markets. While some countries require compulsory nomination committees, restrictions on the scope and power of the committees' operations dilute their effectiveness.

Lastly, none of the markets makes it particularly easy for minority shareholders to nominate candidates for the position of independent director. With the exception only of Singapore and Taiwan, it isn't easy for minorities to remove a director convicted of fraud or another serious corporate crime.

Source: Jamie Allen,
"Weak Rules Hinder Corporate Governance Reform in Asia,"
International Financial Law Review, 23(11), November 2004

We will return to the topic of governance in the specific context of IPOs in Chapter 11.

PARTNERSHIPS AND ALLIANCES

One of the tendencies visible during the dot.com boom and the years that built up to it was a kind of fixation of start-up companies, especially the tech-based ones, on securing strategic partnerships. Now, while it is indisputably true that a judicious partnership can give a new venture a tremendous boost, it doesn't necessarily follow that all such ventures should seek to have one. It has also been observed that between 40% and 55% of such alliances break down prematurely,[8] while research by KPMG Alliances has even indicated a failure rate of as high as 60–70%.[9] So it may be useful to offer some thoughts on the factors that determine whether or not an alliance will be successful.

There are three interlocking keys to generating value from corporate relationships – focus, strength, and trust.[10]

> "...while it is indisputably true that a judicious partnership can give a new venture a tremendous boost, it doesn't necessarily follow that all such ventures should seek to have one."

Focus

Focus is vital from the outset, as more isn't necessarily better in alliances, and it is important to understand that the underlying purpose of an alliance is to create a "repeated game." The first step is to be clear about the logic of collaboration and to ask the question: Why do I need a repeated game with this potential ally? Some examples are:

- *Supply alliance*: to reduce transaction costs between suppliers and buyers.
- *Learning alliance*: to pursue joint knowledge construction, not exchange or transfer.
- *Positioning alliance*: to develop demand or a standard.

Strength

Successful alliances rest on countervailing dependence and reciprocal bargaining power. A truly strong position would be one in which:

- they have few alternatives to you;
- you have lots of alternatives to them; and
- you have control over critical contingencies.

Typical critical contingencies for entrepreneurs would be what might be termed legitimacy and social capital, marketing (especially with long sales cycles), and scaling problems. Those for a large company would include local knowledge, speed of adjustment to change (rather than speed per se), leveraging assets into new spaces, and retaining the very best people.

Trust

Trust-building is largely a matter of a series of small steps, over the span of which a relationship can be established based on reliability, and an avoidance of taking opportunistic advantage. Various studies on the subject have underlined the fact that trust is fundamental to the successful collaboration of entrepreneurial teams. One of these was a working paper produced by INSEAD's Professor Peter Williamson and Research Fellow Sarah Meegan, which looked at the experience of NTT DoCoMo and how its alliances functioned as innovation accelerators (see box). It is true that we are talking here of a large company rather than an entrepreneurial one, but as the authors point out: "The development of a new venture within a large existing firm faces significant obstacles, many of which parallel the challenges faced by smaller entrepreneurial companies."

Alliances as innovation accelerators: The experience of NTT DoCoMo

The emergence of a new, third generation of cellular phones (3G) has led to unprecedented levels of collaboration within the global mobile industry, transcending both international borders and traditional industry boundaries. A particularly notable feature of this wave of collaboration has been the use of alliances to accelerate the pace at which new 3G businesses can be built and to improve their chances of success on a global scale in a highly uncertain environment. NTT DoCoMo, the mobile arm of Japan's telecommunications giant NTT, has been on the forefront of attempts to use alliances in this way, both to build its successful i-mode service and to leverage this platform internationally. (...)

In October 2001, NTT DoCoMo was the first company in the world to launch a commercial third-generation service — FOMA. Internationally renowned for its developments in mobile data services and applications, perhaps the company's greatest innovation was the earlier creation of i-mode, a second-generation service, which provided continuous connection to the internet and redefined the world of mobile communications. Within two years of its launch, in February 1999, the number of subscribers to i-mode exceeded 20 million. By contrast, the introduction of WAP (Wireless Application Protocol), the rival format for providing internet content over mobile phones, had relatively poor reception in Europe, the US, and other parts of Asia. Equally remarkable was the speed with which NTT DoCoMo was able to take these innovations from concept through to venture and, in the case of i-mode, large-scale business. In less than three years, DoCoMo had launched two of the most innovative mobile communication services available anywhere in the world and grown one of these into a significant profit generator. (...)

Rather than forming strategic alliances at the outset, the first step in developing i-mode was to recruit externally to bring fresh and disparate ideas and insights to the new project. However, it soon became apparent that recruiting individuals would not provide rapid access to the depth and range of capabilities, processes, and infrastructure necessary to develop the concept into a profitable business. DoCoMo then turned to alliances to fill this gap. In their more recent innovations (the 3G FOMA and planning for fourth-generation services) they have used alliances from the outset. (...)

The experience of NTT DoCoMo provides clear evidence of the potentially powerful role alliances can play in accelerating innovation. A common thread is the use of alliances to provide access to a more diverse pool of capabilities, knowledge, and resources that exists in any individual firm, thus providing an enhanced vector of inputs to the innovation process. The NTT DoCoMo experience suggests that this role is potentially more significant than traditional risk-spreading arguments for alliances in the context of innovation.

But our analysis also highlights the sharp differences in alliance contribution between different stages of the innovation/entrepreneurial life cycle from co-discovery, through co-learning, co-option, and co-specialization. These differences imply the need for different levels of commitment, different alliance structures, and even a different set of partners as the innovation evolves from an idea to a full-scale business. The use of alliances to accelerate innovation therefore creates a complex dynamic optimization problem of how to maintain strategic and structural fit as an innovation evolves through its life cycle.

Source: Peter Williamson and Sarah Meegan,
"Alliances as Innovation Accelerators: The Case of NTT DoCoMo's i-mode
and 3G Mobile Telecommunications," INSEAD Working Paper 2003/10/ABA

▶▶ CONCLUSION

We have seen, through this chapter, that the transition from new venture to mature organization is a time of turmoil. It is also a time when, to a certain extent, accumulated wisdom is repeatedly turned on its head, as venture management teams discover that they constantly have to reinvent their way of doing things as their company moves along the growth curve. They very often find that what it was that got them to a given point will actually hinder them from moving on to the next level.

For example, it is almost a truism to say that when a start-up commences operations, the first casualty is the business plan. In other words, when reality kicks in, the carefully crafted pillars of the business plan frequently have to be modified, or even abandoned altogether in a sequence that was schematized by Tim Keating, formerly European Director for Intel Capital, as:

1. X was the idea the business plan was based on.
2. Trying to implement X is how we found out about Y.
3. Y is how we got to Z.
4. Now we have to kill X and Y and focus on Z.

Survivors through this phase tend to have a clear understanding of who their target customer is, and what his or her particular "pain point" is. They also manoeuvre through this early "exploration" process keeping their cash outflows to the very minimum.

Once the new company has succeeded in capturing its first customer, what it then naturally seeks to do is find more. This is when it realizes that what got it to this point was extreme attention to the needs of the early customer, whereas what will take it on to the next level involves stepping back from the extreme "tailoring" approach of the first phase to a more "off the peg" approach, seeking to satisfy most of the needs of a specific market segment, rather than all the needs of one specific customer.

Similar inflection points occur all along the growth curve, requiring insight and agility on the part of the management team at each step of the way.

ENDNOTES

[1] This model was developed by Professors Neil Churchill and Randel Carlock, both of INSEAD.

[2] The Deloitte Technology Fast 500 Asia Pacific program recognizes technology companies that have achieved the fastest rates of annual revenue growth in Asia-Pacific during the past three years. It covers those based in Australia, China, Hong Kong, India, Indonesia, Japan, Macau, Malaysia, Philippines, New Zealand, Singapore, South Korea, Taiwan, and Thailand.

[3] Steve Simpson, "Creating a Culture of Service," eCustomerServiceWorld.com, copyright 2001 Keystone Management Services.

[4] Paul Coombes and Simon Chiu-Yin Wong, "Chairman and CEO – One Job or Two?" *The McKinsey Quarterly*, 2, 2004, pp. 42–47.

[5] *Ibid.*

[6] Jamie Allen, Secretary General of the Asian Corporate Governance Association (ACGA), quoted in Chris Leahy, "Asia's Corporate Horrors – Are Lessons from the Crisis Already Forgotten?" *Asiamoney*, 15(8), October 2004.

[7] GMI press release, September 7, 2004.

[8] Jeffrey H. Dyer, Prashant Kale, and Harbir Singh, "When to Ally and When to Acquire," *Harvard Business Review*, July–August 2004, pp. 109–15.

[9] KPMG Alliances, *Alliances and Networks: The Next Generation* (Amsterdam, 1996).

[10] This material was developed by Professor Philip Anderson, INSEAD Alumni Fund Professor of Entrepreneurship; Director – 3i Venturelab; and Director – International Centre for Entrepreneurship, and we are grateful to him for permission to use it here.

Raising
Expansion Capital

*T*his chapter looks at businesses that have already passed the start-up phase and have developed into growing, yet fairly stable businesses. In terms of characteristics, this means they have built up a steady sales stream, with any fluctuations now more related to seasonality, other market issues, or perhaps macro issues such as SARS, rather than to start-up difficulties. From this revenue stream, the business will have stable profitability and positive cash flow. In addition, it will have developed an appropriate infrastructure and management team to support it in its current state.

We shall explore the funding options for these businesses as they seek to expand further either through organic growth or acquisition. In particular, we will look at the market for private equity funding in Asia, which continues to be influenced by both demand and supply side issues.

Finally, we will review two private businesses, one in India and the other in China, that have recently raised expansion capital from private equity funds.

THE EXPANSION CHALLENGE

As we have seen, the numbers of new businesses in Asia are growing at a significant rate. The rate of new business creation is also increasing, and statistics such as the 500,000 new businesses set up in China in 2003 are impressive. The conclusion reached by governments all over Asia is that these businesses are going to be the engine of growth and need to be nurtured if their macro growth targets are to be met. However, once set up and established, the real challenge facing these businesses is their ability to expand. Many will fail, or go into an alternative "face-saving" state often seen in Asia; such businesses are commonly known as the "living dead." Others will survive in a stable state, but while providing a living for the family may not move on to contribute significantly to the economy by generating further employment or wealth creation opportunities. A meaningful proportion, however, will have the opportunity for ongoing expansion. In doing this, they will grow from small companies into medium or larger ones and at the same time make a significant contribution to wealth creation and employment. Clearly, increasing the proportion of these growing businesses must also be a priority – to counterbalance at least the large numbers of new businesses that won't survive.

The opportunities in Asia for businesses to expand certainly look positive, with economic growth rates in China and India in excess of 7–8% going forward and increasing growth trends elsewhere in Asia. But how do these businesses fund such opportunities? The sources of funds for an established company that needs to raise capital to fund expansion are generally different from those used by earlier-stage companies. As we have seen in Chapter 5, start-up companies in Asia source funds from a combination of the founders' own money, family and friends, business angels, government, and venture capital. When established companies embark on an expansion program, their need for capital is just as strong, but the amount required is usually much larger. For example, expansion projects may include an acquisition overseas, setting up an international sales infrastructure, developing a new product, or perhaps setting up a manufacturing base abroad. The money required for this can be in terms of millions of dollars, rather than the hundreds of thousands targeted by early-stage businesses. By the time a business has reached stability, the entrepreneur will already have invested much of his spare cash in the business and is unlikely to be able to contribute significantly to the large amounts needed at this next stage of growth. The issue will be similar for family and friends and business angels. Typically, business angels prefer to invest up to US$500,000 in any one project, for which they will hope to secure a substantial shareholding at an attractive price.

The valuation dynamics of investing in a profitable business are

> **The sources of funds for an established company that needs to raise capital to fund expansion are generally different from those used by earlier-stage companies.**

also very different from investing in a start-up. For start-ups there is little value already in the business except for perhaps an idea, maybe a prototype product, and an entrepreneur. The hook for other investors is that the entrepreneur is prepared to invest his own cash and time into what seems an attractive proposal. In contrast, later-stage stable businesses have already created substantial value in the form of proven products, repeat customers, a management infrastructure, and positive profits and cash flow. The entrepreneur therefore has created value that is now stored in the business. Certainly, by this point, US$500,000 is unlikely to command a substantial minority stake in the business – nor will it be enough to cover the funding needs. Hence, this stage of investing isn't suited to the informal market (individuals such as angel investors) who are looking for high returns from investing early when the risk is still relatively high.

The key providers of expansion capital are shown in Figure 9.1 and include a company's own cash flow, government schemes, debt and other security-based products, private equity, and the public capital markets. This chapter and Chapter 11 will take a closer look at private equity and the public capital markets; however, let us first examine how entrepreneurs decide from where to source the funds.

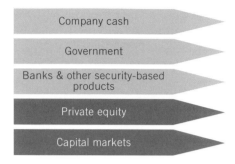

Figure 9.1 Funding Sources for Company Expansion

Assessing funding options the entrepreneurial way

Two key determinants of the attractiveness of different funding options to entrepreneurs are the cost and availability of the funds.

Cost

Generally, entrepreneurs are great negotiators and are always looking for a good deal. They also tend to see cost in terms of the time they need to spend in obtaining the funding. In this sense, using company cash is almost always preferable in that it is cheap and the effort or "hassle" factor involved in obtaining it is minimal – it can be as simple as writing a check. Certainly, the entrepreneur won't necessarily feel the need to write a business plan to convince himself to make the investment.

Government cash is seen as worth the effort if the monetary cost is cheaper than borrowing from a bank – that is, if it is some form of grant or even a low-cost loan. If really necessary, entrepreneurs will take on bank funding, but they worry about being in debt and, of course, resent providing the personal guarantees generally required when banks lend to private companies.

To be realistic, most entrepreneurs the world over dislike using equity to fund growth. They feel it is expensive, because they have to "give away" equity. In addition, entrepreneurs believe that the time and effort spent obtaining private equity is particularly onerous. Raising equity on the public markets by IPO is seen as equally troublesome, but in Asia the perceived benefits of being a listed company can help to tip the balance. These benefits include the prestige of being a listed company, and also the releasing of personal guarantees held by banks that takes place immediately on becoming a public company. The perceived costs of the various types of funding discussed in terms of pricing and "hassle" factor are illustrated in Figure 9.2. For many entrepreneurs, the idea of having to write business plans for "other people" or of involving outsiders in their business in any form is a "put-off," and many SMEs may shy away from projects on principle if they require external fundraising.

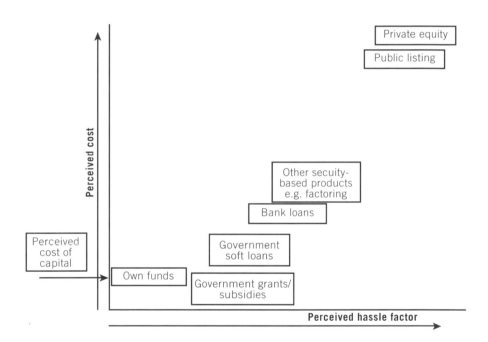

Figure 9.2 Entrepreneurs' Perception of Funding

Availability

Quite apart from an entrepreneur's own perception of the costs of different sources of funding, another key factor is availability. Of course, no matter how attractive a funding option may be, this is of no consequence if access to it is difficult. In many ways, this is linked to the "hassle" factor in that if a particular source of funding is limited, then the provider can be very selective in terms of who to fund and make the hurdles for receiving the funding high. However, the other side of this is the *actual* availability. For example, although most governments provide subsidies and grants, there is some variation across Asia regarding who can apply and who can't. In the same way, the availability of the option to use a business's own cash as a source of funding will be determined by its ability to generate cash. A survey carried out as background for this book of some 100 entrepreneurs and advisors in Asia indicated not only that companies intend to expand over the next few years, but also that the most popular and likely source of funding for this growth is self-generated cash. However, the survey also indicated that the most likely type of growth was organic, which may give some indication of entrepreneurs' preference to grow at a speed at which they can source relatively "hassle-free" capital. This implies that most believe they will have the cash available to fund their plans for expansion – which is excellent. On the other hand, perhaps it demonstrates a lack of ambition – or, alternatively, a strong dose of prudence – in that they will only undertake projects they can pay for themselves.

We need more SME-friendly banks...

Bank debt, despite having a higher "hassle" factor than using one's own cash, is often seen as the preferred source of expansion funds because of its relatively low cost to shareholders. The banking system in Asia is often challenged by entrepreneurs, and sometimes governments, for its lack of interest in supporting SME expansion plans. In particular, entrepreneurs complain that it is difficult to gain bank funding without collateral, and they cite the need for a friendly SME bank that is sympathetic to providing cash in the form of loans to fund growth. This can be to finance working capital needs or perhaps to finance new facilities or development abroad.

> " Bank debt ... is often seen as the preferred source of expansion funds because of its relatively low cost to shareholders. "

Indeed, governments encourage SME lending through incentives such as loan guarantee schemes. There are concerns, however, that this doesn't really increase the amount of funding that banks are willing to provide, nor does it encourage them to adopt a higher risk profile – that is, to loan out to riskier projects. It is a commercial truism that strong proposals will generally receive funding and weak ones generally won't. Below we consider some common reasons why entrepreneurs don't manage to attract bank funding.

Poor cash management

Some SMEs don't display the fruits of good cash management practices. A lengthy, aged debtors ledger together with high figures for receivables or stock in the balance sheet are tell-tale signs of poor cash management. This won't give the bank confidence that loan repayments will be on time or that an overdraft facility will be used properly for managing short-term peaks only.

Lack of proper financial records or information

SMEs don't always have effective financial or management information systems. More likely, the accounts clerk isn't highly qualified and has little function other than to provide statutory information. So, whereas it is normal to provide actual profit and loss figures, it is less normal to see analysis of actual performance against budgeted performance in terms of profit and loss (P&L). The use of cash flow data – either budgeted or actual – is even less common. This means that banks or other lending institutions find it difficult to make proper credit evaluations and, hence, lending decisions.

Lack of track record

This is a particular problem for start-up or early-stage businesses, and will limit the extent to which banks can lend. In these situations, smaller amounts are possible, but they usually require a personal guarantee from the founder.

Undercapitalization

The commitment of the shareholders to the company can be a source of comfort to all types of funders. An SME that has been started with a minimal amount of capital may cause the bank concern, in that the owners could walk away if the situation became difficult and a loan too onerous to repay. This is less of an issue for larger businesses, as the founders have already built significant value for themselves in the business.

Insufficient assets

Entrepreneurs are often heard to complain that banks aren't prepared to lend unless they have some security. Unfortunately, banks, like other providers of funds, have to balance their risk and return and are unprepared to take an "equity" risk on the basis of taking only a small margin return over their cost of funds. If a business needs to raise cash to fund its growth and it has no collateral, then it may be more appropriate to raise venture capital or private equity funding that operates at a higher risk level – and, of course, a higher level of return.

> The Asian entrepreneur ... generally has an aversion to the use of equity in funding growth and often would rather fund everything with relatively cheap bank loans if this were possible.

Overall, a poor business will have difficulty raising funds from most credible sources of capital; however, in many instances the business is sound but the proposal isn't appropriate for bank funding due to one of the above non-operational-type issues. As we have noted, the Asian entrepreneur – perhaps even more than his peers overseas – generally has an aversion to the use of equity in funding growth and often would rather fund everything with relatively cheap bank loans if this were possible. There are still some regions where the banking system remains antiquated in its approach, but generally Asia is well served with a global-standard banking system and with professionals who are well-versed and experienced in the provision of sophisticated products. In addition, and contrary to the beliefs of some entrepreneurs, SMEs are an important market for banks – local regional banks, in particular. They see the competition for their biggest customers intensifying as global banks extend their reach and regulatory barriers are relaxed. As a consequence, lending margins to larger customers are very thin. In contrast to this, interest margins charged to smaller businesses can be much more attractive. This has to be balanced with a higher risk of default, which is why the banks have to have a high-quality benchmark. Entrepreneurs who are unsuccessful in obtaining bank funding may also see this as the banks' reluctance to lend without collateral; however, bankers may see it differently and attribute their lack of appetite to the risk profile of either the business or the expansion situation. In this sense, they are no different from their banking peers worldwide.

Higher-risk situations need equity funding

The cost- and hassle-conscious entrepreneur may call for more SME-friendly banks, but the gap of funding that is left is more appropriately filled with equity. Another way of explaining this is through the matching principle of corporate finance, which matches the risk profile of the project to the return profile of the capital (see Table 9.1).

Table 9.1 Matching Principle for Expansion

Project	Downside risk	Appropriate funding
Building a factory	Market price of building	Mortgage up to a percentage of market price and use equity for the balance
Working capital	Trading may decrease payment default	Flexible loan account or factoring and credit insurance
Acquisition	Acquisition may fail – and may even affect the viability of the core business	Mostly risk capital – equity

The matching principle not only ensures that the provider gets the appropriate return to fit the project risk, but also that the entrepreneur's business is protected in terms of its financial risk profile. For example, if a business uses bank debt to fund an acquisition and the acquisition fails (studies show that some 80% of acquisitions perform below expectations), then the bank debt still has to be repaid and will represent an ongoing burden on the core business. This debt servicing and debt repayment burden is likely to restrict future growth and may even cause the business to fail.

Despite the perceived downsides of using equity to fund expansion, Asian entrepreneurs have a strong history of raising equity funding through the capital markets. But it is clear that public equity alone isn't going to meet the needs of expanding SMEs and the provision and use of private equity should be considered.

To expand or not to expand?

The need to raise 'expensive' equity funding and to go through the perceived onerous process involved can put off many entrepreneurs. But does this mean that projects shouldn't go ahead? Perhaps the biggest competitor for providers of equity the world over is apathy. That is, the entrepreneur always has another option –and that is the choice not to grow. In reality, this generally represents the choice of slower organic growth using one's own resources and/or cheaper money such as bank borrowing. Many believe this attitude may be more pronounced in Asia than elsewhere. One of the big concerns for entrepreneurs when considering raising outside equity is losing control of the business. Raising equity means that an entrepreneur has to "give" a shareholding to a third party in exchange for cash. At this stage, unless the amount raised is very large, the entrepreneur will still be the majority shareholder in his business. But this is only one way of looking at control. For entrepreneurs, any interference in the business, such as a requirement to seek permission before taking certain actions, is also seen as a loss of control. The new investor is likely to require some form of control mechanisms in the shareholder agreement to ensure that their position as a minority shareholder will be protected. This can range from restrictions on future borrowing or expansion, to controls on directors' remuneration, and seats on the board. These are all reasonable requests, but they are a big concession for an entrepreneur used to full autonomy and, perhaps, very little accountability.

Clearly, when raising public equity through IPOs, the controls are more defined; however, whether raising public or private equity, there is some transfer of control involved. An entrepreneur generally looks at control in two dimensions. First, how much of the business does he own in terms of equity? In this instance, more than 50% can be a magic figure for them. Second, how much interference does he receive from others in terms of the day-to-day running of the business? Studies indicate that Asian entrepreneurs are significantly more concerned about this issue than their peers in the Western economies. Figure 9.3 indicates that almost 70% of Asian entrepreneurs are either concerned or very concerned about losing control if they finance growth, compared with less than 50% elsewhere in the world. This would indicate that perhaps the current level of private equity financing for Asian SMEs may be influenced not only by the availability of funds, but also by the appetite of entrepreneurs to raise equity funding.

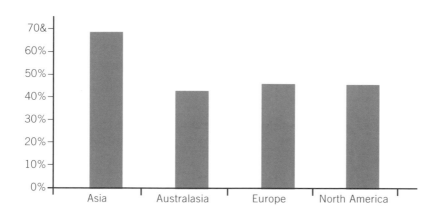

Source: Grant Thornton, PRIMA Global Research Report, 2004
(based on a global survey of 8,728 private business owners).

Figure 9.3 Percentage of Respondents Concerned or Very Concerned about How They Will Finance Growth and Retain Control of the Business

PRIVATE EQUITY IN ASIA

Private equity provides equity capital to enterprises that are private – that is, not quoted on a stock market. As these investments are normally for a minority stake in a private company, they are seen as illiquid and therefore the expected holding period is generally medium to long term. Investors in private businesses will aim to receive their return in one of the following ways:

- IPO (public listing of the shares);
- a sale or merger; or
- some form of share buy-back or recapitalization.

Private equity is a general term covering all types of investments in private companies, from start-ups to expansion capital to management buyouts (MBOs). In this sense, venture capital – capital for investing in start-ups and early-stage businesses – is one form of private equity. Expansion capital is another. All these forms have their own distinctive characteristics in terms of risk, return, instruments used, involvement of investors, and so on. We cover venture capital and MBOs in more detail in Chapters 5 and 13, respectively.

Expansion capital is private equity provided to private companies for the purposes of funding, or helping to fund, expansion projects that have the characteristics of being relatively high risk together with the potential for matching attractive returns. Good examples of these situations are accelerated organic growth, or acquisition. Despite its association with private companies, expansion capital is also provided at times for publicly listed companies. This seems strange, as one of the benefits of being a listed company is the access it brings to public funds. However, as we discuss in Chapter 11, becoming a listed company in Asia doesn't always work out this way and therefore, particularly in Asia, we are also seeing

> " Expansion funding has been attracting a declining proportion of the total private equity funds invested in Asia for some years. "

examples of private investment in public entities (PIPE) transactions. Unfortunately for Asian entrepreneurs, there seems to be a relative lack of interest in investing in expansion opportunities compared with other funding opportunities. In fact, expansion funding has been attracting a declining proportion of the total private equity funds invested in Asia for some years (see Figure 9.4). In 2004, over 60% of investment went to MBO opportunities, with a large proportion also being invested in restructuring and turnaround situations.

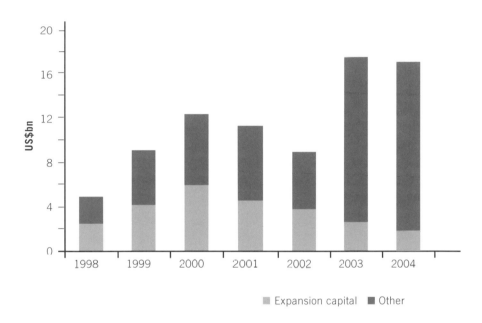

Source: PricewaterhouseCoopers/3i Global Private Equity Review, 2003/2004/AVCJ statistics

Figure 9.4 Proportion of Expansion Capital Invested in Asia, 1998–2004

With the strong economic growth rates being recorded in Asia relative to the rest of the world, we might expect that Asia leads the world in expansion funding. This isn't the case. In 2003, Asia only accounted for four places in the top 20 countries globally in terms of private equity investment in expansion capital: Japan (9), Korea (11), India (14), and Hong Kong (16).[1] The apparent lack of interest in funding expansion situations is compounded when we split the technology and non-technology businesses. Private equity funds typically have a specific focus. For example, there are several large buyout funds operating in Asia, and any mergers and acquisitions (M&A) opportunity of appropriate size will attract the attention of these players even when operating a long way from home. The sale of Singapore Telecom's Yellow Pages business is a good example of this. Private equity players from all over Asia showed interest in the business, which was sold to CVC Asia Pacific Ltd, a buyout specialist fund for over S$200 million. In the same way, there are many smaller technology-focused funds operating all over Asia. While some of these may target particular sectors such as biotech or communications, they have a common thread in that their targets are all technology-related. For non-technology SMEs and start-ups, there are fewer takers. This gap in the funding market, illustrated by the gray star in Figure 9.5, is one that is being taken more seriously by governments around Asia, which are seeking to attract more private money to help fund SME growth.

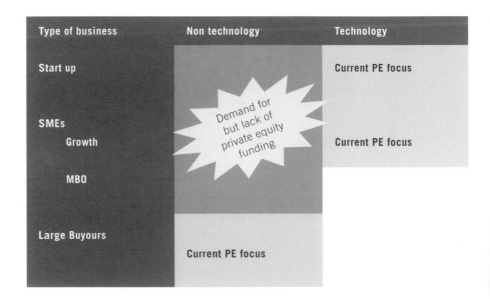

Figure 9.5 Snapshot of PE Focus in Asia

Much of the issue is seen as a supply-side problem – that is, the supply of private equity, rather than the supply of opportunities, as can be seen by the adjacent recent quotation from Thailand.

But as we discussed earlier, the supply of interested investors may be only half of the problem. The other part may rest on the psyche of the Asian entrepreneurs themselves. If they are seen as difficult and unwilling customers, the private equity fund pool will flow to easier and more receptive investing opportunities, such as MBOs and situations involving corporate distress.

RECENT EXAMPLES OF EXPANSION FUNDING

The figures so far paint quite a depressing picture both in terms of the willingness of entrepreneurs to seek equity funding for expansion

> " Even though Thailand seems to attract both foreign direct investment and capital market investment, private equity investment is still a very different story. Despite government money in SME VC fund (Baht 1 billion) and Thailand Equity Fund ([US]$245 million), it is very difficult to raise private equity money in Thailand. "
>
> VIRAPAN PULGES, PRESIDENT, THAI VENTURE CAPITAL ASSOCIATION, APRIL 2004

and the availability of such funding. However, there *are* instances in Asia where entrepreneurs have made the choice to raise expansion capital with equity. These are entrepreneurs who see the opportunity to build a much bigger business as being worth accepting some dilution of their equity holdings and the introduction of accountability and controls. To some this is seen as positive in that it helps to start the process of professionalizing the business. In addition, they are attracted by the idea of having a financial partner who will be able to provide other valuable non-financial support and experience. The case studies below profile two such businesses – one is a retail business and the other is technology-based.[2] Vandana Luthra's Curls and Curves is a chain of beauty and fitness centers based in India which has raised some US$10 million of equity capital to fund its aggressive geographical expansion plans, while CSMC Technologies Corp. is a semiconductor fabricator based in China which has raised substantial further equity funding to pay for its capital expenditure requirements.

CASE STUDY

Vandana Luthra's Curls and Curves, India

After being a housewife for six years, Vandana Luthra put into action her idea of setting up a business to provide services and advice on beauty and health. She believed that this industry had much potential, but that the services being offered to customers were limited. At the time, the main option for people keen to achieve weight loss was joining a gym. Vandana felt that a more personal service was needed, providing good advice, support, and access to modern methods and practices. In 1989 she opened up her first slimming, beauty, and fitness center in Delhi. Her husband was very supportive, although she recalls her father-in-law saying, "*Hamaare ghar ki bahu naai nahi banegi*" ("The daughter-in-law of our house will not become a barber").

Since then, Vandana Luthra's Curls and Curves (VLCC) has become an Indian entrepreneurial success story and one of that country's most successful branded retail businesses. By 2004, VLCC health and beauty centers cover some 40 cities throughout India and are visited by almost 100,000 people each year. This represents annual sales of approximately US$20 million. VLCC has a staff of over 2,500 doctors, nutritionists, and health and beauty professionals. It specializes in Ayurvedic products and therapies, which provide a holistic approach to slimming. VLCC's slimming and beauty centers provide a growing demand for health trainers, as well as an effective distribution channel for beauty and health products. To support this, Vandana Luthra has added two more elements to the business, which now has three divisions.

Slimming and beauty

This is the core business consisting of some 70 health and beauty centers throughout India.

Personal care products

VLCC runs two manufacturing units at Gurgaon and Dehradun, which make various products marketed by VLCC, including skin care, body care, hair care, and foot care products. Approximately 30% of these are sold by the network of slimming and beauty care centers, while the rest are sold through some 6,000 outlets across India, including leading department store chains.

Training institutes

VLCC runs two institutes that have produced around 2,500 trainers. About half of these have been absorbed into the VLCC slimming and beauty center network.

Further growth plans

VLCC's strong brand recognition and operational success has presented it with an opportunity for further rapid growth, not only within the Indian beauty and slimming market, which is expected to continue its double-digit growth, but also abroad. VLCC sees the advantage of rapid growth to further secure its position in the market and aims to:

- operate 100 beauty and slimming centers by the end of 2004;
- open a further four training institutes; and
- set up beauty and slimming centers abroad, including a joint venture in the United Arab Emirates, as well as marketing products and setting up centers in other parts of the Middle East and the UK.

This represents a significant step up in company growth. Whereas the business had grown to almost 70 centers over the previous 15 years, it now intended to open 30 more in one year, as well as to set up the infrastructure for more training institutes and an overseas division. In the past, growth could be supported from cash generated from the business and other local sources; however, this new, rapid spurt of growth would require a substantial amount of cash to be raised from a source that would be comfortable sharing the risks and rewards of VLCC's rapid growth strategy. Management were also looking for commitment from a funder for the whole plan, rather than have to raise funding center by center. VLCC looked to Asia's private equity market for a partner.

VLCC attracts private equity

In 2004, VLCC reportedly became the first Indian retail business to attract investment funding from a foreign institution. In July 2004, VLCC announced that it had secured a US$10 million investment from a fund managed by CLSA Private Equity, based in Hong Kong. It is expected that the investment will be delivered in tranches over two to three years and in the form of preference shares. These will then be converted into a minority stake before the company's planned IPO. VLCC's managing director reflected on the perceived benefits that raising private equity investment would have for the business: "VLCC has set itself ambitious targets. We plan to be a 100-centres strong company by the end of this financial year with a foray in international markets... Overall, CLSA's investment in our company would help us achieve this rapid growth and targets ahead of time." (Mukesh Luthra, *The Hindu Business Line*, July 15, 2004)

Benefits to VLCC of raising private equity

Commitment

CLSA's Private Equity (PE) fund has provided a commitment of US$10 million, which VLCC can utilize to accelerate its growth plan. This is a much better situation than moving step by step, not knowing if there will be enough money for the next stage or needing to embark on successive fundraising programs in order to reach the objective.

This not only saves a lot of management time, but also enables the business to establish a defensible market position more quickly.

Risk sharing

The private equity fund provider becomes a partner with the founder shareholders. This means that instead of focusing on collateral and covenanted repayments, as would be the case with bank finance, the private equity fund has "bought into" the vision of the business's founders and, along with them, will either benefit from the success, or suffer from the failure, of the plan.

Experience and contacts

The benefits from private equity are not just money-related. In this case, VLCC will gain from the benefit of the PE fund's experience of growing businesses, as well as from their contacts abroad. In addition, VLCC will have more credibility as it ventures outside India if it has an internationally recognized PE partner.

Attractiveness for IPO

It is likely that having an international PE fund as a shareholder will help to increase VLCC's attractiveness to public investors when the business applies for a public listing. This is because investors may feel that the PE fund has not only carried out significant due diligence on the market and the prospects of VLCC before investing, but also that the standards of corporate governance required by the fund will ensure that VLCC is well-run from a shareholder viewpoint.

What makes VLCC an attractive PE investment?

Strong track record

We described earlier in the chapter the difference between venture capital and expansion capital. VLCC provides an excellent example of an established business with a track record. Prior to the PE investment, it had sales of some US$20 million, with already wide coverage through its 60-plus outlets. Although the numbers are not publicly available, it can be expected that the business has a strong cash flow. The management team had clearly not only proven the business model, but had created a widely recognized brand that in itself would have significant value. Indeed, the business only needs the investment of US$10 million to *speed up* its growth plans.

To look at this another way, the founders of VLCC could easily choose a slower growth path and not raise any money at all. So, whereas early-stage or start-up businesses need capital to help establish the business, larger businesses choose to raise the money because of a growth opportunity. This makes it very attractive for the PE investor, as the normal risks associated with "will the business actually work?" are already minimized. Hence, while the risk that VLCC will fail as a business in opening its first 10 beauty and slimming centers is high, the risk of failure of increasing the number of centers from 70 to 100 is relatively low. Perhaps the biggest risk with this investment is the development of the international side of the business. However, the international plan appears to be a relatively low-profile one and its small size relative to the core business will help to mitigate the risk of failure.

Credible growth opportunity

VLCC already has 70 centers and some 100,000 customers; however, we can imagine that, given the size of India in terms of population, there is still some way to go. In addition, the market itself is growing at quite a rate. As Josephine Price, managing director of the CLSA PE fund, notes: "We think the sector's got tremendous growth ... beauty is growing at about 8%, Ayurvedic is growing in double figures, and slimming at around 13–15%."

In addition, the business has developed other growth areas, including the manufacture and sale of products. A credible growth opportunity is an important aspect for expansion capital, both for the entrepreneur and the investor. Why should VLCC be prepared to use equity in the business to raise money if they don't believe that the business will grow significantly quicker and bigger as a result? Growth-oriented entrepreneurs are happy to have less equity in a much larger business than more equity in a smaller one. In the same way, how will the private equity investor make its returns unless quantum growth in value is possible?

Clear exit route

A way to realize the investment at some point is always a consideration for private equity, whether the situation is a start-up, early stage, expansion, or MBO. PE funds generally have a life of five to 10 years, by which time the investors in the fund itself expect to recover their initial investment plus the capital return. The concern with making minority investments in private companies is that the investor has little say in driving the business to an exit and has the prospect of being stuck a minority investor forever or until the majority shareholders decide to sell the business. In VLCC's case, there is a clear plan to IPO the business within two to three years. In addition, due diligence by the investor could include discussing the viability of a listing with some Indian investment banks. Of course, the majority investors may still block a sale, but it is interesting to note in this case that the structure of the investment provides some protection and leverage to the investor on two fronts. First, the investment appears to be in several tranches. This provides the investor with a lever in that, if performance or progression to IPO isn't satisfactory, subsequent draw-downs may be withheld. Second, the investment is in preferential shares with the ability to convert prior to IPO. This enables the investor to have some control through special preferential share rights up until the point of IPO. These rights may include measures that are designed to ensure that the company proceeds to an exit situation such as increasing dividend payments or demanding redemption of shares after a certain time interval or, indeed, the ability to convert to a higher proportion of the equity if certain events don't happen. There is a further twist in that, in many Asian countries, a listing doesn't necessarily mean an exit for the PE fund, particularly if liquidity – or demand for the shares – is poor. This is discussed in Chapter 11. Again, if the PE fund isn't happy that a listing can bring a proper *cash to cash* return, then they may use the preferential share rights to cause the company to find other exit routes.

This is an interesting example not only because it was one of the first private equity investments in this sector in India, but also because it illustrates that private equity can be attracted to businesses that are not technology-related. While it is clearly early days, the investment in VLCC provides a clear example of the potential benefits for both sides in terms of using private equity for expansion plans.

The next brief case study is selected to provide an interesting contrast. First, from a business viewpoint, the company was set up by professional entrepreneurs, and backed by venture capital from the outset, to meet an opportunity that was developing in the semiconductor industry – that is, manufacturing products (semiconductor wafers) based on mature technology for the growing electronics market in China. This type of business creation works on the basis of rapid growth to get to an established position in the market. This then allows the investors to exit the investment via a trade sale or IPO. In this case, it would always be necessary for one or two rounds of funding to meet the large capital expenditure needs of a growing semiconductor foundry business. These would be at increasing valuations and would take the business to a stage where it was large and interesting enough to list and allow the investors to realize their investments. At IPO, the start-up VC investors would receive a high return in compensation for the high risk they took back in 1997 when the company was set up. The later-stage expansion round, or "pre-IPO" round, investors would receive a lower return given that their investment was taken at a stage when the business model was already proven and the IPO and exit already in sight. Second, CSMC is a chip manufacturer and is clearly dependent on the technology market. As is typical of successful technology-based businesses, it has experienced a much higher growth rate than a company such as VLCC.

CSMC Technologies Corp., China

CSMC was founded in 1998 by an experienced team of international semiconductor industry professionals led by Dr. Peter Chen, who himself has some 30 years in the sector. The business operates open semiconductor foundries in China and targets the market for integrated circuits (ICs) requiring six-inch wafers. Although this is relatively old technology, ICs in this range account for over 70% of the China market. CSMC has now developed into the leading six-inch IC foundry services provider in China. Dr. Chen and his team saw this as an exceptional opportunity that had certain advantages. First, operating in the relatively old six-inch wafer area meant that the business wouldn't come into direct competition with the large foundry businesses such as UMC and TSMC in Taiwan, which concentrate more on providing semiconductors for leading-edge technologies. Second, CSMC has been able to buy secondhand equipment from other foundries that have already moved away from producing six-inch wafers. With the significant ongoing capital investment needed in this type of business, this has been a real benefit. By 2003, CSMC had six of the 10 largest Chinese fab-less design houses as its customers and was starting to provide open foundry services to integrated device manufacturers (IDMs). Dr. Chen and his team believed that CSMC's business model was a strong one: "We have US technology, Taiwan entrepreneurship and operational expertise, backed by international capital. Place these within the cost structure and market opportunity in China now and we've got an unstoppable formula."

CSMC's sales and operating profit to 2001–03 is shown in Figure 9.6.

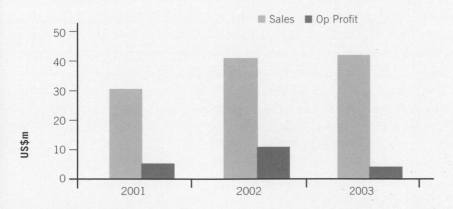

Figure 9.6 CSMC Sales/Profit, 2001–03

At its inception, Dr. Chen had set up the business with the aid of venture capital investment from a number of investors, including Walden International. The founders realized that a foundry business would need significant continuing capital investment to fuel growth, and that subsequent rounds of financing would be inevitable. Although it had plans to move upwards into eight-inch wafer manufacture once the Chinese internal market demand for more leading-edge ICs developed, CSMC felt there was still more demand to service at the mature technology level. With the benefit of two strong years of growth in sales and profitability, and cash flow, the CSMC team commenced discussions with private equity funds with a view to raising capital to build another six-inch foundry. During 2003, management secured commitment of approximately US$50 million expansion funding from a new large group of investors led by Crown Crystal Investments Ltd (CCI) and 3i, a leading UK venture capital group. This was seen as a precursor to a planned IPO on the Hong Kong Stock Exchange in 2004. Despite the general cyclical issues associated with the semiconductor sector and the ongoing need for high levels of capital investment, the growing Chinese market for the products, together with the business model adopted by the management team, was compelling to investors. In addition, the team and its large number of investors were committed to a listing in Hong Kong within 12 months. This would provide a quick capital gain for investors and a method of realizing their return.

As CSMC prepared for its listing in 2004, it was hit by a number of issues. First, its results for 2003 were below expectations and the exciting trend of sales over the previous two years leveled together with a fall in operating profit. Second, CSMC suffered from a decline in investor sentiment toward Chinese IPOs in general. Finally, there was a general slowdown in the momentum of the global semiconductor industry. In June 2004, a listing planned to issue 621 million new shares at a price of between HK$0.73 and HK$1.10 was called off, reportedly due to lack of sentiment in the market and disagreement among its recent investors over the possible eventual share price. The need for new funds, and a method for the investors to monetarize their shares, still remained. First, cash was required to meet CSMC's continuing growth plans, which included the establishment of a next-generation eight-inch wafer fabrication plant. Second, the investors needed an exit – in particular, the early-stage VCs had been investors for some seven years and wouldn't be keen to remain locked in for a further period. In August 2004, the company revived its IPO plans and finally listed on the Hong Kong Stock Exchange. Despite the poor investor sentiment, it achieved this by cutting the IPO price to HK$0.50 and raising less than half the original amount of US$80 million. In addition, existing shareholders agreed to purchase some 50% of the new stock. After listing, the shares traded at a discount to the listing price.

It isn't our intention to give the impression that expansion capital investments in non-tech companies are more successful than those in technology-related businesses. There are plenty of examples of successful and non-successful ones of both types. Although the listing for CSMC hasn't so far been successful for investors, particularly those that provided the later-stage expansion capital and who may subsequently find their shares trading at below their original purchase price, sentiment on the stock market is unpredictable and usually accepted as a risk by investors. As long as CSMC continues to implement its plan and deliver a positive trend in terms of growth, profitability, and cash flow, then it should benefit from a change in public sentiment either toward the semiconductor sector, China, or even better, both. This case does demonstrate, however, that a listing doesn't always provide an exit for investors – unless, of course, they are prepared to sell and make a loss. Either way, the change in timing does affect the return in that for every year an exit isn't achieved, the extra uplift needed to maintain past returns is more challenging. Dr. Chen and his team at CSMC have successfully used private equity to build a significant business, and their own return, having set up the business, should be in good shape. In VLCC's case, it is also early days and problems may develop in many areas. However, its market looks solid. We, as individual customers, are capable of putting on weight all year round and for years at a time, which ensures that businesses in the health and slimming market are relatively non-cyclical. In addition, the capital expenditure requirements are not so huge, and the market risk is spread over a wider area, as opposed to technology-related investments that tend to depend on the fortunes of a small number of customers. As mentioned earlier, it isn't our intention to make a judgment on tech versus non-tech investments, but rather to demonstrate some of the differences in risk profile between them. We often hear that the tech sector is more interesting because of the higher returns, but we can forget that this is justified because of the higher risks involved. The non-tech-related opportunities such as VLCC may not promise such high returns, but the risks tend to be lower and more manageable. Over time, given the different risk profiles, the returns to either should converge. There is just as much a need for non-technology businesses in Asia to receive expansion funding, but this is an area that probably doesn't get as much attention as it deserves.

▶▶ CONCLUSION

Asia's need for expansion funding to fuel its continuing economic growth is already significant and is likely to continue to grow for some time. It is also unlikely that this need will be satisfied by the provision of government grants and subsidies, banking products, or from the public capital markets. The development of a private equity market, therefore, with willing suppliers (investors) and customers (entrepreneurs), will be fundamental to supporting the projected growth of SMEs in Asia going forward.

ENDNOTES

[1]   PWC/3i *Global Private Equity Review, 2003/2004.*

[2]   The material for both studies is gathered from press reports and other public domain sources.

CHAPTER

10

Going
International

---

*B*usiness operations on an international scale are widely held to
be a major contributing factor to company growth and
profitability. In this chapter we look at what normally constitute
the different phases of the internationalization process, its attendant
problem areas, and best practice experience.

We go on to consider how Asian companies have historically fared
in this process, and why the situation may well be changing rapidly
during these opening years of the 21st century, with some thoughts as
to why there might be real advantage to be derived by Asian companies
from coming late to internationalization.

We end the chapter with a case study in which the CEO of a young
Hong Kong company recounts his firm's experiences in the process of
going international.

THE "FEAR OF FLYING"

During a chat one of the authors had with Narayana Murthy in late 2003, he asked the question: "What is the biggest single issue facing Indian entrepreneurial companies at the present time?" The answer came back with no hesitation: "Taking their companies international." Indian companies, he explained, are perfectly well equipped to compete within the boundaries of their own country, but are seriously lacking in the will and the know-how to extend their operations beyond those boundaries. (As with any generalization, of course, there are exceptions to this statement, Narayana Murthy's own company, Infosys, being a shining example.)

However, a similar line of thought came up during a talk with another Murthy, Mahesh Murthy this time, CEO of PassionFund in Mumbai:

> Indian companies tend to have a kind of inferiority complex when they try to sell their products overseas. The approach tends to be "my product is different from IBM's and that is why it is half the price," rather than "my product is different from IBM's and that is why it is 20% more expensive."

This is clearly a phenomenon that will tend to disappear over time, and as it does, the implications for competition around the world are enormous.

Consider, for example, the situation in China. Right now, an impressive quantity of Chinese manufactured goods is already being offered for sale around the world, but in the vast majority of cases, under a non-Chinese brand. And yet within China itself there is a plethora of local brands that have strong positions in their domestic market – for example, Panda in home electronic equipment, and TCL and Ningbo Bird in mobile phones. Indeed, the market share of local mobile phone handset manufacturers jumped from 5% in 1999 to nearly 40% in 2003.[1] Sooner or later, the managers of these companies are going to want to capture a larger chunk of the value chain in overseas markets for themselves, as indeed Haier has already done in household appliances. As they start to do this, so plenty of mistakes will be made. However, over time, they will become increasingly good at it, with inevitable consequences for currently dominant international brands (see box).

China's power brands

How do you get rich in China these days? Build a brand. That's what 35-year-old Huang Guangyu has done. The Guangdong native started out at 18, renting a market stall in Beijing and hawking cheap plastic appliances. Today, his GOME Electrical Appliances is China's top consumer-electronics chain, with well over 100 stores, US$2 billion in annual sales, and the kind of high-plateau brand recognition that Circuit City and Best Buy enjoy in the United States.

And thanks to a back-door stock listing in Hong Kong in mid-2004, Huang's net worth is now at least US$830 million. There's just one hitch, though. China's domestic retail players, including GOME, are already worried about the impact of foreign competition in 2005, when Beijing will open the entire country to retailers from abroad.

This little tale neatly sums up the story of China's emerging brands today: there is tremendous excitement about the brands, but a good dose of fear about their staying power. Global business executives are certainly agog at the prospect that the next stage of China's super-fast development will be the establishment of power brands in everything from retailing to white goods to autos and more – brands strong enough both to dominate at home and to thrive overseas. "They are definitely going global," says Glen Murphy, the Shanghai-based managing director of ACNielsen in China. "With their resources and production base, they are large enough to reach out to the world."

Source: Business Week, November 8, 2004, pp. 50–56.

The comparison that comes immediately to mind is the progression of Japanese cars in overseas markets through the 1980s. At first considered as something of a joke ("low price, low quality, low design"), over time they built up a reputation for stylishness, dependability, and innovation that made them in many cases market leaders.

In similar fashion, a handful of South Korean brands, such as Samsung and Hyundai, have made the transition from local to global, something that was virtually impossible to envisage 20 years ago.

With this prospect on the horizon, then, it is interesting to look at internationalization activities and attitudes currently prevalent in Asia. However, before doing so, let's take a brief look at what have historically been considered as the various stages of an internationalization process.

ENTREPRENEURSHIP ACROSS BORDERS

A question that could legitimately be asked at this point is: why should a firm ever want to go international? After all, by doing so it inevitably ventures into unknown territory, fraught with problems and sometimes even dangers. So, why bother?

The answer is simply that, as various studies have found over the years, one of the features that characterizes successful SMEs is a strong overseas presence. Take, for example, Hermann Simon's study of the SMEs that he called the "hidden champions" of the German economy.[2] Simon identifies nine "lessons" he found as common characteristics in successful small companies, one of them being that they "combine a narrow market focus with a global orientation involving worldwide sales and marketing."

> ...one of the features that characterizes successful SMEs is a strong overseas presence.

Academic research strongly supports this idea. For example, Oviatt and McDougall, in a study published in 1997, were already asserting that international expansion positively influences new ventures' survival, profitability, and growth;[3] while more recently, Zahra et al. concluded their study on the topic with these words:

> The results (...) emphasize the importance of international business operations for successful new venture performance. These operations are largely associated with more growth and profitability.[4]

However, other studies have highlighted that the benefits deriving from international business operations are by no means linear. Exactly how they evolve over time is still the subject of debate, but one recent study of Japanese companies would suggest that there are three phases in the internationalization process:

...our findings (...) suggest that managers need to take a long term view of internationalization. At initial stages, there might not be immediate positive returns from foreign expansion, and a firm can even suffer a decline in profits in its initial forays. During this stage, declining profits need not halt internationalization efforts...[5]

A second phase is reached during which firms reap the full benefit of their international operations, but they need to stay alert for the third phase...

As well as being resolute during early stages of international expansion, managers need to be cognizant of the potential downside of excessive international expansion and to be proactive in the design and implementation of international strategies by optimizing the configuration of subsidiary networks to keep the scope of internationalization activities at an optimal level.[6]

Patterns of internationalization

The way firms develop an international activity has been the subject of academic interest for nearly 40 years already, and certainly the best known and most widely accepted model of international expansion is that advanced in the 1970s by what has come to be known as the Uppsala school.[7]

The model proposes four different steps or stages that describe a firm's level of internationalization, as follows:

1. Direct exporting to a foreign country, often in response to an unsolicited order.

2. The firm decides to actively seek export orders with the help of independent representatives or agents abroad.
3. The establishment of a sales subsidiary or affiliate in a foreign country.
4. The creation of a production/manufacturing facility abroad.

A basic assumption of the model is that one phase constitutes the input of the next. This implies that the present state of internationalization is an important factor in explaining what will be the next step.

The underlying assumption of the Uppsala model is that, by and large, the internationalization process will be an unplanned affair, at least in its early stages, with firms responding to stimuli coming from abroad, as opposed to implementing a structured plan of attack. Implicit in this assumption is a degree of unplanned improvisation, especially in the early stages, wherein lie the seeds of, if not outright disaster, then at the very least some unexpected upsets.

Typical problem areas

Consequently, the smaller-sized firm's path to internationalization isn't trouble free but is beset by many obstacles of variable severity and significance. Leonidas Leonidou, a professor at the University of Cyprus, published an article in 2004 addressing just this topic.[8] Professor Leonidou undertook a systematic review of 32 empirical studies conducted over a period of 40 years, with the objective of extracting, collating, and consolidating existing knowledge on the nature of barriers and their association with small business exporting. He also sought to analyze the characteristics, content, and impact of each barrier on export management decisions in smaller firms.

One fascinating output of his research was a consolidation and ranking according to level of impact of all the many barriers and obstacles identified in the empirical studies he reviewed (see box).

Ranking of export barriers

Very high impact
- Limited information to locate/analyze markets
- Inability to contact overseas customers
- Identifying foreign business opportunities
- Difficulty in matching competitors' prices
- Excessive transportation/insurance costs
- Different foreign customer habits/attitudes
- Poor/deteriorating economic conditions abroad
- Political instability in foreign markets

High impact
- Offering satisfactory prices to customers
- Accessing export distribution channels
- Obtaining reliable foreign representation
- Granting credit facilities to foreign customers
- Unfamiliar exporting procedures/documentation
- Unfavorable home rules and regulations
- Foreign currency exchange risks
- Strict foreign rules and regulations

Moderate impact
- Problematic international market data
- Lack of managerial time to deal with exports
- Inadequate/untrained personnel for exporting
- Shortage of working capital to finance exports
- Providing technical/after-sales service
- Complexity of foreign distribution channels
- Adjusting export promotional activities
- Problematic communication with overseas customers
- Slow collection of payments from abroad
- Lack of home government assistance/incentives
- Keen competition in overseas markets
- High tariff and non-tariff barriers
- Unfamiliar foreign business practices
- Different socio-cultural traits

Low impact
- Meeting export product quality standards/specs
- Lack of excess production capacity for exports
- Verbal/non-verbal language differences

Very low impact
- Developing new products for foreign markets
- Adapting export product design/style
- Meeting export packaging/labeling requirements
- Maintaining control over foreign middlemen
- Difficulty in supplying inventory abroad
- Unavailability of warehousing facilities abroad

Some of these obstacles are associated with internal weaknesses – for example, shortage of working capital – while others relate to external factors, as in the case of different customer habits. Moreover, there are also problems that arise within the domestic sphere of the exporter – for example, lack of government assistance/incentives – and others that occur in the foreign market where the company operates or is planning to operate, such as keen competition. In general, internal barriers found within the country base of the exporting firm are more controllable and easier to manage than external problems occurring abroad.

The analysis also showed that the frequency, intensity, or importance of export barriers can vary according to different time, spatial, and industry contexts. This highlights the fact that the impact of barriers on exporting is situation-specific, largely depending on the idiosyncratic managerial, organizational, and environmental background of the firm. Irrespective of the influence of these factors, certain barriers, such as those pertaining to information inefficiencies, price competitiveness, foreign customer habits, and politico-

> " In general, internal barriers found within the country base of the exporting firm are more controllable and easier to manage than external problems occurring abroad. "

economic hurdles, have a systematically strong obstructing effect on the export behavior of small firms.

Best practice

All of which has given rise to an abundant supply of horror stories illustrating how *not* to do it, and an accompanying and equally abundant literature addressing how it should be done. An excellent example of this latter is the best practice list that emerged from a study carried out by the UK Department of Trade and Industry (DTI) in 1997.[9] The DTI studied a cross-section of British SMEs that were active internationally, and concluded that the following were characteristics shared by all the successful firms:

- having a truly international outlook;
- showing real long-term commitment to export markets;
- researching new markets thoroughly;
- building close, long-lasting relationships in export markets;
- recognizing and adapting successfully to different cultures;
- achieving error-free documentation; and
- building an international reputation for quality.

THE ASIAN EXPERIENCE

Internationalization is a challenge for all companies, but in particular for Asian companies which, with the possible exception of Japan, don't have a tradition of international activities, as in Europe or the United States. So, we now turn our attention to internationalization as seen through the Asian experience. In 2002, two INSEAD professors,

> " Internationalization is a challenge for all companies, but in particular for Asian companies which, with the possible exception of Japan, don't have a tradition of international activities, as in Europe or the United States. "

Arnoud de Meyer and Peter Williamson, wrote a very thoughtful working paper on precisely this topic.[10] The following two sections are reproduced, with minor changes, from that document.

Background

Despite their region's long trading history, most East Asian and Southeast Asian companies[11] have pursued only limited internationalization, in the sense of building multinational networks through foreign direct investment (FDI). However, there are many signs that this historic pattern might have begun a period of rapid change.

The reasons for hypothesizing that such a sea-change may be taking place goes beyond the oft-repeated descriptions of the "globalization wave" that has swept the world economy over the past decade. There appear to be at least three reasons why the pressures and opportunities for internationalization facing East Asia might be both stronger than and somewhat different from those operating in other parts of the world.

First, following the Asian financial crisis of 1997, the IMF and other international bodies exerted pressure on the governments of many East Asian countries to gradually open up their markets to international competition. Singapore has probably implemented the most far-reaching and rapid changes in this direction, but similar liberalization processes have been initiated in Thailand, South Korea, Taiwan, and even in Indonesia and Malaysia. These have included the liberalization of restrictions on inward FDI and cross-border acquisitions, as well as moves to reduce intra-Asian trade barriers. Examples of trade liberalization include plans to turn ASEAN into a free trade area, Singapore's pursuit of bilateral free-trade agreements with its main trading partners, and China's entry into the WTO.

Where trade and cross-border investment barriers had already been removed, MNCs such as Shell, Toyota, GE Capital, and Citibank's card services tended to dominate their respective market segments across Asia. Local companies such as banks in Malaysia, telecommunications companies such as Singtel, automobile assemblers such as Astra in Indonesia or Hicom in Malaysia, not to mention the numerous state-owned enterprises in China, could succeed in the past because they operated in protected sectors and in many cases acted as "national champions." These protective barriers are obviously not being removed overnight. However, gradual liberalization of trade and investment will inevitably result in the incumbent "national champions" coming under increased competitive pressure from multinational players, both through imports and new entry via expansion or acquisition. In response, East Asian companies may themselves be forced to further internationalize in order to remain competitive.

Second, the Asian financial crisis revealed the weakness of the horizontal diversification that had been pursued by many East Asian companies as a way to leverage their resource- and relationship-based advantages in their local markets, including preferred access to capital, raw material supplies, and licenses. Companies whose core competencies were spread too thinly across a multitude of different businesses were among the most severely impacted by the crisis, because they lacked the depth of knowledge and managerial capabilities to compete across such a wide variety of businesses in the tough market conditions that ensued after the crisis. This had led a number of East Asian companies to turn their attention to opportunities for growth through geographic diversification and cross-border expansion of their core businesses where they enjoy a depth of specialist capabilities. Such a shift in strategy would lead directly to greater internationalization among East Asian firms.

Third, prior to the late 1990s, the profitability of many East Asian companies had arguably been heavily underpinned by their ability to leverage the information asymmetries that abounded in an environment characterized by underdeveloped information and communications infrastructure and lack of transparency. Where much of the current investment in information and communications technologies (ICT) in the US, Europe, and Japan will have an incremental impact in much of East Asia, embracing ICT is likely to result in a step-change in transparency and accessibility of information. This will put pressure on the ability of East Asian firms to profit from information asymmetries that have underpinned their competitiveness in local markets. One result may be to look for opportunities to use the new ICT infrastructure to exploit the cross-border synergies available from internationalization to restore margins and open up new profit streams.

It is arguable that the recession which began in the second quarter of 2001, and which was aggravated by the September 11 terrorist attacks in the US, may act as a brake on these forces for the internationalization of Asian firms. East Asian countries may opt for protectionist policies that create a favorable environment for local champions. Malaysia's industrial policies, for example, show some evidence of moving in that direction. On the other hand, the 2001 recession has acted as an uncomfortable reminder of how dependent Asian firms remain on sub-contract orders from multinationals. This dependence amplifies the impact of the recession in the US, Europe, and Japan. In order to become less exposed to major recessionary waves, Asian firms will have to diversify their geographic portfolio of activities and may well seek greater control over their end markets by increasing their international spread through FDI.

Possible "latecomer" advantages in the internationalization game

Climbing the internationalization staircase clearly presents a formidable challenge for East Asian companies, and they start with significant handicaps. As latecomers to the internationalization game compared with many of their Western or Japanese counterparts, however, East Asian companies do have a number of potential advantages they can exploit.

The first, and perhaps most obvious, advantage is that East Asian companies have examples to learn from and to follow. While the impediments to internationalization outlined in the preceding section are typical for East Asia, they are not unique. Japanese companies, such as Sony or Toyota, have successfully wrestled with overcoming the difficulties of a knowledge-management process that depends on co-location. Many former "national champions" from Europe – smaller companies, in particular – faced similar capability gaps. French companies, for example, often began with more resource-based advantages than system-based advantages when they started down the road to internationalization. In each national case there are success stories of companies that overcame their specific hurdles. Documenting these lessons and adapting them to the specific East Asian situation should be a priority for East Asian companies (and academics).

Companies coming late to the internationalization game can also benefit from a second advantage: talented and successful East Asians have preceded their companies overseas. The best universities of the US, Australia, the UK, and to some extent continental Europe, are populated with East Asians. Some of these best and brightest have stayed; others have returned home. If cleverly exploited, this group can be an enormous advantage to internationally expanding cooperation. Those who have stayed overseas form a potential network of allies; the ones that have returned bring home potentially a vast wealth of know-how about foreign markets and culture. But this repository of contacts and know-how is often under-exploited. Those who went abroad will have changed in attitude and behavior. When they come back, they may face proverbial "tissue rejection" if they don't suppress these changes – we at INSEAD have often seen this problem with MBA students returning from Europe to Asia. Rejection amounts to foregoing enormous opportunities to speed up the internationalization process. But a prerequisite to leveraging this potential advantage is an appreciation that today it is knowledge, and not just resources, that will be decisive in future international competitive battles.

A third advantage that shouldn't be underestimated as a potential contributor to speeding up the internationalization of East Asian companies is the underlying power of their local economies from which these companies can draw strength. China is big and, from an economic point of view, very well managed. India is equally big and has the advantage of a reasonably strong infrastructure for business and education. But also Southeast Asia shouldn't be underestimated. Together the major Southeast Asian countries comprise 450 million potential consumers, currently with a higher spending power than consumers in either China or India. If internationalization must be built on company-specific competitive advantage, then if and when a company has such an

> "...today it is knowledge, and not just resources, that will be decisive in future international competitive battles."

advantage, it is likely also to be strong in its home market. The sheer size and relative robustness of these major home markets consequently provide an advantage for East Asian internationalizers. Hong Leong of Singapore is a prime example: having built strength in the local hospitality industry, it has successfully expanded with hotel acquisitions to build a strong network in Europe across which it can leverage its system-based advantages.

Hong Leong's experience suggests a final bright spot: we should not underestimate the potential of the distinctive, system-based advantages that the East Asian economies have already developed. The combination of an efficient transshipment port, an excellent airline, a top-class airport, very professional shippers, and an IT industry that has developed skills specifically to transport, has created both in Hong Kong and Singapore a systemic knowledge in integrated logistics. Based on this rich foundation, both Hutchinson from Hong Kong and PSA of Singapore have internationalized and now manage ports worldwide. The sub-contracting of assembly of electronic products and of the fabrication of micro-electronic components has become a specialty of several Taiwanese, Singaporean, or Chinese companies, such as Flextronics and Taiwan Semiconductor. Fish farming, endemic to Taiwan, Vietnam, and Thailand, among others, is another example of a locally developed, system-based advantage – subsequently picked up and further developed by Chareon Pokphand of Thailand as a basis for its expansion into fish farming in India. Too rarely, however, are these capabilities recognized for what they are: distinctive locally developed competitive advantages. It is perhaps a lack of ambition,[12] and a certain complacency based on the resource-based advantages, that hinders the international deployment of these advantages.

Specific examples: Hong Kong, Singapore, and Australia

Hong Kong and Singapore both have long experience as city-states, and both have been transformed from small fishing villages into major financial and commercial centers in just over a century. Given their similarities, it would be tempting to speculate that both would have followed a similar path to internationalization, driven by the very limited size of their respective home markets, and yet such a speculation wouldn't be justified.

In a fascinating book,[13] Henry Wai-chung Yeung identifies the differences in developmental patterns between the two city-states, and in so doing makes the important point that the speed and nature of internationalization of entrepreneurial companies isn't common across all countries, but owes a lot to differing ethnic and societal factors. In particular, he has this to say about the differences between Hong Kong and Singapore:

> "...the speed and nature of internationalization of entrepreneurial companies isn't common across all countries, but owes a lot to differing ethnic and societal factors."

...they have indeed very different dominant forms of economic organisation in relation to business organisations, industrial structures, labour organisations, and capital markets. These institutional differences are an outcome of the differential role of the state and entrepreneurship in driving economic development. (...) In particular, Singapore's developmental state has taken over the primary responsibility for economic development from private entrepreneurs. The state has therefore become a public entrepreneur in its own right and invited global corporations to locate their production facilities in Singapore. Put in their different historical contexts, the two city-states have evolved into very different business systems in which pre-existing configurations of institutional structures have differential impacts on entrepreneurial activities. (...)

These institutional differences in home country business systems are directly translated into quantitative and qualitative differences in outward investments ... (which) ... from Hong Kong tend to have a longer history and geographical reach, compared with those from Singapore.

The reason for this contrast in development is succinctly given by Lee Kuan Yew, for many years Singapore's prime minister and now its "Minister Mentor," in his memoirs:

> We did not have a group of ready-made entrepreneurs such as Hong Kong gained in the Chinese industrialists and bankers who came fleeing from Shanghai, Canton and other cities when the communists took over. Had we waited for our traders to learn to be industrialists we would have starved.[14]

It is fascinating to see, in a totally unrelated study, that in Australia similar factors appear to have been at work:

> ...few Australian firms have ventured beyond the bounds of the domestic market. Easy and popular explanations appeal to the tyranny of distance, which depict Australia as marooned in a psychically distant Asian region, isolated from the richer markets of Europe and North America. (...) an alternative view: multinational growth by Australian firms was constrained primarily by domestic factors, rather than the lack of external opportunities. The scale of inward technology flows, which were largely controlled by foreign-owned affiliates, constrained the evolution of domestic technologies and brands that could be taken out to the world market.[15]

In other words, the massive presence of large foreign multinationals has historically put a brake on the development of "home-grown" brands and products that can be taken into international markets, and what overseas trade there was tended to be with traditionally close nations, such as the UK and the US.

All this would tend to confirm that in order to successfully embark on a process of internationalization, firms must of necessity have some unique resources and capabilities, and firms in countries in which these are largely in the hands of foreign firms will have greater difficulties in internationalizing.

Government support schemes

Since the early 1990s the Australian government has encouraged Australian companies to consider Asian markets as "natural" destinations for their international activities; and in similar fashion, the Singaporean government has also undertaken an energetic series of actions designed to encourage Singaporeans to be more entrepreneurial and to seek foreign markets. There is even a statutory board (International Enterprise Singapore, or IE Singapore) responsible for taking SMEs overseas. With 36 centers in various countries around the world, IE Singapore's mission is to help Singapore-based companies to grow and internationalize successfully, and to be an expert agency in firm-level growth, market intelligence, and internationalization strategies.

Other government internationalization support schemes around the region include:

- the Korean Small and Medium Business Administration, which offers a comprehensive export support system to provide SMEs and venture firms with an export base, including representative offices on both coasts of the United States;
- New Zealand Trade and Enterprise, a government agency, which provides a range of international consultancy services for New Zealand exporters; and
- the Malaysian SME Information & Advisory Centre, a government agency, which has established a new program called HeadStart 500, designed to provide SMEs with support services needed to accelerate their transformation from domestic-oriented to global manufacturers.

C A S E   S T U D Y

Outblaze, Hong Kong[16]

Outblaze, a Hong Kong company marketing email services, is an excellent example of how a young Asian company approached the process of going international and coped with the difficulties it met, all of which reflect those listed by Professor Leonidou. Founded in August 1998 by current CEO, Yat Siu, Outblaze set out to tap into the seemingly lucrative market for internet advertising. The original idea was to create portals for companies on an outsourcing basis, and then split the advertising revenue generated by co-branded sites 50–50 with its customers. However, by mid-2000, internet companies worldwide were crumbling, and limited growth in revenue projections had prompted a vital change in the company's business strategy. Rather than offer email and other portal services for free in the hope of tapping advertising revenues later, the company began to charge its customers, albeit at a fraction of what it would cost them to set up and maintain the services themselves. The revised mission was to become the leading service provider of information, communication, marketing, and commerce platforms for e-businesses and portals. Within months, Outblaze was selling its new services to international firms.

Outblaze's internationalization process was a faithful reflection of the Uppsala model described earlier. First came direct exporting to a foreign country, in response to unsolicited orders. CEO Yat Siu takes up the story.

Come 2000, we started getting a lot of customers coming to us from abroad. We weren't really looking for them; they were coming to us, from the US, Europe, Africa, South America, just about everywhere. Then, when we made the shift from free to chargeable services, that's when we realized which of the markets would make money for us. We focused on that, and essentially the markets were the US and Europe.

I chose to grow geographically. If we were a company based in China, you could argue that we could just focus on China to grow. In our business, the email space, Hong Kong, was too small a market. The population is 6–7 million, and only 1 million were online. Email is a scalable, commodity business. You need millions of subscribers to become a dominant player. Although it's a utility business, it's not like electricity. Electricity is very localized; you cannot trade electricity the way you trade email. It must be international. We had a lower cost structure than our US and European counterparts, so we leveraged that and grew our business internationally. A lot of people in Asia are building businesses to sell overseas to exploit their competitive advantages. If we hadn't internationalized the business to sell to the US and Europe, we wouldn't be here today.

If there was any issue that outlying offices complained about, it was support. Issues in Hong Kong got more attention, but that had to change. Another problem that still persists is that Hong Kong may not want to do a deal that a country manager wants. In China, for example, we have highly varied customers. Outblaze supports what they need, since they are starting from scratch and the customer wants to do a number of things. But we can't do some things alone, and co-promoting or co-bidding [with complementary service providers] isn't workable or popular. No one wants to share, even though customers want a one-stop shop. But Outblaze can't respond to that, today. That's why the telecom groups are easier for us to target.

Being from Hong Kong didn't make any difference, as long as we could accommodate the client's schedule. So, sometimes we came in at 11 a.m. and stayed until 4 a.m. It didn't make any sense for us, in Hong Kong, to focus on Asia. The US clients did prefer that we have a US presence, so we had a US "office," but it was a shell. Basically, it answered the phone. All of the US activities were managed and sold from Hong Kong. The only difficulty was getting a foot in the right door, assuming that language is not a barrier.

We've had some peculiar success in Latin America. It's one of those markets that we had assumed wouldn't be that significant, but ended up having significant fee-paying clients coming from there, and some of our biggest opportunities are still in that region.

Our most recent deal [December 2003], Univision, is a US-based company focused on the Latin American market with Hispanic broadcasting. It's testament to the fact that the Latin American market's very important to us. We didn't target that market; it came to us. They went to our staff, some directly to Hong Kong. They were price-conscious, so they were probably looking at a number of vendors and doing research on who they wanted to use. Peru, for example, is a fast-growing market in terms of revenue size. They kept coming to us, and we had so many opportunities that we established a reseller there.

We have business coming in from the Middle East, and you might ask what we are doing there. We are not an American company, and that turned out to be a big advantage in places like Syria. It was good to be an Asian company.

The next stage was that the firm decided to actively seek export orders with the help of independent resellers abroad.

We look at markets where we see the lowest-hanging fruit: large portal operators with high-cost infrastructure. If they outsource services to a company like Outblaze, it makes a lot of sense. We used cash flow to expand local operations in the US and Europe, and built direct sales. We hire resellers until we close enough deals or a major deal, then we open an office of our own.

But the process was by no means without its problems. For example, in France... I talked to people there, had a reseller there, and we decided to go into that market.

But it turned out that France was an even more relationship-driven, guangxi-based market than China. If you didn't come from the same technical "école," graduate from the same polytechnic, forget it. And here I was thinking Europe would be a little bit more open.

In Germany, we had some cultural issues in the early days. If there was a problem, our Chinese engineers would articulate it so it didn't sound like a real problem. People in Germany were more accusatory in their style. The Chinese thought the Germans were rude, and the Germans thought the Chinese were incompetent, so they never got anything done together. I haven't good things to say about the Central European business style. I don't mean to be critical and can't claim to be very knowledgeable, but I have found it is a very rank-conscious society that also (from a business perspective) suffers from the Asian problem of not being direct about a problem. The American business style is much more direct: address the problem head on. That doesn't work well in Asia, but if I would adopt anything from the West, it would be getting people to take responsibility and dissolving the hierarchy that is so apparent in Asian companies, to promote more knowledge sharing.

Early on, we approached everyone. Here are the yellow pages, so hunt. Now, attention is based on revenue share. It's not just a market. It's also a market focus, so we have a very focused approach in terms of who we want to target.

We used to just do business with anyone. Now we actually request deposits for service fees in advance, especially for markets that we consider a little bit more risky. Of course, the maturity of our business allows that. Three years ago, it would have been a different story. The competitive market has changed, too. Now there are really only two choices for outsourced email: Critical Path or Outblaze. Three years ago we had 40+ competitors.

The following stage was the establishment of a sales subsidiary or affiliate in a foreign country.

China is very different – it's more software sales-driven, one-off software sales and very heavy sales on the anti-spam/anti-virus suite. China has a very big spam problem, so we're approaching it on that level. The opportunity is with SMEs, and we've been selling software solutions to address that sector with some success. We've developed a product on a CD that can be distributed. It's a completely different model than we use anywhere else.

We have suffered from turnover in Beijing in a pretty bad way. We've managed to retain the key people, but not our support staff. Basically, what we need to do is to establish reseller channels in China to sell our products. In China, the attracting and retaining of personnel in the IT sector is very hard. It's where Hong Kong was at the end of 2000. And it's not just in our sector; I've heard of some companies that have had 100% turnover. Because we're small – we had 7–8 people, then some left and we had to rehire – and investing in people is also hard because you give them a raise, and it's not enough. It's very difficult.

We also calculated whether it's cheaper to hire someone in China rather than Hong Kong. We thought, maybe we should establish a larger base there, even an R&D center. We tried that, but it didn't work. We had the space, and we got a group of QAs (quality assurance specialists) and programmers in China, and we decided to do some of our development there. We sent up some of our guys to try and train them and bring them to the next level. We had around 10 people there and, basically, they all left. It was just impossible to keep them.

You could say it was bad management, but the job market opportunities were just too strong and, in the end, we would have had to pay as much as we do people in Hong Kong to keep them. We tried to make it more attractive via the management style, a relaxed environment, flexible hours if they did their job, lots of free food, a party environment. The emotional attachment would be lost if you quit. I hired someone with the official title of "Office Mother," whose job was to tie up people on a personal level. She put on birthday parties and things. That worked when we were smaller, but not when we got to 50 people. But the bubble had burst then and we were able to be more realistic about compensation.

Maybe China is OK for manufacturing, which is a streamlined process. But our business is very human capital-intensive. We have to invest in our people, send them for training; they have to study our products. It's a three-month process and, once we educate them on our system, they can probably go somewhere else and use that skill. On top of the training investment, taxes in China make hiring a large staff in China prohibitive in terms of cost. Maybe the base salary is only RMB3–4,000, but once you load on all the costs, you're maybe looking at RMB6–7,000/month. Now in Hong Kong, you can hire a similarly skilled person for HK$8,000/month (RMB9,000) because the market's been so depressed. So, the savings don't justify the costs and risk.

There were a number of areas where I sensed potential. It was based on my discussions with people, but certainly not research on a Gartner level. I went to the marketplace, I went to a conference, I talked to a few people, and I made a gut decision that this is a market we should be in.

The fourth and last stage in the model is the creation of a production/manufacturing facility abroad.

> We've ended up with multiple operations in different countries that focus on different areas. Hong Kong remains our R&D base. We can attract international developers from around the world here, and the tax structure also benefits us. Project management stays here. In India and China, we have specific, focused development, e.g. anti-spam. These are labor-intensive, since we get 100 million emails and 70–80% is spam. A robot analyzes it, and a human has to analyze samples to create anti-spam libraries. It requires a lot of attention to detail, and you can't do that effectively out of Hong Kong. Customer support is done out of Manila, because it is cheaper and they have very good English skills, which we can't really find, even in Hong Kong. They are not good engineers compared to other areas, but they are good at solving problems and serving international markets.
>
> We don't foresee very strong sales in either Manila or India, but you can't argue with the cost involved. We couldn't provide half as good services as we do offer if we didn't have operations set up in India. Hong Kong is double the cost, and that's still talking about hiring fairly inexperienced people, not top-level, because they're going to be expensive in a city like Hong Kong.
>
> When we're going to the US or Europe, do they necessarily care about a company from Hong Kong with 70–80 employees and a market cap which is perhaps what people pump into seed investments on that side of the ocean? There's always that kind of issue. So traction in the press and marketing efforts are very important while keeping costs "reasonable," which means "very low."

▶▶ CONCLUSION

We have seen in this chapter that the internationalization of companies in some Asian countries has been slowed by an important presence in those markets of affiliates of overseas firms that have put a brake on the development of "home-grown" brands and products that could be taken into international markets.

This slow rate of development has inevitably created a situation in which relatively few SME management teams have experience of operating in overseas markets, and this fact has compounded the problem, as it has meant in turn that the internationalization instinct, if we may put it that way, isn't there.

However, governments around the region are making every effort to try to overcome the problem, and there can be no doubt that as Asia-Pacific managers mature in an international sense, so their companies will become more redoubtable on the international stage.

And, as we saw right at the beginning of the chapter, when Chinese (and also Indian) firms reach that point, they will be a major force to be reckoned with in world trade.

ENDNOTES

1   *The McKinsey Quarterly*, 2, 2004.

2   Hermann Simon, *Hidden Champions: Lessons from 500 of the World's Best Unknown Companies* (Boston: Harvard Business School Press, 1996).

3   Benjamin M. Oviatt and Patricia Phillips McDougall, "Challenges for Internationalization Process Theory: The Case of International New Ventures," *Management International Review*, 1997, 37, pp. 85–99.

4   Shaker A. Zahra, R. Duane Ireland, and Michael A. Hitt, "International Expansion by New Venture Firms: International Diversity, Mode of Market Entry, Technological Learning, and Performance," *Academy of Management Journal*, 43(5), 2000, pp. 925–50.

5   Jane W. Lu and Paul W. Beamish, "International Diversification and Firm Performance: The S-Curve Hypothesis," Academy of Management Journal, 47(4), 2004, pp. 598–609.

6   *Ibid.*

7   See Jan Johanson and Finn Wiedersheim-Paul, "The Internationalization of the Firm: Four Swedish Cases," *Journal of Management Studies*, October 1975, pp. 305–22; and Jan Johanson and Jan-Erik Vahlne, "The Internationalization Process of the Firm: A Model of Knowledge Development and Increasing Foreign Market Commitments, *Journal of International Business Studies*, 8(1), 1977, pp. 23–32.

8   Leonidas C. Leonidou, "An Analysis of the Barriers Hindering Small Business Export Development," *Journal of Small Business Management*, 42(3), 2004, pp. 279–302.

9   "Export Winners," a report from DTI Overseas Trade Services (www.dti.gov.uk/NewReview/ nr32/html/exporting_successfully.html).

10 Arnoud de Meyer and Peter Williamson, "Internationalisation of East Asia Companies: A New Era?", INSEAD Working Paper 2002/68/ABA.

11 Based on companies from ASEAN plus Greater China and South Korea.

12 This exactly mirrors Narayana Murthy's comment quoted at the beginning of this chapter.

13 Henry Wai-chung Yeung, *Entrepreneurship and the Internationalisation of Asian Firms* (Cheltenham: Edward Elgar, 2002).

14 Lee Kuan Yew, *From Third World to First: The Singapore Story: 1965–2000* (Singapore: Times Editions, 2000) (quoted in Yeung, *op. cit.*).

15 Elizabeth Maitland and Stephen Nicholas, "Internationalization of Australian Firms in Asia," *International Studies of Management and Organization*, 32(1), Spring 2002, pp. 79–108.

16 This section is based on, and quotes extensively from, the INSEAD case study "Outblaze: International Entrepreneurship" written by Sarah Harper, Research Fellow, and Steven White, Professor of Asian Business at INSEAD. Copyright © INSEAD 2004.

Let's Go
IPO

*L*isting on a public exchange is one option chosen by entrepreneurial
businesses that need to raise cash for expansion. The practice of
carrying out a public listing has long been popular for Asian
entrepreneurs for a variety of reasons, but raising cash for expansion
has recently become a fundamental driver of the growth of Asian
exchanges. In this chapter, we first take a look at the relative growth in
importance of the Greater China region in respect to Europe and the
United States in terms of company listings. Next a brief case study,
Sunset Components, considers the expansion issues facing an Asian
SME and its decision to become a public company. As a follow on from
this, we take a closer look at the decision to go public in Asia in terms
of the perceived costs and benefits. We then briefly review two currently
topical issues: corporate governance, and life as a small-cap company.
Finally, we return to the China growth phenomenon and take a look at
the issues surrounding the growing queue of Chinese SMEs seeking IPOs.

INTRODUCTION

While setbacks such as recession, September 11, SARS, and bird flu have dampened investors' appetites in the last few years, they don't seem to have derailed Asia's growth in terms of supply of businesses to the public markets. By far the key driver of this has been the growth in importance of China. Figure 11.1 shows the relative growth in terms of numbers of listings between Greater China, Europe, and the United States. Table 11.1 lists the stock exchanges included in the three regions.

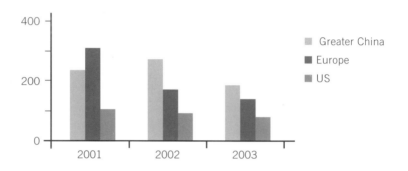

Source: PricewaterhouseCoopers, Greater China IPO Survey Report, May 2004.

Figure 11.1 Numbers of Listings, Greater China versus Europe and the United States

Table 11.1 Regional Exchanges included in Figure 11.1

Greater China	Shanghai, Shenzhen, Hong Kong, Taiwan
Europe	15 EU member states plus Norway and Switzerland
United States	New York, Nasdaq

The picture changes if we look at the total amount of funds raised in these years. In terms of amount raised, the US is almost equal to China and Europe added together. This, of course, is a reflection of the actual amount of funds raised per company, which tends to be large in the US.

However, from Table 11.2 we can see that Greater China is growing in relative importance globally and, since 2002, has been able to raise more public money from listings than Europe. Indeed, Greater China was responsible for almost 50% of capital raised worldwide in 2003 and produced the world's largest IPO that year – the insurance company China Life, which listed on the New York Stock Exchange, raising over US$3 billion. A third trend has been the increase in the size of the listings. Figure 11.2 shows that the amount of IPO funds raised per company in China has been growing over the last three years, whereas in the US and Europe it has declined. Of course, the China listings have started from a low base, but by 2003 they were raising more on average than European listings.

Table 11.2 IPOs: Amount Raised (US$bn)

	2001	2002	2003
Greater China	10.62	13.51	13.93
Europe	34.92	12.03	7.00
United States	41.49	25.48	17.67

Source: PricewaterhouseCoopers, Greater China IPO Survey Report, May 2004.

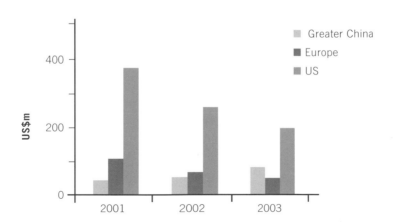

Figure 11.2 Trend in Average Size of Listings

This is positive from many aspects. It demonstrates that IPO candidates in China are becoming more effective in their ability to raise funds. This is a reflection on business size as well as plans for growth. Also, listings are becoming more efficient. The fees and expenses associated with listing a company have a large fixed element and therefore, if a business raises a small amount, a relatively large proportion of this will be used to cover fees, rather than to fund projects that will grow the business. With the high growth rates and business opportunities available in Asia, it seems intuitive that Asia will produce companies that are capital-hungry and are likely to attract more and more of the available global pool of public capital. In a perfectly competitive world, the capital will flow to those companies that promise more exciting returns in terms of dividends and capital appreciation, wherever they are. The world, of course, isn't perfect, and inefficiencies and blockages in the system will serve to slow the process. Examples of this in Asia include:

- the ability of Asian exchanges to cope with the pipeline of candidates for listing;
- the availability of enough advisors and brokers to cope with the large numbers of businesses wishing to embark on the listing process;
- concerns by international institutional investors that Asian companies can comply with global standards of corporate governance and transparency; and
- a general concern of investors that the Chinese economy may be growing too fast, and about the potential knock-on effect of a slowdown on Asia-related stocks.

> Asia is growing in stature as a provider of businesses to the capital markets and this trend is expected to continue.

As we can see, Asia is growing in stature as a provider of businesses to the capital markets and this trend is expected to continue. However, on a more micro scale, we will now look at some of the issues facing Asian SME entrepreneurs as they make their decisions to list. To set the scene, the case study on Sunset Components is based on a real-life situation, although some details and descriptions have been adapted to protect the anonymity of the business, which is still listed on an Asian exchange.

Sunset Components

Dominic Tan and Bryan Yeo founded Sunset Components (Sunset) in Singapore in the early 1980s with the aim of sourcing and distributing electronic components to subcontract manufacturers (SCMs) in the region. They both used their savings to set up the business, which amounted to some US$10,000. Initially, the business mainly involved buying printed circuit boards from small suppliers in Hong Kong and selling them to SCMs in Singapore.

A breakthrough

By 1990, and after much hard work, the two partners had built Sunset to a level of US$100,000 sales per month. On the back of this success, in 1991 they secured distribution rights for a major branded component manufacturer. This contract was a major turning point in the growth of the business, as it not only gave Sunset exclusivity for Southeast Asia, it also brought with it the responsibilities of growing and supporting the customer network. A key element of this was providing credit terms and ensuring the availability of components at short notice. Of course, this meant that Sunset would need to hold a broad range of stock. The provision of credit terms and holding extra stock meant the business would need extra working capital. With sales expected to grow to some US$6 million and the need to offer credit terms to customers of 60 days, the company estimated it would need a facility of some US$2–3 million to cover the working capital fluctuations.

Finding cash for growth

Yeo, as financial officer, considered the options. He approached the banks, but quickly discovered that they would need security to cover the facility. As the business was light on assets – save for the stock – this wasn't going to work. There weren't many other options available for a company at this stage of its development. However, the partners considered the use of factoring. This was a practice relatively new to Asia, but its focus on a company's debtors (or accounts due for payment by its customers), instead of on Sunset's ability to provide security, seemed to be a neat solution to the problem. The other benefit was that as the business expanded, the amount that Sunset could draw from the factoring company would also grow to fit the corresponding growth in customer debts due at any one time. This solution did have some drawbacks, though. First, it was more expensive than bank debt; and second, due to the nature of this type of factoring, the factoring company would have direct contact with customers in collecting payments. This worried Tan and Yeo, because Sunset was heavily dependent on strong customer relationships and many of the slow payers were actually strong and faithful customers. Despite this, they had little alternative and went ahead with the factoring contract.

The business successfully used factoring to fund its growth over the next three years. By 1994 the business had accumulated enough cash to provide a security deposit to take a bank facility. The factoring had taken Sunset through a critical stage of growth, and their success during this period enabled them finally to replace the factoring with a cheaper line of credit. Over the next five years, the company grew its sales to over US$10 million.

A changing marketplace

By the late 1990s, the partners had become particularly worried about the future of their core business of sourcing electro-mechanical components for their SCM customers in Singapore. The root of their concern was the growing trend of manufacturing operations moving to lower-cost areas such as Malaysia, Thailand, and China. In addition, the margins on their components distribution business were experiencing pressure as the large SCMs were placing increased focus on component cost savings.

Tan and Yeo considered their strengths as a business. They had built Sunset through developing strong relationships with large numbers of both suppliers and customers, and by providing value-added services such as working with external design houses to help "design-in" the components to their customers' end-products. To manage this large customer network, the business had also developed a reliable set of distributors not only in Singapore and Hong Kong, but also in other countries such as Malaysia and the Philippines.

First, they felt that they should focus their customer base away from the large SCMs and end-product manufacturers to include smaller SCMs. This would help them deal with margin pressure on a more equal basis. Second, they felt that their coordination experience of suppliers, designers, and end-product manufactures, together with their distribution channels, provided a new potential market opportunity for Sunset to launch its own brand of modular components.

Developing the brand

The partners set up an initial project in 1998 and launched their first range of components, which included mechanisms for electronic products such as VCDs and printers. This new business area saw strong early promise, with sales in the first year of US$4 million and growth of 100% in the second year. It was clear that the market for the own-branded components was going to be exciting, and Tan and Yeo considered how they could make the most of this opportunity. Very quickly, they realized that to grow this area they would need more cash. In a way, they were facing a more acute challenge than before. This time, they would need to fund a stock of high-value modules rather than only low-value components. They calculated that they would need some US$4 million in total to use as working capital to support this new product line, and wondered where they could raise this amount of money.

They considered various sources, including venture capital. There were several active VC funds at the time, but their focus was more on high-growth, technology-related businesses, and Sunset's profile as an electronics distributor didn't fit into their target market. Private equity funds were also considered, but the partners were advised that the amount required would be too small to attract their interest.

The partners turned to their bank, which didn't feel inclined to increase the lines of credit, as not only did the project seem too risky to be funded by debt, but Sunset still lacked collateral to provide as security. The bank introduced the founders to its brokering arm to discuss the possibility of raising public money through a listing. At the time, there was a lot of appetite for public investment in exciting new companies in the region, and the bank felt that Sunset's pitch as a local company with a long track record of serving blue-chip customers, along with its early success in developing its own modules for distribution in Asia, would be an interesting story for investors.

A public listing looks attractive

The advisors suggested that because of these positive factors, and with their assistance, the business could achieve a price-earnings multiple of 14 on a listing. The founders were attracted by this; it meant that, although they were using equity to raise the money, it would be introduced at a valuation that wouldn't result in too much dilution. As well as the opportunity to raise the money they needed, Tan and Yeo were also attracted by the other benefits of listing:

- *Profile*: As they grew the business in Asia, being a listed company in Singapore would be of immense help in providing confidence to new business partners.
- *Personal guarantees*: For over 10 years, the founders had been providing personal guarantees to their bankers, and although they never had doubts that they could meet their obligations, it would be a relief to have these dissolved.

They did have concerns, though, about the process of listing, its cost to the business, and how to set up a process of corporate governance, which would be required once they were a listed company. Their advisors assured them that while the costs of listing would seem high, the value they would bring to the process would be worth it — not only would they be able to help the company to achieve its aspirations in terms of a high valuation, but they could also underwrite the listing from their own network. The founders felt that this would be worth the fees others charged and the costs of the listing, and also didn't feel the need to talk to other brokers in Singapore to benchmark the approach and the deal. In mid-1999, they agreed to start the listing process.

The listing process proved a lot more difficult than the founders had envisaged. The first big surprise was the amount of time they had to put into producing the listing manual. They believed that the brokers would take a bigger role in this, but the drafting, re-drafting, and checking of information involved almost became bigger than the day-to-day activities of running the business. Finally, the application for listing was submitted late in 1999, but because of the backlog of listings, the actual listing was delayed for a further six months. This was a big disappointment for Tan and Yeo after all their hard work and anticipation. However, after the New Year, the company started gearing itself up for a listing in early 2000.

Apart from the delays, the founders were to meet with other disappointments as the listing drew nearer. Their advisor, who had agreed to underwrite the whole amount of US$4 million, seemed to be having difficulties with the original valuation and adjusted it downwards from 14x earnings first to 10x and then finally to 8x. This was a serious blow to the founders, as the dilution of equity necessary to raise the US$4 million was increased considerably. The final shock, however, came with only three weeks left before the listing, when the broker announced that it wasn't now in a position to underwrite the listing and could only find 70 new shareholders – out of a minimum 1,000 needed for a main board listing. It felt too late to pull out – particularly as the company needed the money for expansion and a withdrawal would potentially create bad publicity. The founders and their colleagues got to work to find the new shareholders required and, from among their friends and contacts, were able to find an additional 430 shareholders by the listing date. It wasn't enough for the main board, but it was sufficient to enable the listing to go ahead on the second board. By this time the listing fees, which amounted to 13% of all the funds raised, now felt expensive.

One other area was the requirement for more transparency and accountability going forward. The new listing status would require Sunset to conform to the new guidelines on corporate governance. This involved setting up a formal board structure with two extra board members who would need to meet the requirement of being independent. The company had used family members in the role of non-executive director in the past, but taking on outsiders to sit on the board was a strange concept. How would they find suitable candidates? Would Tan and Yeo be able to form a good working relationship with them? There seemed to be many independent directors already appointed to listed companies in Singapore; however, finding and appointing such a person was new to the team and they didn't really know where to start. In the end, as they were up against a time deadline, they decided to take two independent directors nominated by their bank.

Despite the trail of broken expectations and hard work, Tan and Yeo had achieved their listing. They also had new capital in the balance sheet to support development of their new product line in terms of branding, working capital, and building a presence in new markets. In addition, the founders felt quite fortunate in retrospect. The recession that followed their listing hit their markets badly, and with money in the bank Sunset was more fortunate than most in being able to weather the difficulties this produced.

Four years later, the founders are again in need of cash to grow the business further, and they are finding their status as a listed company more burdensome than they expected. The recent introduction of quarterly reporting in Singapore has provided much more work, and has become one of the key discussions at board meetings. Tan and Yeo feel that this has the effect of leading them to look for short-term fixes rather than longer-term strategies. In addition, they estimate that being a listed company now costs the business some US$150,000 per annum.

As for the challenge of raising new cash, Sunset's status as a public company isn't making this any easier. Like other small-cap businesses in Asia, it attracts little or no interest in its tradable shares and therefore it is very difficult to raise cash by offering new shares to the market. Indeed, the share price hasn't moved for over 18 months and is languishing at some 70% discount to the original listing price. In the meantime, Sunset continues to grow by making its working capital work as hard as possible and by looking for opportunities to expand through making small acquisitions.

Sunset is a good example of where the public markets have been useful in raising a one-off sum to fund expansion plans. However, it also illustrates that for many SMEs, becoming a listed company can be a one-off fix only and doesn't necessarily provide access to a continuing source of further funds. We can also see that along with its obvious benefits, becoming a public company has its drawbacks, which sometimes can be lost in the excitement of early listing discussions.

THE DECISION TO GO PUBLIC: BENEFITS AND COSTS

What is the attraction of going public?

Why is it that taking their businesses public has been and remains so popular among Asian entrepreneurs?

Access to capital for growth

This is usually the main reason for listing a business. To this point, it will have fueled its growth using a combination of its own resources, angel financing, venture capital, banks, and so on. However, an opportunity may present itself that needs a significant injection of equity capital. Examples of this may be the launch of a new product, expansion abroad, acquisition of another business, and so on. All of these projects are growth-oriented and not only bring the likelihood of an attractive return, but also introduce an element of risk to the business. Because of this, they are not appropriate for debt funding. (Debt ties the company into a servicing and repayment contract regardless of whether or not the project is successful.) There are other options in terms of private equity that we cover in Chapter 9, but a more normal route in Asia to date is to seek a listing.

A market for the company's shares

As a business grows, the value of its shares may also grow. Those in private family businesses who have experienced facilitating the sale or purchase of shares between friends and relatives know that this can be a complex, and often emotional, process. A listing on a public exchange creates a market for the shares, setting a price at which shareholders can buy or sell and in theory makes the process so much simpler. Often this can also be seen as an exit route for third-party investors such as business angels and VC funds, who may wish to crystallize their capital return by selling shares.

High profile and visibility

Having the profile of a listed business is seen to bring benefits in terms of a business's standing with its customers and suppliers. This can be particularly important if the business is dealing with large businesses, is expanding abroad, or is marketing a consumer product or service. It can also help in terms of attracting high-quality employees.

Increased corporate transparency

Listed companies are expected to have a more effective level of corporate governance and transparency. This gives comfort to financial stakeholders in the company such as banks and credit companies, who may offer more competitive terms as a result. Of particular importance to the entrepreneur is the issue of personal guarantees. It is usual for banks and other credit companies to require the owners of private businesses to provide personal guarantees in addition to the normal security requirements for all lines of credit. This is particularly uncomfortable for the entrepreneur who knows, despite the limited liability status of his company, that he may face personal financial ruin if disaster befalls his business. Once companies list, it is common practice for banks to release these personal guarantees. This in itself can be a strong motivator to list a business.

Recognition/vanity

Many entrepreneurs see listing their business as the end game. Meeting the requirements of listing, and attracting the funds from outside investors, can provide the ultimate recognition that they have achieved success. This can be enhanced by the publicity that generally surrounds every listing, not only in the media, but also in the hundreds of wonderful glossy booklets that are distributed. The prospectus is the story of the entrepreneur in print – wonderful. The business of printing these large booklets is hotly contested, bringing attractive margins and making up over 15% of the listing costs.

> **Many entrepreneurs see listing their business as the end game.**

THE COSTS OF LISTING

The costs of going through a listing process are two-fold. First is the time and physical resources and share of mind the process takes; second is the actual financial cost of listing.

Time/process

It is normal for entrepreneurs to underestimate the amount of their time that will be taken up with the listing process.

Listing expenses

Listing expenses can be substantial and consist of management, underwriting, placement, and brokerage fees, as well as other expenses. In addition, fees are paid to the IPO manager for preparing the prospectus. The prospectus is a required document that essentially explains the business and its plan to potential investors. The information it contains has to be accurate, and it is the job of the IPO manager not only to coordinate its compilation, but also to manage the verification process of all statements of fact it makes. Consequently, the cost tends to be fairly flat regardless of the size of the company being listed or the amount of money raised. The underwriter or broking firm charges a percentage of the proceeds for placing out the shares to its clients and for underwriting the issue. Other expenses include fees charged by the lawyers and accountants who carry out due diligence on the business and its assets, and fees paid to public relations agencies.

CONGRATULATIONS, YOU ARE ON THE TICKER BOARD

The end of the listing process can't come too soon for entrepreneurs, who long to get back to what they enjoy doing: building the business. Life, however, isn't quite the same afterwards, and although some entrepreneurs adapt well to the higher profile and accountability, others find the transition difficult – particularly if the benefits of being a listed company are only transitory. Two aspects of this post-IPO experience – corporate governance, and life as a small-cap business – are discussed below.

Corporate governance in Asia

One of the biggest changes entrepreneurs experience on completion of the listing process is in the area of being accountable to their new shareholders. This is embodied in the process of corporate governance, which over recent years has developed a higher level of enforcement by most regulatory regimes in Asia. When running a private company, the entrepreneur will have become used to full autonomy in terms of decision-making. Apart from needing to ensure that obligations to creditors are met, and of course that customers are well looked after, the founder has been able to run the company without "interference" from outsiders. Listing brings with it a new accountability both in terms of reporting and decision-making. Board meetings, which in the past may have been token rubber-stamping sessions, are now expected to become more formal affairs with minutes recorded. In addition, the introduction of independent directors brings a new layer to the decision-making process. The extra cost of being a listed business in Asia is now calculated to be at least US$150,000 per annum and is a factor to be considered, particularly for SMEs.

The business environment in Asia doesn't fit easily with the introduction of corporate governance procedures. Historically, much of the capital for business, and hence most of the shareholding, rests with governments, banks, or families. For example, in Japan, banks have been dominant; in China, the government still holds the majority of listed shares; and in Singapore, it is a combination of government and a small number of families. The strong growth experienced by Asia has created a demand for capital that surpasses the ability of these traditional providers to service, and the need to attract foreign capital is driving convergence toward global standards of corporate governance.

The Asian financial crisis in 1997 further highlighted the weakness of the existing financial structures and systems, and the specific issues in Asia were again put under the spotlight in 2002 when CalPERS, the California Public Employees Pension Fund and one of the world's largest institutional investors, listed several Asian countries in which it would not invest, citing lack of corporate disclosure and corporate governance ethics among the key reasons.

> " The business environment in Asia doesn't fit easily with the introduction of corporate governance procedures. "

Since 1997, significant strides have been made in Asia toward improving corporate governance practices, and although there remains much discrepancy between countries, basic progress is being made. The introduction of independent directors and the formation of audit committees represent two of the fundamental pillars of establishing a process of good corporate governance. In 1997, only Singapore and Malaysia had implemented these practices. However, by 2003 most Asian countries were complying with these basic principles (see Table 11.3).

Table 11.3 Progress in Basic Corporate Governance, 1997–2003

	1997		2003	
	Independent directors	Audit committees	Independent directors	Audit committees
China	•		•	•
Hong Kong	•		•	•
India			•	•
Indonesia			•	•
Malaysia	•	•	•	•
Philippines			•	•
Singapore	•	•	•	•
South Korea			•	•
Taiwan			•	•
Thailand			•	•

Source: Asian Corporate Governance Association data

This progress is encouraging, but it should be noted that it has mainly been in the area of establishing corporate governance processes. This can act as a corporate governance *veneer* and doesn't always mean that the spirit of corporate governance is being applied. Asia is already developing its own "Enrons." In December 2004, China Aviation Oil (CAO) – a Chinese business listed in Singapore – was beginning to emerge as a strong candidate. In CAO's case, the business ran up huge losses of over US$500 million in its oil trading arm. This in itself is a bad result for investors, but the bigger discussion has centered around how the company's audit committee managed to sign off an upbeat third-quarter results statement in mid-November at a time when the trading arm had already built up a loss in excess of US$200 million. Examples such as CAO demonstrate that process-driven corporate governance procedures may provide only false security and hopefully will increase the focus on developing the role of independent directors.

The drive to improve corporate governance in Asia has in some ways been complicated by "failures" such as Enron and WorldCom in the so-called global standard economies. With international standards themselves being challenged, it makes it more difficult to persuade companies in Asia of the benefits of implementing good corporate governance practice. In particular, SMEs seeking public capital are unlikely to get on the radar screen of international institutional funds regardless of how effective their corporate governance practices are and tend to see their implementation as more of a cost than a benefit. Efforts are being made to demonstrate that investors are willing to pay a premium for transparent and well-governed companies – a benefit that may provide some attraction for entrepreneurs. However, the evidence remains weak and this route may only bear fruit when private investors make their presence and views matter. The increasing interest of media and analysts in corporate governance issues will also play a part.

Is it worth it? The small-cap experience

There is a growing concern in parts of Asia that the poor performance of many businesses – and their stock prices – after their IPO is undermining the credibility of new listings among potential investors. As we have discussed above, the process itself can have a big drag on the resources and focus of the business.

Many small company listings do seem to have more downside than upside. Because of their small size at the time of listing, the amount they can raise – without diluting the founders too greatly – can seem hardly worth the effort. A good example is Gates Electronics, which listed on the Singapore Stock Exchange in June 2004. With a target of raising S$2.8 million to fund expansion, it was left with only S$2.1 million after expenses. A massive 25% of the proceeds went on management, underwriting, brokering, and placement fees, printing, and other expenses including lawyers, accountants, and public relations. A study of five similar listings during 2004 in Singapore showed listing expenses ranging from 14% to 27% of gross money raised. The average amount raised by these businesses was S$6.54 million, of which a significant 19% was spent on listing expenses, as shown in Figure 11.3.

> " For some companies, this strain on their resources can sometimes cause them to lose focus of their long-term business development efforts, which are critical for achieving their growth strategies, and this inevitably impacts their bottom line. "
>
> TAN CHIAN KHONG,
> PARTNER, E&Y ASIAN PRACTICE,
> *THE STRAITS TIMES*, AUGUST 30, 2003

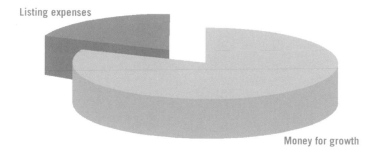

Listing expenses

Money for growth

Source: The Straits Times, June 8, 2004

Figure 11.3 Listing Expenses Bite.

IPO managers will argue that the risks involved with listing a small business are the same as a large one and therefore there is a base level of preparation and due diligence costs incurred that is unavoidable.

Despite the costs of listing, many SMEs in Asia often don't have many other options. Ang Kay Tiong of Stirling Coleman, a boutique corporate finance firm, believes that for "many SMEs in Singapore and China, other than selling a stake to investors or [taking on] bank loans, there is little alternative for them to raise capital."

For many entrepreneurs, whether or not a listing was worth it remains a debatable point. Unfortunately, this is usually decided retrospectively. Those entrepreneurs who have been successful in using the new cash raised at listing to grow their business as expected will look back in satisfaction at their decision. They know that without the money, they probably couldn't have achieved their development plans for the business – or certainly not as fast as they have. For these businesses, it is a virtuous circle. The local media will talk of their success, they will be lauded and cited by all the advisors involved in the listing as a success story, bankers will be keen to develop better relationships with them, and the invitations to lunch will continue. Interest in the stock will grow, and trading volumes will be healthy. The entrepreneur may even welcome the experience of the independent directors who have joined the board as the business moves into uncharted and exciting territory. The quarterly or half-yearly reporting regime, whichever is appropriate, although still a chore will not be so unpalatable if the business meets or beats its prospectus expectations. Better still, the entrepreneur will feel that he has fulfilled the confidence that friends, colleagues, employees, and other individual buyers of his stock placed in him at listing.

The opposite scenario is just as real, and the virtuous circle turns back on itself. There are a significant number of stocks on the Asian exchanges that, perhaps after an initial flurry, have sunk into mediocrity. The share price hasn't lived up to initial expectations and trades below the initial offer price. Furthermore, trading volumes – or stock liquidity – are low, with little interest in the market for buying the stock. As an example, a quick review of the 32 new listings in Singapore during the first five months of 2004 shows that by the end of November

> " The IPO gravy train continues to roll in Asia and is expected to increase in importance as a key source of funds for growing businesses. "

in the same year, over half were already trading at a discount of more than 20% to their original offer price (see Figure 11.4). To put this into perspective, the Singapore Straits Times Index actually rose some 14% over the same six-month period (May to November 2004).

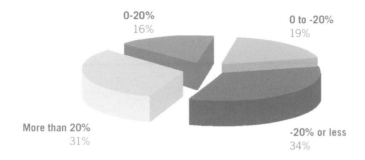

Note: Segments indicate end November 2004 trading in terms of premium or discount to offer price.

Source: Singapore Stock Exchange data.

Figure 11.4 Performance of New Listings on the Singapore Stock Exchange, 2004

In a more lamentable position are those entrepreneurs who may have used up the money raised at listing, but haven't seen the growth plans bear fruit. They are left only with the costs and ongoing burden of being a listed business. This includes the ongoing cycle of disclosures and public reporting, and accountability to a board containing independent directors who now seem expensive for their input. Moreover, there can often be the loss of face associated with investors who are facing a capital loss. An entrepreneur can feel this intensely when investors include family, friends, colleagues, and employees. The annual general meeting now becomes something of an ordeal as third-party owners of the business demand explanations and changes.

Despite these pitfalls, the IPO gravy train continues to roll in Asia and is expected to increase in importance as a key source of funds for growing businesses. The consequences of listing for individual businesses and entrepreneurs can clearly be significant, and therefore the decision to go ahead needs to be carefully thought through and evaluated. Unfortunately, few entrepreneurs have ever been through a listing process before, and accepting this key weakness in experience should determine how they will evaluate the options available. Entrepreneurs are encouraged to seek advice from other entrepreneurs who already have listing experience – good and bad – to put alongside the flattering assessments of hungry listing advisers and brokers.

CHINA'S CAPITAL MARKETS: THE KEY TO UNLOCKING GROWTH

One of the key challenges for China in terms of promoting continuing economic growth is the funding of SMEs. Private SMEs have been a key driver of the Chinese economy, but, as in many countries, they may find it difficult to raise funding from banks and other equity sources. After two decades of restructuring the national economy, the size of the Chinese capital market was still only US$500 billion by the end of 2003. Figure 11.5 puts this in perspective by comparing it with the London, Hong Kong, Singapore, and Malaysian capital markets.

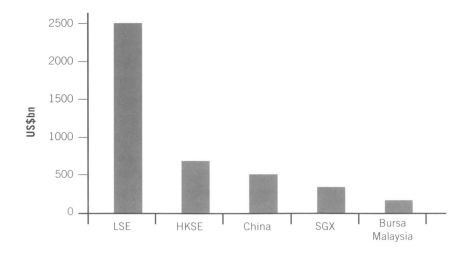

Sources: Data from individual stock exchanges

Figure 11.5 Comparison of Total Market Capitalization at end 2003

In addition to the relatively small size of the capital market, liquidity is low, and some two-thirds of the shares are government-owned and non-tradable. With China's current growth rates, it is clear that its entrepreneurs are going to need a more efficient access to capital than at present. The impact of SMEs on the Chinese economy isn't lost on the Chinese authorities. SMEs together account for 50% of GDP and for some 60% of exports, and provide 75% of the total jobs in urban areas. In February 2004, China's central government issued a policy paper calling on regional governments to coordinate and promote the capital markets. It outlined its keenness to promote and develop the capital markets, but with the guiding principles of ensuring that a stable market environment is also created. At the same time, Li Qing Yuan, an official from the China Securities Regulatory Commission (CSRC), referred to the development of China's capital market as an "urgent need" in order to support China's ongoing economic growth.

Catching the China overflow

The difficulty that entrepreneurs experience in accessing the public capital markets in China has created a substantial backlog of companies waiting to list. One of the key outlets for this build-up has been Hong Kong, which attracted almost all the 76 overseas listings of mainland companies in 2002. Its proximity to the Chinese market, together with its standing as an internationally recognized financial center with its abundance of professional resources, well-established legal system, sound regulatory framework, tax advantages, no capital restrictions, and access to a broad investor base – both local and international, makes it a favorite with mainland businesses. As such, it tends to rival Shanghai in attracting many of the larger mainland listing candidates.

With Hong Kong concentrating on the large state-owned enterprises (SOEs) such as the US$3 billion listing of China Life at the end of 2003, Singapore is attracting the privately owned SMEs. These businesses are in need of funds for expansion, but find themselves languishing in the queue for listing in Shanghai as the large SOEs take priority. Chinese entrepreneurs are attracted by the lower costs and shorter processing time associated with a listing in

Singapore, as well as by the opportunity to be a larger fish in a smaller pond. Singapore is generally seen to be about 25% cheaper in terms of listing expenses than Hong Kong, and the long queues forming in Shanghai and Shenzhen mean that looking abroad for a more straightforward listing process makes sense. In 2003, the Singapore Stock Exchange completed the listing of 55 companies of which 13 were from China, and this trend is expected to continue with 11 already listed in the first half of 2004. Celestial Nutrifoods Limited was the first of the 2004 vintage and is profiled in the following case study.

> The difficulty that entrepreneurs experience in accessing the public capital markets in China has created a substantial backlog of companies waiting to list.

Celestial Nutrifoods: A Chinese listing in Singapore

Celestial Nutrifoods Limited (CNL) is a manufacturer of soybean-based food products. It is based in Beijing, but has production facilities in Daqing, Heilongjiang province. The business was set up in 1997 and quickly established the Sun Moon Star brand of nutritional soybean-based products. By mid-2003, CNL had some 40 distributors covering 10,000 supermarkets located in more than 130 cities in mainland China. Customers include Wal-Mart and Carrefour. The products include health beverages, soy protein isolate (used to enhance the nutritional value of end-products such as meat and dairy products), and soybean oil (used in the production of margarine, soft spreads, and so on).

According to CEO Ming Dequan, who comes from a poor farming family, but worked his way up by attending university and studying food engineering, the competitive advantage of CNL is its proprietary production technology, which enables it to produce health beverages with high protein concentrations. Since its formation, the business has experienced very high growth (see Table 11.4). The growing demand, together with the increasing brand recognition of the products and the increasing trend toward consuming healthy foods, led management to seek new funding for extra manufacturing facilities. In fact, the business calculated that it would need to triple its capacity to keep up.

Table 11.4 Celestial Nutrifoods' Financials (RMB m)

Y/e 31 Dec	2000	2001	2002	2003	2Q 2004	2004F	2005F
Sales	51.0	131.2	226.4	288.5	165.3	372.7	591.8
Profit before tax	15.0	49.0	92.5	121.0	45.4	141.9	229.4

Source: Figures from Kim Eng Securities, KELIVE Research, May 14, 2004.

According to an interview with *The Straits Times*, the company was told it would have to wait at least two years before it could list in Shanghai. Ming Dequan said, "When your production capacity isn't big enough and you can't meet market demand, who can afford to wait two years?" In the end, it took CNL only six months from the time it submitted its IPO application to the day the stock made its debut on the Singapore Stock Exchange, making it the first Chinese enterprise to list in Singapore in 2004.

The business announced its offering of 118 million shares priced at 28 cents each, raising gross proceeds of S$33 million. On its January 9 debut, the share price closed at 51.5 cents, an 84% premium on its offer price of 28 cents. In August 2004, the company issued its half-year results, which showed that the business has traded slightly below expectations, mainly due to a combination of lower gross margins and higher administration and selling expenses – although management believe they are still on track to achieve the forecast figures. The initial surge in share price to 51.5 cents hasn't been maintained; however, at the half-year point in June, the stock held up well and was trading at 35 cents, although by October 2004 it was trading at slightly below the offer price.

Notwithstanding fluctuations in the share price, the IPO of Celestial Nutrifoods appears to have been a win–win for all concerned. The most important factor is that the business, with funds for expansion in its bank, has been able to continue on its entrepreneurial high-growth path despite the pipeline of listing candidates in China. The Singapore Stock Exchange also demonstrated its ability to accommodate a mainland business in terms of speed and access to the right funding.

Easing the bottleneck: The Shenzhen SME Exchange

In 2004, the CSRC finally approved a long-awaited proposal to set up an SME exchange in Shenzhen. The Shenzhen second board is the successor to the Nasdaq-style high-tech board that was scheduled in 2000, but which was shelved after the bursting of the dot.com bubble. The new SME board is designed to attract growing SMEs with strong track records and has a preference for high-technology content. It has the same listing requirements demanded by the main Shanghai exchange, including a minimum of three years of operating history with a positive earnings track record. The exchange officially opened in May and started trading at the beginning of July 2004, and by September it had 10 listings. Potentially, this new exchange may be a blow to Singapore, in particular, which has been attracting many of the high-growth private SMEs to its own capital market. However, with a queue for Shenzhen listings believed to be already some 1,000 companies strong, it is likely that the phenomenon of Chinese companies seeking overseas listings will continue for some time.

▶▶ CONCLUSION

Raising funds on the public capital markets is an important source of capital for entrepreneurs as they seek to grow their businesses. With the private equity industry still in its infancy in Asia, going public has been the traditional way for Asian entrepreneurs to raise funds, as well as gaining other perceived benefits such as an increased profile and a market for their shares. The opening up of China in particular is providing large numbers of high-growth businesses eager to tap the public market. This, together with the restructuring of large state businesses, is significantly raising the profile of Asian stock markets with international investors.

On the other hand, the cooling of investor interest in smaller listed businesses, together with the increasing demands in terms of meeting the increasingly complex regulatory and governance requirements, has increased the costs and reduced the benefits of listing. Notwithstanding the increasing costs, there are few viable alternatives, and the queues of entrepreneurs who wish to fund their growth opportunities are getting longer. Asian governments recognize that releasing the expansion plans of these businesses is crucial to reducing supply-side issues as the economic growth rates continue at their high level, and are starting to address some of the bottlenecks.

Quite apart from the blockages in the system, the process can be further complicated by unforeseen movements and changes in public sentiment. There may have been a window of opportunity in 2003/04 for companies with a strong China growth story, and those businesses at the front of the listing queue will be able to make the most of this. However, the public markets are fickle and already interest is moving away from a potentially overheated China market toward businesses with growth stories involving South Asia. The challenge going forward, therefore, is how to make public capital more accessible to high-growth businesses in Asia, while continuing to improve the regulatory and governance environment necessary to attract a broader and more international pool of investors.

SECTION IV

Themes of Maturity

*T*his section covers issues relevant to more established businesses – that is, businesses which have not only successfully left behind their start-up phase long ago but also have grown to a stage where they have steady, or perhaps still growing income, profits and cash flow. These businesses can be either listed or private.

We have chosen two themes that, in Asia, are becoming a more important feature of the business landscape. The first, "Handling Succession," reviews the issue of survival of entrepreneurial family businesses beyond the exit – through retirement or otherwise – of the founder. The large numbers of family businesses in Asia where the founder is at or nearing retirement age make this a serious and growing issue.

The second theme, "Releasing Entrepreneurial Potential: MBOs," considers the growing phenomenon in Asia of the management buyout. The need to restructure in some of the more mature Asian economies is creating new opportunities for frustrated management teams to acquire their businesses in syndicates with private equity funds and banks. The numbers of completed MBOs in Asia are increasing year on year, and indications are that this will grow in importance as a tool for revitalizing tired and unloved subsidiaries of large businesses. In addition, MBOs are helping to release the entrepreneurial talent of more mature but professional management teams.

12

Handling
Succession

*T*he topic of entrepreneurs and entrepreneurship generally centers
around business and value creation. However, a key issue for
entrepreneurs – particularly those who have presided over the
development of their business for many years and seen its value grow –
is how to manage their own retirement. This is, of course, an ongoing
issue for entrepreneurs globally, and is certainly not new. However, in
Asia, the topic of succession is becoming more and more critical as a
business issue to be resolved.

Asia has large numbers of businesses that are still owned and
managed by founding entrepreneurs who are either approaching, or
have already entered, normal retirement age. One of the challenges,
therefore, for family businesses in Asia is survival beyond the retirement
(or otherwise) of the founding entrepreneur.

In this chapter we will discuss the common approaches to
handling succession in family businesses and review them in the Asian
context. A case study – Lim's Metal Hinges – is included to illustrate
many of the points covered, along with initial analysis of how succession
in this instance might be approached.

INTRODUCTION

There is plenty of evidence to show that succession in Asia is a growing issue; however, there is little evidence that the solution has progressed much beyond the traditional method of passing on to the next generation.

Japan is an excellent example of the growing significance of this issue. In April 1997, IBJ Research reported on its review of over 100,000 SMEs in Japan that over 40,000 of the businesses had owner-managers aged 60 years or over and that some 10,000 of these had owner-managers aged 70 years or more. Despite the relative advantages that the Japanese seem to have in terms of longevity, it is clear that succession will be a rapidly growing issue in Japan. This is supported by MITI (the Ministry of International Trade and Industry, now METI), which revealed in its survey of SMEs in July 1999 that about one-third of such businesses see succession as a major business issue.

In short, there are large numbers of businesses in Asia that will be facing some kind of succession issue over the next decade.

The brief case study below highlights succession issues in the empire of Hong Kong's Li Ka-shing.

> " There are large numbers of businesses in Asia that will be facing some kind of succession issue over the next decade. "

CASE STUDY

A high-profile Asian succession

A difference between Asia and the United States is the sheer number of elderly CEOs at the region's largest companies, many of which are family-run. The generation of entrepreneurs that built Asia's business titans after World War II are now in their seventies and eighties. Most of them are still at the helm and plan to stay there until they die. Two-thirds of publicly traded companies in Asia are controlled by a single shareholder, very often the founder, compared with just 3% in the US, according to the World Bank.

Some of their children boast business degrees from US universities and are ready to take over; some are playboys waiting to get their hands on another toy. With no succession plan in place, there is no certainty for investors, business partners, or employees.

Hong Kong's richest man, 75-year-old Li Ka-shing, is still at the helm of two of Asia's biggest companies, Hutchison Whampoa and Cheung Kong Holdings. Mr. Li, a 1940s' wartime refugee from mainland China, founded Cheung Kong in 1950 as a manufacturer of plastic goods such as toys and flowers. The group's interests now range from telecommunications operations in Asia and Europe to the world's largest network of shipping ports, including terminals at both ends of the Panama Canal.

Mr. Li has never publicly announced his succession plans, which are the source of constant speculation in Hong Kong's financial circles. His elder son, Victor Li Tzar Kuoi, is managing director of Cheung Kong Holdings and often cited as the likely heir. But the reclusive 36-year-old is viewed by many as merely a competent caretaker.

That leads bankers and others who have worked with Mr. Li's companies to wonder about a possible role for his second son, Richard, whose entrepreneurial acumen helped him build a personal fortune in satellite television and telecommunications valued at more than US$1 billion. Without a succession plan in place, the company risks a crisis of confidence.

Often, Asian corporate chiefs are even more reluctant than their US counterparts to discuss who should replace them. "It's kind of taboo," says Raymond So, a finance professor who studies the issue at Chinese University of Hong Kong. To the founder, "it means, 'Hey, you want to get rid of me'."

Source: Excerpt from Sarah McBride, "In Corporate Asia, a Crisis over Succession is Looming," Association of Executive Search Consultants Management Library, 2003

SOLUTIONS FOR SUCCESSION ISSUES

Western practice

In the more advanced Western economies, the issue of succession is generally dealt with in one of the ways discussed below.

Handing down

Handing over to the next generation is the traditional method of dealing with succession. It not only preserves the business within the family, but also maintains all the existing relationships and as much of the status quo as possible. Founder entrepreneurs often favor this method, as they are able to extract themselves gradually from full-time involvement and, in the meantime, continue to involve themselves in the business in the way they enjoy most – often tinkering with the machines on the factory floor.

Selling to second-tier management

Another method of dealing with succession is to sell the business to the next tier of management backed by private equity and/or bank funding (a succession management buyout – or MBO). Succession MBOs combine the benefit of realizing cash from the business with being able to provide faithful long-term employees with the opportunity also to create some value for themselves from the business as it moves forward. At the same time, the retiring entrepreneur may have the opportunity for continuing involvement with the business – at least for a time – as a chairman or in some other honorary-type role.

Professionalizing the business

A third method is to recruit a professional manager and list on a public exchange, or sell the business either to the manager or to a competitor. This method takes some advance planning and culture change to accommodate the new CEO. In addition, it can be quite a difficult process, as the founder remains the majority, and perhaps the only, shareholder. The challenge with this route is that the owner often finds it hard to let go, and continuing in his role as owner will give him plenty of opportunity to interfere. An appropriate incentive package for the new manager, and good chemistry with the owner, are usually fundamental to the success of this option.

Selling the business

Selling to a competitor or other trade buyer with a strategic interest in the business is yet another succession method. This is an effective method for realizing cash, and provides the entrepreneur with the financial means to experience a relaxing and often very comfortable retirement. On the other hand, selling the business isn't always favored by the entrepreneur, who may be concerned that he will be seen as "selling out" his loyal and faithful long-term employees, who may now face an uncertain future.

Whatever the preferred method, there are a number of tried and tested solutions for resolving succession issues, and advisors to family businesses are generally well versed in ensuring that the business prepares in good time.

Asian approaches to succession

Although these solutions are relatively commonplace in the mature Western economies, they are not yet fully accepted in Asia where succession issues have carried a greater expectation of family-oriented solutions.

> " In Asia, succession issues have carried a greater expectation of family-oriented solutions. "

Handing down

This is still seen as the preferred route for Asian family businesses. A 2002 Grant Thornton *PRIMA Global Research Report* survey of nearly 9,000 privately owned businesses around the world provided some useful insights into the way Asian owners view succession in comparison to their European and North American counterparts. As far as management succession is concerned, there seems to be a much stronger feeling in Asia that successors should be chosen from the family. Figure 12.1 indicates that 39% of Asian entrepreneurs believe they should be succeeded by family members, compared with less than 25% of entrepreneurs in Europe, North America, and Australasia.

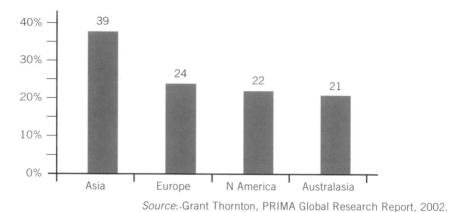

Source: Grant Thornton, PRIMA Global Research Report, 2002.

Figure 12.1 Percentage of Owner-managers who Believe that Management Successors Should be Chosen from the Family

In support of this belief, the survey also reveals a stronger intention in Asia that children should not only join the family business, but also that a child's education should be geared toward the needs of the business. Figure 12.2 again shows that Asian entrepreneurs are significantly different from their peers elsewhere in this respect.

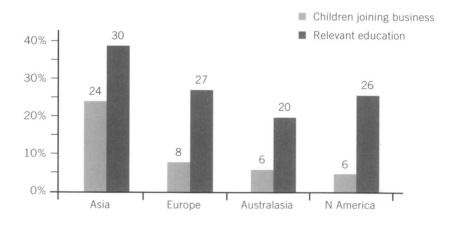

Source: Grant Thornton, PRIMA Global Research Report, 2002.

Figure 12.2 Percentage of Owner-managers who Intend for their Children to Join the Family Business and who Gear their Education to Business Needs

One of the succession issues already discussed is the entrepreneur's general desire to have some ongoing role in the business after retirement. This can be true of entrepreneurs all over the world, but it seems from the study that it is especially true of Asia where almost half of the respondents felt that the older generation should always have a formal role in the business. This contrasted with less than a third of respondents in Europe, Australasia, and North America and perhaps gives us an indication of the form that succession solutions in Asia may take. Of course, the best-laid intentions don't always mean success. The relative preoccupation that Asian entrepreneurs have with grooming their children as successors also leads them to worry more than their counterparts overseas in terms of what will happen if their children don't perform well in the business and how they will provide for their children if they don't join.

Despite the stronger expectation in Asia that businesses can be kept within the family, the next generation – like their Western counterparts – are increasingly unlikely to want to follow in their parents' footsteps. Many have gone abroad to study at university and would rather enter into the professions, such as the law or accounting, than take on what they may see as the unexciting task of managing the family business.

Selling to second-tier management

A family company in Asia typically has a weak second level of management. The entrepreneur not only prefers to keep hold of most of the management tasks and decision-making, but is also very cost-conscious. Why pay good money for an experienced production or marketing manager, when the entrepreneur can do the job perfectly well himself? In this sense, the Asian entrepreneur is often the architect of his own indispensability. The drawback with this route is that often the second-tier management don't have the ability or experience to step

> " The Asian entrepreneur is often the architect of his own indispensability. "

up to the CEO/strategic-level role. The success of the founder in running the business single-handedly often creates a weak second-management tier.

Professionalizing the business

Introducing a professional manager into the family business is a tough process for any entrepreneur. However, supposing this is the preferred route, it does depend on the availability of suitable candidates. In the economies of North America and Europe, the vibrant mergers and acquisitions market, which facilitates the continuous expansion, contraction, and restructuring of business groups, provides a ready pool of experienced and professional managers and CEOs looking for their next job opportunity. In Asia, unfortunately, this isn't yet the case. As restructuring gathers pace this situation will change, but for the moment professional CEOs will continue to be a scarce resource for succession situations.

Listing the business

A more typical route – although not particularly helpful – is to list the business. A listing can take the pressure off the founding entrepreneur(s) by releasing them from any personal guarantees; however, given the low level of liquidity in the capital markets, the real issue of succession is seldom addressed. Indeed, we see large numbers of listed family businesses where the original founders still hold a majority of the shares. Given the lack of liquidity, any attempt to download the founder's shares sticks out like a lighthouse and can destabilize the stock. One of the benefits, perhaps, is that as a listed company the business will generally have added some non-executive directors to the board who may be able to bring further experience to bear to the succession issue. The subject of IPOs is discussed in Chapter 11.

Selling the business

This method is seldom seen in Asia, for two key reasons. First, the idea of "selling out" is seen as even less culturally acceptable than it is by entrepreneurs in other parts of the world. Second, even if the aging entrepreneur can get over the stigma of selling, the lack of a vibrant M&A market in Asia means the opportunities are few. In addition, after three months spent on the golf course, entrepreneurs often find that they don't adapt well to a life of leisure and that an abrupt exit – no matter what the price – isn't what they really want. As a result, it may be some time before this becomes a normalized and acceptable exit for Asian family businesses.

> " After three months spent on the golf course, entrepreneurs often find that they don't adapt well to a life of leisure and that an abrupt exit – no matter what the price – isn't what they really want. "

SUCCESSION CASE STUDY

Introduction

The discussion earlier regarding the succession issues facing Hong Kong's Li Ka-shing reflects the situation in many large corporate family groups in Asia. However, the bulk of the succession issues in terms of sheer numbers in Asia going forward lie with the smaller family businesses. The entrepreneurs involved generally don't have the corporate resources and infrastructure enjoyed by Mr. Li, and their situation can become more desperate more quickly due to the sheer lack of experience, understanding, and resources available to resolve the issue. The Lim's Metal Hinges case study, below, draws out some of the issues discussed. The study follows how in 1969, Lim, an entrepreneur from Taiwan, set up his small metal-stamping business which grew to be of significant size by 2003. The study is based on a real-life Asian situation, but it has been disguised to protect the business as the issues described remain unsolved.

Lim's Metal Hinges

In 1969, Mr. Lim, a 30-year-old Taiwanese, set up a metal-forming business to provide hinges, which he sold to local furniture makers. He called the business Lim's Metal Hinges (LMH). To set up, he invested US$20,000 he had been loaned by his father, which, along with a small bank loan, provided the funds to buy the initial tools and machines, along with a stock of raw materials. The venture proved successful, and Lim gradually grew his sales to over US$2 million by 1975, with a net profit of US$200,000 after personal drawings of US$50,000.

Although this provided a comfortable living for Lim and his family, he saw new opportunities ahead. Over the next few years, Lim gradually broadened his expertise to be able to form more complicated metal parts, including mechanisms for tape recorders. This, in turn, enabled him to broaden his customer base, which started to include suppliers to large original equipment manufacturers. This was a very competitive market, and the tough competition meant that keeping costs low was a priority. To this end, Lim kept a very tight management structure. He had two account clerks and an office administrator only – his large extended family helped to cope with any bottlenecks. He did, however, hire and train a set of trusted operating managers, all of whom answered directly to him. Lim had two sons: the elder son showed no interest in the family business but was very strong academically; while the younger son enjoyed helping at the plant and, in particular, was interested in the IT side of the business.

This kind of structure suited Lim's management style. He was keen to ensure that customers had the best service, so he always dealt with them directly. In addition, most of the R&D was led by Lim, so he was best placed to understand the requirements of his customers and how his company could provide appropriate, and profitable, engineering solutions. In fact, his happiest times were spent using his experience to develop engineering solutions for customers. He adapted the standard machines in the factory not only to improve their capability in terms of what they could do, but also to make them run more efficiently. Indeed, at any point in time, all the machines would have at least three to four modifications or add-ons made by Lim himself.

By the beginning of the 1990s, the business had a turnover of US$10 million and net profit of US$1.3 million after Lim's own salary of US$200,000. About 80% of the sales were with two main customers who were keen for Lim to become a major supplier to support them in the growing PC market – in particular, in making disk drives. This was an important project and, over the course of the next 10 years, involved Lim setting up a major new plant in Taiwan as well as a further two plants in China. Lim approached this in the same way as he had the previous 20 years and ensured that he recruited good factory managers who reported directly to him. Again, he continued to manage all the customer relationships and to run the business with his small team of administrative support staff.

By 2001, Lim, who was now 62, ran a business with sales of US$78 million and net profit of US$8 million after Lim's own drawings of US$500,000. The strong cash flow – now approximately US$12 million per annum – had enabled Lim not only to expand without the use of bank funding, but also permitted a healthy dividend which supported a comfortable lifestyle and ensured that his sons could pursue their interests. Both sons were now in the United States – the elder son studying law at Harvard, and the younger one now involved in a promising dot.com business in California.

The year 2002 proved to be a tough one for Lim and LMH. The recession in the electronics market, along with problems caused by the combination of the effects of 9/11 and the SARS epidemic, had led to LMH almost experiencing its first year of losses. Lim's strong relationship with his suppliers and customers helped during this tough time, but it wasn't enough; it was only through making some drastic cost cuts that a short-term cash crisis was averted. However, the laying off of some workers who had been with him for over 20 years had had a profound effect on Lim. This, together with the worry over the final failure of his son's dot.com business into which Lim had recently injected US$4 million of rescue money and the drop in value of Lim's other stock-market investments, also made him feel that perhaps he was overstretching himself.

In 2003, the leaner cost base, along with a strengthening market recovery, helped LMH to return to strong profitability. The business turned in record figures of US$85 million in sales, a US$10 million net profit, and cash flow of US$14 million. On top of this, in the third quarter of 2003, one of Lim's key customers put a new and exciting proposal to him. This proposal would make LMH its lead supplier, with the potential to grow sales to over US$150 million within three years. For this, the customer was looking for a commitment from LMH to a five-year plan that would involve more capacity – two new factories in China and Malaysia – and setting up a joint design operation in Mumbai. Lim celebrated the proposal over dinner with his customer and afterwards at a karaoke bar and promised to review it quickly. Beneath the euphoria, however, Lim's heart sank.

On his way home from the celebrations, several thoughts were going around and around in his head. He remembered how he used to enjoy the buzz of being at the hub of everything that happened in the business. He would return from meetings with customers and call his key managers in for a discussion. Together they would work out how best to meet the customers' requirements. Although he was in charge, he was able to enjoy the closeness of working with the team.

The development of the business over the last few years had been exciting, but it had also brought drawbacks. Lim's original customer relationships had changed; the new ones seemed more intent on achieving cost savings for long production runs, than on reaping the benefits of customized engineering solutions. His country plant managers were very competent, but they seemed too distant to be able to give any input into some of the bigger issues facing the business. He once used to know the name of every employee, but they now numbered over 2,000 and were spread over several countries. He also thought about the cuts he had recently needed to make to keep the business profitable. Most of the cuts had been in the original factory due to its relatively out-of-date practices and high running costs. He knew the names of all those he had made redundant and he missed them.

Lim reflected on his customer's proposal. Ten years ago he would have been excited, but now he wondered if he actually had the stomach to commit to the next five years. He was now 64 and realized that he hardly knew his family and was worried about a deterioration in his health due to the extra stress.

With the bad experience of the 2001–02 years, Lim was for the first time in his life concerned about the risks involved with expansion. On the other hand, he worried what it would mean for the business if he didn't agree to partner his customer on the new proposal. He knew that the business had significant value as it currently stood. This value wasn't only his pension fund, but also the inheritance for his children.

Lim considered his options…

It is often at points such as this, where personal preferences and business needs come into conflict, when entrepreneurs realize the importance of timely succession planning. This is, of course, a strategic and fundamental decision point for the business, but unfortunately it is also one area where many entrepreneurs have little experience. The other drawback of this situation is the emotional dimension associated with succession in family companies, which can obstruct objective decision-making. For both these reasons, entrepreneurs need to seek help and advice from outside on what their options actually are and how to choose between them.

> It is often at points such as this, where personal preferences and business needs come into conflict, when entrepreneurs realize the importance of timely succession planning.

The size of the problem

A few facts about the situation generally help as a start. Below, we will take a look at the potential value of the business as it stands. We will then review its strengths and weaknesses. Let's see how much Lim's original US$20,000 investment is worth now.

Price-earnings ratio basis

This ratio calculates the value of the business in terms of a multiple of its net earnings after tax – or, in other words, after all expenses have been deducted from the sales revenue. For LMH, its last year's net profit after tax was US$10 million. To calculate the value of the business, or of Lim's shares, we use the following calculation (for this example, we will use a multiple of 10):

Value in US$m = Net profit * Multiple (e.g. 10)
= 10 * 10
= 100

Cash flow basis

This method calculates the value of a business on the basis of its annual operating cash flow. Again, a multiple is applied to this value. We would expect the operating cash flow to be bigger than the after-tax earnings of a business – this is because non-cash items such as depreciation are added back. This also means that the multiples applied when using the cash flow valuation method will be lower.

The multiples used in both cases will vary and, in practice, will only be fixed when a final price is agreed between buyer and seller. They can then be applied to this price to allow the buyer and seller to judge if they feel the valuation seems fair or not. However, they are useful as a guide. Key determinants of how high a multiple you might expect for a business include:

- comparison with other similar businesses which are publicly listed;
- non-financial issues which contribute to the attractiveness of the business, such as quality of the management team, defensibility of market position, length of contracts, quality of customers, and so on; and

- negotiation strength of both the buyer and the seller – in other words, how much does the buyer want for this particular business, and how much does the seller need to complete the deal?

To illustrate this, Tables 12.1 and 12.2 show values over a range of multiples for LMH using both methods.

Table 12.1 Price-earnings Ratio Valuation

Multiple	8	9	10	11	12
Valuation (US$m)	80	90	100	110	120

Table 12.2 Cash Flow Multiple Valuation

Multiple	5	6	7	8
Valuation (US$m)	70	84	98	112

If we take a sensible range from both valuation methods, we can imagine that Lim's original investment of US$20,000 is now potentially worth somewhere in the range US$80–100 million. Although this is a rough estimation, it is important that Lim is aware of the potential value of his equity stake. We have seen entrepreneurs in Asia who approach this type of issue as though they are still dealing with a stake worth US$20,000 – this can show itself in terms of the effort and resources they commit to the process. In Lim's case, the issue he is dealing with in this instance is a US$60–80 million question. For almost all family businesses, succession is likely to be the biggest commercial issue in terms of dollar value they have ever dealt with. It is also an area where they have little or no experience. To this end, the early use of outside-advisors who are well-versed in understanding and resolving succession issues is a sensible step in all family succession issues. Paying money for experienced advisors

> **The early use of outside advisors who are well-versed in understanding and resolving succession issues is a sensible step in all family succession issues.**

– for example, legal, accounting, and corporate finance – is also frequently a new experience for family businesses, but this is definitely a time to break with the past.

Understanding the strengths and weaknesses

Another useful step is to outline the business's strengths and weaknesses (see Table 12.3).

Table 12.3 Strengths and Weaknesses of LMH

Strengths	Weaknesses
• Customer base and relationships	• Reliance on two major customers
• Manufacturing capabilities in low–cost Asian countries	• Management structure and bandwidth
• Reputation for providing effective engineering solutions	• No succession plan
• Strong cash flow and profitability	
• Opportunities for further growth	

What are Lim's options?

So, pulling all these together, we can identify a range of possible options for Lim.

Maintain the business in its current state and decline further growth opportunities

This may appear the more manageable option for Lim, but he needs to consider two key issues. First, he already feels the business is becoming more difficult to run and he won't be getting any younger. Second, the demands of the market today mean the business will still need to develop and grow just to keep up. Failing to keep up is also likely to result in an erosion of business value as customers leave to team up with other suppliers who are prepared to grow and develop with them. This not only puts off the inevitable issue of succession but may create an environment that brings more stress for Lim than before.

Take the business forward and develop the new opportunity

There is a real opportunity for LMH to enter a new stage of growth in tandem with the needs of its current customers. The issue here is that the business doesn't have the management infrastructure – or experience – to take this next step. If Lim is keen to keep the business independent, he will need to build the senior management team and either nurture a CEO or recruit an experienced one to lead it. As far as his sons are concerned, it is unlikely that they will be ready – or willing – to lead the business. This means recruiting from outside, which again will be a new experience for Lim. He should get the best advice and engage an experienced headhunter to help him identify the right candidate.

Sell the business

We have established that the business has a potential value of US$80–100 million. A well-managed sale process would have a good chance of attracting near the top end of this bracket, particularly if there is a buyer who sees that the business has a strategic value. For example, a similar business but with different customers may acquire LMH to broaden its customer base and in so doing reduce dependency risk and provide opportunities for cross-selling of services. Returning to Table 12.3, the lack of management infrastructure may even be attractive to a trade buyer, which may prefer to install its own people in key positions. A key element of the due diligence, though, may be the importance to the business of Lim himself. Many founder-entrepreneurs are responsible for some key elements of value in the business, such as customer relationships, intellectual property, and so on. The acquirer will need to establish the reliance of the business on Lim himself and how this may be mitigated. Lim may need to be part of the "package," in that he could be asked to remain with the company for some time until the acquirer is comfortable that he has transferred his contacts and knowledge. It may even propose holding back an element of the payment until this is completed. This may suit Lim in that he is able to continue working with the business on a part-time basis while he gets used to the idea of retiring.

Other options or combinations of options do exist, but these three are the key ones. For example, Lim may consider some kind of strategic alliance or joint venture — although these may increase the complexity of his current position, rather than alleviate matters. Another option would be to sell the business to management backed by outside funding in an MBO. However, while Lim's next tier of management is capable operationally and good at their jobs, they haven't been recruited or nurtured as management successors and would find it difficult to attract private equity money to back them. In Western economies, a hybrid option could be possible where the private equity fund brings in a professional CEO from outside to strengthen the existing management team – this is called a management buy-in (MBI). While there is a growing cadre of experienced buy-in candidates in Europe and the US, this is still a relatively new concept in Asia and there is a lack of suitable and available candidates. The second option, which involves the recruitment of a professional CEO for the business, will still be challenging in this respect, but the quality and experience of the candidate required for straight recruitment as a CEO designate is different from that required of a candidate who needs to lead an MBO/MBI. The latter needs to be much more experienced as a CEO and credible enough to convince a private equity fund and banks to provide some US$80 million to finance the acquisition.

> **While there is a growing cadre of experienced management buy-in candidates in Europe and the US, this is still a relatively new concept in Asia.**

Choosing between the options

If we assume that all three options are possible, then it all depends on Lim's own preferences regarding how he sees his and his family's future in relation to the business. There is no hard and fast rule here, as all entrepreneurs are different and have different family circumstances. Key considerations for Lim will include:

- *His own health*: How much longer does he want to be in charge?
- *His sons*: Is it likely that they will want to return from the US to work in LMH, with one of them perhaps eventually taking over as CEO?
- *Lim's appetite for further involvement in the business*: The three options are placed in descending order of involvement by Lim, in Table 12.4.

Table 12.4 Lim's Options

Option	Lim's involvement
Maintain business in current state	Full involvement – no change
Take the business forward and develop new opportunities – recruiting/nurturing a professional CEO	Initially full, but decreasing as the CEO designate develops into the role
Selling the business	Some part-time involvement generally required by the acquirer for one to two years post-sale - negotiable

Those working to find succession solutions for family businesses often find that price isn't always the key determinant. The matrix of family needs, emotions, and constraints in these situations requires a flexible solution, whether the option chosen is selling the business or some other combination. This means that for the more pragmatic acquirers, buying a family company can present a strong value proposition. In addition, the opportunities afforded to professional managers who are willing to join family companies can be attractive. Although pay and perks may not quite match those offered by MNCs, the prospects for capital growth through equity packages can more than offset any perceived short-term differences.

▶▶ CONCLUSION

Lim and many hundreds of founder-entrepreneurs like him all over Asia will be facing critical succession issues over the next decade. Many will continue to rely on handling the issue within the family, but sadly this approach will be optimal for only a small fortunate number of family companies.

We must be careful not to put the relative differences with Western entrepreneurs down to culture alone. From our experience of entrepreneurs and family businesses, the issue of succession and how to involve children is always a concern. However, the options available to European and North American entrepreneurs in terms of vibrant M&A markets, the supply of professional managers, succession MBOs, and public market liquidity all help to make the issue a manageable one. Asian entrepreneurs generally have experience of and access to only one option, and only the lucky few will have children of the right experience, capability, and ambition to be able to take the reins of leadership.

Like other fundamental business challenges, the succession problem cannot be solved without a careful review of the options and objective decision-making. *Unlike* most other business challenges, however, the inevitability of succession as a business issue means it is one that can be planned for several years in advance. Although we are starting to see a number of cases where advance planning is taking place, unfortunately this is generally not the route chosen by many entrepreneurs in Asia to date. This, together with developing alternative options such as those available in the more advanced economies, will be important challenges to face to ensure the orderly survival of many Asian businesses beyond the founder entrepreneur.

13

Releasing Entrepreneurial Potential: MBOs

*T*he idea of an entrepreneur is generally associated with new venture or business creation. However, through the medium of management buyouts (MBOs), the economies of North America and Europe have developed a new breed of entrepreneur – the corporate manager transformed into business owner. The late 1990s saw the emergence of MBOs in the relatively developed and structured economies of Japan and South Korea. Since then, the number of MBOs in Asia has grown steadily and their contribution to unlocking entrepreneurial potential is increasing. This chapter looks at the still embryonic, yet growing, phenomenon of MBOs in Asia. From describing what MBOs are and how they work, we look at the challenges involved in developing new MBO markets and review the example of Japan in particular. A case study of a recent MBO in Japan – Vantec – helps to put the key points of the chapter into perspective.

INTRODUCTION

The idea of management buying their own business supported by banks and private equity first evolved in the US in the 1970s. It was eagerly adopted and developed in the UK from the 1980s onwards as a tool to help restructure an economy heavily burdened by nationalized industries and wieldy conglomerates that were beginning to look at the benefits of core strategies. It was also an economy that needed to inject a new vein of entrepreneurialism at all levels of business. The MBO helped to provide both of these. A by-product of this was the development of a new breed of entrepreneur. This new entrepreneur came from the cadre of corporate managers many of whom had long-term careers working in large companies as employees, but were transformed into entrepreneurs through circumstance and opportunity. The circumstance is that they held senior positions in subsidiaries of larger companies or conglomerates, but felt they could develop the business more effectively without the baggage of being part of a larger group. The opportunity was that head office had little interest in developing the subsidiary they managed and decided to divest, as it would rather have the cash to invest in its core business.

This position is illustrated by the example in Figure 13.1.

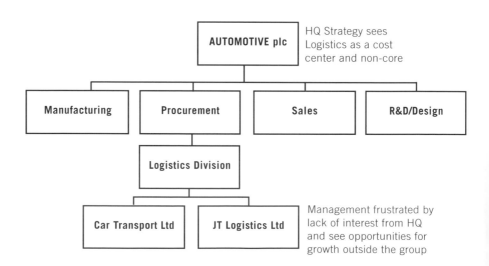

Figure 13.1 Life as an Unloved Subsidiary

In short, MBOs are where the management of a business acquires the business from the owner by raising a mixture of their own funds, private equity, and bank debt. Once the business is acquired, it becomes an independent business with new shareholders and objectives. The shareholders usually include private equity funds and the key management team. These buyouts – especially if they are large and the proportion of management equity involvement is relatively small – are also sometimes known as institutional buyouts (IBOs) or leveraged buyouts (LBOs). The common thread, however, is that all of these aim to reward incumbent management teams either through substantial equity holdings or attractive stock options. This has the effect of incentivizing management to think as entrepreneurs and business owners, rather than just as employees. For the purpose of this chapter, we will refer to all these variants under the generic term "MBO".

Developing a vibrant MBO market doesn't happen overnight, however – as has been evident in the economies of Western Europe. The conditions that need to be in place for an MBO market to thrive are many and include cultural considerations, regulatory and legal environments, availability of capital, and a healthy M&A market, to name a few. The ease of creating these conditions varies from country to country.

Later in this chapter, we will be looking in more depth at the case of Japan where, in recent years, the development of its MBO market is becoming a strong contributor to the introduction of a more entrepreneurial culture. First, however, we will look at the overall picture in Asia with respect to MBOs.

THE GROWING IMPORTANCE OF MBOs IN ASIA

If we take Asia as a whole, the growth in importance of MBOs has been a very recent phenomenon. A useful indicator of the development of an MBO market is the level of investment of private equity funds in MBOs. The growth of investment in MBOs in Asia in relation to total private equity investment in Asia is illustrated in Figure 13.2. From a very low base in the mid-1990s, funds invested in MBOs have grown and by 2004 represent 60% of all venture capital and private equity funds invested in Asia. This proportion is approaching global norms, although, when compared with the total amount of funds invested in Europe and the US, Asia is still relatively insignificant. For example, funds invested globally in 2003 – in all situations including start-up, expansion, MBO, and so on – totaled US$155 billion. Asia accounted for approximately only 10% of this total. Despite this, international investors in MBO funds see a bright future for the continuing and successful growth of the MBO market in Asia. A 2004 survey of over 100 international institutional investors in venture capital and private equity funds revealed that Asian MBOs were seen as providing the second-best opportunities for investment in the near future. In the survey, MBOs in Asia ranked behind MBOs in Europe, but ahead of North American MBOs and also ahead of venture investing in any geography.[1]

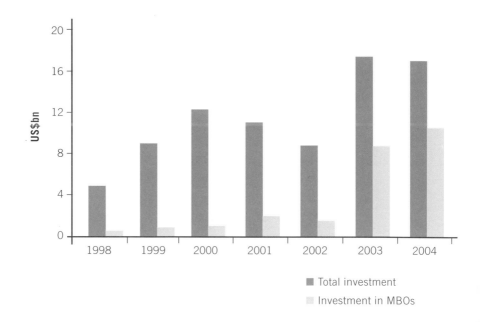

Source: PWC/3i Global Private Equity Review, 2003/2004

Figure 13.2 MBOs in Asia Compared with Total VC and PE Activity in Terms of Investment Amount, 1998–2004

MBOs may not, on the face of it, seem particularly entrepreneurial as they involve businesses that are already established, rather than creating new ones from scratch. But if we remind ourselves of an early definition of entrepreneurship – "the activity of organizing, managing, and assuming the risks of a business or enterprise"[2] – then these MBO managers are indeed being entrepreneurs. Those who have seen the birth of an MBO from close quarters – perhaps as MBO managers, or perhaps their families and friends, private equity practitioners, corporate finance advisors, and so on – will know that the decision to carry out a management buyout isn't taken lightly. Start-up entrepreneurs are often at an early stage of their life and wealth creation, and the cost of failure isn't so high – particularly as they will have plenty of time to develop other opportunities or careers. On the other hand, managers undertaking MBOs tend to be in the latter part of their careers and risk throwing away much, including their career, hard-earned savings, and reputation.

In the past, these downsides have been cited as some of the key reasons why the idea of MBOs wouldn't be adopted in Asia. Taking part in an MBO raises many challenges for managers. In essence, they are not only investing their own cash in an opportunity, but it is an opportunity that will depend heavily on the manager's skills and abilities if it is to be successful. Some of these elements are discussed below.

Money invested, or "commitment money"

An important element of the MBO equation is the money invested in the opportunity by the managers who will run the business once it is independent. This investment is important in order to give the institutional providers of funds to the MBO confidence that the managers are attracted by the upside opportunities of the business. The amount can tend to be anything from one year's salary upwards, depending on the financial position of the manager. This is a *real* commitment for managers, as by the time they are over 40, a lifestyle has been established which needs to be maintained and the needs of a family have to be taken into account. For the long-term salaryman, putting his well-planned financial future at some risk is a major consideration.

Secure employment

When an MBO completes, the senior management team voluntarily severs its employment with the parent company or group. This can be a big decision for long-term salarymen and is a huge demonstration of commitment in itself. In today's environment, long-term secure employment is no longer taken for granted; however, when the MBO was developed in the 1970s and 1980s in the US and Europe, this system was still firmly in place. The perks associated with corporate life are attractive, and leaving them behind is seen as a significant opportunity cost of carrying out an MBO. This type of culture has remained strong in economies such as Japan and is seen as a significant obstacle to the development of MBOs.

Confidence in own ability to operate independently

The reputation and achievements of long-term employees are often intrinsically aligned with their company. There is a risk that without this association – which may include the benefits of working under a well-known brand name – the employee's true ability may become exposed … with good or bad results.

Adapting to a more entrepreneurial culture

A separate issue for MBO managers is the loss of being part of a large organization with its significant infrastructure and support. There always seems to be someone to take care of everything, from expense claims, marketing, and treasury services, to IT support and human resource issues. Hence, moving from a large company infrastructure to a small company culture after implementing an MBO isn't easy, and there is a risk that the manager may not adapt.

THE BENEFITS OF MBOs

The benefit of the MBO phenomenon is that it releases hidden or suppressed entrepreneurial energy. More than this, these newly created entrepreneurs have the benefit of professional management training and experience – both qualities which early-stage business creators often lack. These management teams are often frustrated in their corporate jobs and long for the benefits associated with independence in terms of the decision-making freedom, flexibility, and relative lack of bureaucracy that a small company culture can bring. Along with this comes the opportunity to be a shareholder (or owner) of the business, and this in itself can bring a change in mindset toward being more entrepreneurial.

So, why was it, for example, that Japan from the mid-1990s was keen to encourage the concept of the management buyout as one of the tools that could help to revitalize its heavily structured and stagnating economy? Although the leveraged buyout developed in the US in the 1970s, it was in the UK and later in mainland Europe that the mechanism was used to help restructure tired and rigid economic structures. At the beginning of this period, the UK not only had huge nationalized industries, but also large conglomerates each with a diverse and often unfocused portfolio of companies. The development of M&A as a normal method of divesting non-core businesses brought with it the growth of MBOs, where entrepreneurial management teams – backed by private equity and bank funding – joined in alongside other businesses or competitors as potential acquirers. These MBOs were believed to bring real benefits to the economy: they provided a relatively smooth way for vendors to raise cash and put the money to work in more productive parts of the group; also, after MBO, the newly independent businesses became more entrepreneurial and made more positive contributions to economic growth and employment. In short, tired and unloved subsidiaries could be transformed into independent enterprises with highly incentivized and shareholder value-focused management teams.

A survey published in 2001 by the European Venture Capital Association (EVCA)[3] reviewed MBOs and MBIs carried out in Europe from 1992 to 1997 to establish the benefits of MBOs in terms of entrepreneurial value creation. The survey provided strong evidence that not only did MBOs have a significant impact on the overall survivability of businesses, but also that after the MBO, these businesses were more likely to increase their total number of employees (see Figures 13.3 and 13.4). It provided strong support for those lobbying European governments to relax some of the legal and regulatory blockages to permit the faster development of the MBO market. Indeed, this study has been studied by and referred to extensively by policy-makers in Asia.

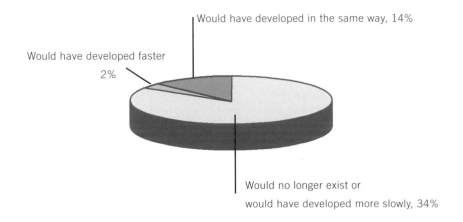

Source: CMBOR/EVCA

Figure 13.3 The Overall Impact of MBOs on the Survival and Growth of Companies

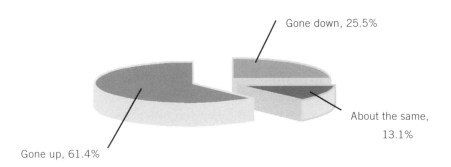

Source: CMBOR/EVCA

Figure 13.4 Change in the Total Number of Employees after an MBO

The benefits don't stop here. Post-MBO companies were also found to be more likely to increase turnover and operating profit, as well as to spend more on training, capital expenditure, marketing expenditure, and research and development. Overall, MBOs have been seen to play a key part – in tandem with the growth of M&As in general – in helping to unwind the cumbersome and often unfocused large business groups in Europe.

For most of the 1990s, Japan experienced widespread economic stagnation. The structure of its economic landscape was shaped around heavily entrenched industry groupings, or *keiretsu*, which, like the conglomerates and nationalized industry groups of the UK in previous decades, were standing in the way of change and release of entrepreneurial flair. As we will see, in the case of Japan, the issues and obstacles are perhaps more entrenched. Before examining Japan's experience of MBOs, it will be useful to understand the fundamentals of how MBOs work and, from this, what the key drivers are in terms of developing a new MBO market.

HOW DO MBOs WORK?

In simple terms, management buyouts combine a mixture of clever financial engineering with the introduction of a new entrepreneurial and shareholder value culture into the business. This combination enables fair prices to be paid for businesses and the buyers to make an attractive return. Let's demonstrate this by a straightforward example. Unloved Ltd. is being sold by its parent, Focused plc, at a price of US$100 million. The four senior Unloved managers have confidence in the future of their business and are keen to invest US$250,000 each, totaling US$1 million in its future. However, this is clearly not enough to purchase the business, as it only represents 1% of the funds required. This is where the MBO financial structure helps to transform the situation. Attracted by the keenness of the management team to invest and commit to the opportunity, a private equity fund, IR^2, is happy to provide a large amount of funds and at the same time incentivize management by providing them with 10% of the equity in return for their US$1 million commitment. IR^2 and management approach a number of banks, who also express a keenness to provide some long-term senior debt to the business.

Apart from the management investment, the amount that IR^2 provides will depend on the amount of debt funding that can be obtained from the banks. In this example, let's assume that the bank is comfortable providing 50% of the total funding package of US$100 million. The balance of US$49 million is provided by IR^2 and will be split US$9 million for 90% of the ordinary shares, and US$40 million in the form of some repayable or redeemable instrument such as debt or preference shares. This structure can be seen in Figure 13.5. The left-hand column represents the structure of the MBO company at the point of purchase.

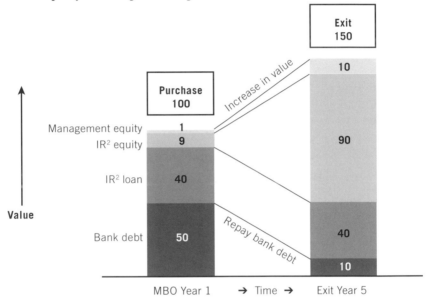

Figure 13.5 How MBOs Work

The MBO makes its return in two ways: first, by repaying as much as possible of the bank senior debt and IR^2 subordinated debt from its operating cash flows; and second, by selling the business at a higher price than what was paid at initial acquisition. An increase in value from either route accrues directly to the holders of the equity and hence increases their return. A combination of the two methods of debt reduction and increasing final sale or IPO value is the normal approach to making a return. However, it is possible for MBOs to make an attractive return through the gearing effect only

– that is, just by repaying bank and IR^2's debt. Table 13.1 illustrates two scenarios. The first shows the returns to management and the private equity fund if there is no change in the final exit price, whereas scenario 2 shows the impact of increasing the valuation at exit by 50%. The returns in scenario 1 are adequate, but those in scenario 2 are much more attractive. Both assume that US$10m of bank debt and all the IR^2 debt is outstanding at exit which takes place in Year 5.

Table 13.1 MBO Returns to Shareholders

		At purchase	Scenario 1 Exit at $100mn		Scenario 2 Exit at $150mn	
	Figures in US$	Amount invested	Amount realized	IRR	Amount realized	IRR
Returns	Management	1	5	50%	10	78%
	IR^2	49	85	15%	130	28%

The MBO consortium would ideally plan to achieve scenario 2 or better, although the downside scenario 1 still assures a healthy return to management and an acceptable return on funds deployed by the private equity fund. One of the fundamental principles of MBOs is also demonstrated in this return table – that is, the best return goes to management. The private equity subordinated debt allows managers to take a larger proportion of the equity and proportionally more of the upside benefit. IR^2's return is lower than that of the managers, as it is a blended return of both its equity proportion of US$10 million and its subordinated debt instrument of US$40 million.

WHAT ARE THE KEY DRIVERS OF MBOs?

The explanation of MBOs in the previous section allows us to determine the key drivers of successful MBOs. These are discussed below.

An established business with strong cash flow

First and foremost, the business that is to be acquired needs to have a strong and sustainable cash flow. If the business has a weak or unstable cash flow, then it won't be possible to pay back the bank senior debt – indeed, it won't be possible to persuade a bank to provide the debt in the first instance as the banks will see the business as having too high a risk profile. Not only does the business need a strong cash flow; it also needs to be a sustainable one. This implies that the business is able to function independently from the group once divested, that it is well established in its sector, and that there are high barriers to entry.

Opportunities for value growth

On-target returns mean that the value of the business should also be enhanced after the MBO. This can be achieved by increasing profits/cash flow, or by selling the business on a higher multiple than that paid on acquisition – or, ideally, some combination of the two. The earnings of the business can be improved by a number of strategies, including increasing sales, improving margins, and reducing costs. The sale multiple on exit will be higher if either the buyer has a particular strategic need for the business or if the general strategic value of the business is enhanced. Examples of an increase in strategic value could include improving the business's position in the market, or perhaps reducing customer or product dependency. The important factor here is that there is scope to increase the value after MBO. More often than not, the MBO managers will have lots of ideas for increasing the value of the business – but in the past, they will have been frustrated that these couldn't be implemented. The MBO helps to release the frustration that has been built up over the years and to channel it into positive action.

Strong management team

A high-quality and broadly based management team is essential to the success of MBOs. In particular, this team needs to be capable of taking the business from a position of relative dependence within a group structure to one of independence. All key positions need to be filled with competent directors. The finance function is often a source of weakness in these situations. Although the financial controller or finance manager is comfortable collecting the figures and sending them to the CFO at head office, they may be less confident or capable of making the step up to being an independent CFO after the MBO. Experience of MBO successes and failures has shown that a competent and independently minded CFO is a necessity.

An exit

Return scenarios remain fictitious unless there is an actual recovery of investment cash for cash – commonly termed "an exit." The most common forms of exits are sale to a trade buyer or to another MBO consortium, or a public listing. The best exits involve an outright sale for cash. A public listing isn't ideal, as there are often lock-in periods for the key shareholders. Even once these have expired, it can be difficult to sell large amounts of equity without destabilizing the share price.

WHAT IS NEEDED FOR A NEW MBO MARKET TO DEVELOP?

As in the case of most new market development, there are some fundamental drivers which need to exist before an MBO market can begin to take root. The key drivers include a supply of businesses for sale (that is, a mergers and acquisitions market), the existence of management teams keen to take entrepreneurial responsibility, the availability of funding – both equity and debt, and an appropriate legal, financial, and regulatory framework. These drivers are discussed below in more detail.

The existence of a healthy M&A market

Clearly, the first prerequisite for MBOs to take place is that there are businesses for sale. An MBO consortium may still have to compete with other trade buyers of businesses – for example, competitor businesses wishing to expand – but the opportunity of a business for sale is needed to set off the process. As we have seen above, a business needs to have strong cash flow and attractive growth prospects for it to be an appropriate MBO candidate. In this sense, the M&A market needs to include good-quality businesses, and not just businesses that are being sold because they are weak. Weak financial structures and some management or organizational issues can be resolved in the process of carrying out an MBO, but fundamentally weak businesses are poor candidates. A mature approach by vendors to core business strategies is therefore required, where they understand that selling a non-core subsidiary – even if it is a good business – can release cash that can be invested in its core business area and, through this, enhance returns to the group. Nationalized industries can also be a source of interesting MBO candidates if it is government policy to embark on a divestment program.

A strong M&A market is also important to facilitate the final exit for the shareholders of the MBO company. As discussed above, trade buyers are one of the preferred routes for releasing the value created by the MBO managers and their financial backers.

Entrepreneurial professional managers

At the core of a successful MBO is a group of managers who are able to put their corporate careers and everything they stand for aside – including job security, perks, and benefits associated with working for a large organization – because they see and are excited by the opportunity to take full responsibility for the business they run, and to develop it in ways they previously only dreamed of. They will also be prepared to invest alongside the other fund providers in the business, not only to demonstrate their commitment, but because they genuinely believe they will make an attractive capital gain.

The similarity of these managers to entrepreneurs is that, for them, the possibilities and opportunities that an MBO can bring outweigh the risks involved. And this, together with their own self-belief, enables them to make the jump. It is usual that these MBO managers have started to experience much frustration while they have been running non-core divisions or subsidiaries of large companies. While their business may not have been officially labeled "non-core," they will have been experiencing the non-core treatment by head office. This manifests itself in many ways, including the general lack of interest in agreeing plans put forward to invest in opportunities to grow or develop the subsidiary. Indeed, it can be more blatant in that head office's only interest in the subsidiary is as a provider of cash to the rest of the group. These frustrated managers who see exciting opportunities for their businesses if only they were independent make excellent MBO candidates.

Availability of private equity experience and funding

Apart from the input of management funds, which tend to be a small percentage of the overall money required to finance the acquisition of the MBO company, the rest of the risk money – that is, the funds with no tangible security – is provided by private equity funds. These funds are similar to the venture funds discussed in Chapter 5, but because they are targeting larger, more established businesses with professional and experienced management, their risks, and therefore expected returns, are lower. Their importance lies not only in the provision of funds, but also in their experience of both carrying out MBOs and working with the business after the acquisition to help make it successful. While the MBO managers are expected to be able to run the business on an operational level, the strategic input and experience of the private equity practitioners at the board level can be invaluable. Both the MBO managers and the private equity funds are co-shareholders in the new business, and it is important that their working relationship is strong and their objectives are fully aligned.

Availability of debt funding

At least half the funds used to acquire the MBO business are provided by the banks – often termed "senior debt." (This is because there may be other types of redeemable or debt instruments in the financial structure that may be unsecured and junior in terms of security and control to the bank.) The appetite of banks for this type of funding is important. Often, the banks may need to go beyond their normal comfort levels in terms of the amount of low-yield debt they provide in order for the private equity fund to make its return – this is particularly true if the business was bought at a full or high price. The US and Europe are blessed with a banking sector that is very experienced in working with MBO companies. They are happy to provide a large amount of flexible, long-term, and low-yielding debt for MBO structures, as they believe that the strong cash flows make up for any lack of security, and are comforted by the addition of private equity funding that is experienced in and motivated to drive the business to repay debt as a first priority.

An appropriate legal, regulatory, financial, and cultural framework

There are various obstacles in terms of legal, regulatory, and financial frameworks that can serve as a blockage to the development of MBOs. These tend to differ by country and can vary from the ability of private equity funds to set up limited partnership funds, or of banks to lend to MBO acquisition vehicles, or even to create different classes of shares. Other similar impediments may involve common local practice or culture – for example, the provision of representations and warranties by vendors when selling businesses or, perhaps, local due diligence practices. A general lack of transparency in terms of company information can make acquisitions in general very difficult.

INTRODUCING THE MBO TO ASIA: THE CASE OF JAPAN

Japan has for decades exhibited the potential to develop a strong MBO market. As the second-largest economy in the world, Japan has thousands of established businesses with professional management teams. The development of the *kereitsu* system of business groupings has produced mega-conglomerates with diverse portfolios of subsidiaries. These subsidiaries not only stretch vertically, with ties into associated companies that are able to provide almost all the needs of component sourcing for the front-line manufacturing businesses, but also horizontally in terms of different products and businesses. It isn't our intention to go into detail to describe the *kereitsu* system here, but only to highlight that reform of this system – or a move to core business strategies – had the ability to create a vast M&A market of which MBOs would very likely take a significant share. It was also believed that many of these businesses had the potential to perform much better if they were released from their life of corporate bondage. In 1999, Japan's Ministry of International Trade and Industry (now METI) carried out a survey of over 30,000 domestic subsidiaries of manufacturing companies in Japan (with more than 50 employees and ¥30 million in share capital). Of these, it identified that some two-thirds could be considered *non-core* – or not directly related to the central business of the parent company.

Japanese MBO market: Obstacles to growth

The existence of these large numbers of potentially non-core businesses could provide the basis of a very large MBO market, yet why, unlike in the US and Europe, didn't the 1980s and 1990s see the development of MBOs in Japan? Some of the answers can be found in the unique characteristics of Japan's economic and business structure which, until the late 1990s, held back the acceptance of MBOs. These include the following:

Lack of businesses for sale

Until recently, the Japanese have not had a domestic M&A culture. During Japan's rise as an economic power from the 1960s we have been used to seeing Japanese companies buying businesses and real estate abroad; but unfortunately, Japanese business culture only developed the *buying* half of the equation. Expansion and market share have been a central objective of Japanese companies, rather than shareholder value. Selling a business, in the Japanese context, can be seen as failure – that is, if a business needs to be sold, then it will mean either that the decision to buy or develop it in the first place was a bad one or that those running the business have failed to make it successful. A major element of this is also the sense of betrayal that would be felt by the loyal and faithful employees of the business. So, even bad businesses wouldn't be sold. Even admitting that these underperforming businesses existed would bring too much shame to the group and their employees. The historical M&A figures are therefore not surprising. The numbers of M&A transactions involving Japanese companies in the decade up to 1995 are small compared with the US (see Figure 13.6). Of the Japanese figures, less than 2% of the total transactions involve "OUT-IN" transactions – or non-Japanese companies acquiring domestic Japanese businesses.

Source: MAR/Thomson Financial

Figure 13.6 Number of M&As, Japan versus United States, 1985–95

Management culture

In the mid- to late 1990s, when interest in the restructuring of Japan began to attract private equity practitioners and funds to the region, one of the key concerns was the management culture. It was believed that managers of subsidiaries would find the concept of leaving their group extremely difficult. A Japanese salary worker, and to some extent also his family, takes pride in being part of the large extended family of his company and of the *keiretsu* to which it belonged. For example, a worker from the Fuyo *keiretsu* would have his bank accounts with the Fuji Bank and would likely drive a Nissan car. It is also likely he will have met his spouse at his workplace. The bond between employer and employee was more than just a service contract; it was a pledge of allegiance that would work both ways and would be for life. Removal or dismissal for poor performance, for example, would be unheard of – the worker would simply be assigned a different job, or perhaps be moved to a subsidiary. In other words, the "problem" would be dealt with quietly and without loss of face to anyone involved. Selling off part of the business to a competitor – a business from another *kereitsu* – would also be unheard of. Selling to a foreign business, unspeakable. To have to contemplate either would be seen as a last resort – and something that would need possibly resignation and apology at the highest level. Also part of the culture was the perceived lack of entrepreneurial motivation. "Japanese salarymen won't want to invest their own money in an MBO" was a frequently heard objection to the development of MBOs.

Quality of management teams

The management development structures in Japanese companies have been adept at developing generalists, rather than specialists. The top companies in Japan have historically attracted the best candidates from universities to join their management programs. These high-flyers will embark on a career track that involves a broad spectrum of two- to three-year posts within the group structure. At times they may be sent on secondment to another major group within the *keiretsu* – for example, it has been normal for banks to send managers to assume senior positions with client businesses. This is seen as good for relationships and also for broad experience. As time moves on, the best candidates will be groomed for the small number of top posts in group headquarters. Those who don't quite make it either continue to fill one of the large number of peripheral posts – or perhaps some of the less important overseas postings – or take a senior post in a subsidiary. The latter route has been termed "descending from heaven." This is a good result for a manager who hasn't quite made it to the top, but instead is rewarded by being appointed *shacho* (president) of a subsidiary business with all the perks of staff, car, salary, and so on that the post brings. Unfortunately, they bring little specialist understanding of the business nor, indeed, much drive to improve the performance through change.

Although this is a general description and there are exceptions, it does raise two issues. First, senior managers of subsidiaries were typically those who hadn't quite made the grade, rather than those who relished the opportunity to run their own operation. Second, it is likely to catch the notice of those in management positions at head office that selling subsidiaries would put an end to this rather pleasant consolation or pre-retirement perk. In many cases, this has provided an amount of natural inertia or middle-management blockage in terms of advancing the idea of divestment programs in Japanese business groups. It is unlikely that middle management will recommend divestment of subsidiaries, in the same way that turkeys are unlikely to vote for Christmas. Finally, a challenge often voiced in Japan in the late 1990s was that management teams wouldn't have the appetite to take part in MBOs, let alone invest their savings in them. Why should they invest in the company that employs them?

> " In many ways the MBO structure suits Japan – it exploits low interest rates and keeps established personal relationships in place. However, it may take more than altered incentives to transform salarymen into entrepreneurs. "

FINANCIAL TIMES, JANUARY 15, 2001

Their commitment is investment enough. Also, this would make them different from their other salarymen peers in the group – which would be in conflict with their in-built desire for uniformity.

Lack of acceptance and experience of global-standard due diligence

For any type of M&A activity to develop, there needs to be a mutual understanding between buyer and seller regarding the process involved, including due diligence procedures and standard legal agreements. Global-standard legal agreements regarding M&A are fairly comprehensive in scope. While it is normal for vendors to negotiate these documents to reduce their own exposure, in Japan the word of a company president has been enough to provide cover for third-party transactions. Any ensuing problems would be sorted out quietly to everyone's satisfaction. Thick legal documents aren't necessarily a good thing – except for lawyers, of course – but fund investors as well as shareholders do expect both private equity executives and public companies to seek adequate assurances and protections when carrying out third-party M&A transactions. The good word of a company *shacho*, while probably historically more effective in seeking redress in Japan than a legal agreement, wasn't generally acceptable in modern M&A particularly at a time when Japanese companies were experiencing financial difficulties and public apologies – the accepted get-out clause – for not being able to meet commitments, verbal or otherwise, were becoming more commonplace. Local legal and

> **Japan's new accounting rules and disclosure requirements were a major step forward in terms of corporate transparency. However, Japan has proportionally less accountants than in the US: whereas there are 350,000 accountants in the US, there are only 13,000 in Japan.**
>
> DEAN YOOST, CEO,
> PRICEWATERHOUSECOOPERS
> FINANCIAL ADVISORY SERVICES, JAPAN

financial advisors are also relatively few in number and generally not experienced in dealing with the sale or acquisition of a business. An increase in the availability of these advisors is necessary to facilitate the growth of the M&A market.

Legal, regulatory, and accounting blockages

The Japanese commercial framework wasn't geared to facilitate actions such as restructuring and unwinding cross-company shareholdings, management stock incentives, use of holding companies to buy other businesses, and so on. Moreover, the lack of a requirement to consolidate company accounts meant that it was easy to hide poor-performing subsidiaries.

Lack of appropriate debt financing

Another broadly held belief was that Japanese banks would have little precedent for or interest in the concept of providing large amounts of gearing to MBO vehicles. As we saw above, for MBOs to work, some 50% or more of the funding needs to come from banks in terms of long-term flexible debt. Bank lending in Japan has been driven traditionally by assessment of security, rather than cash flows and the ability to repay. In hindsight, Japanese banks may have been in better shape if the latter had been their guiding principle over the previous decade or so; nonetheless, it was felt that bank credit committees would find it extremely difficult to agree to MBO-type structures.

Poor visibility regarding exit opportunities

As we mentioned earlier, returns to investors in MBOs don't count until an exit – in the form of cash – has taken place. Even IPOs are not effective exits, as it isn't always possible to sell shares immediately. The lack of an M&A market therefore reduces the opportunities to make a final return for MBO investments. An important source of exit for MBO businesses in the vibrant M&A

markets of the US and Europe is foreign multinationals, who are often willing to pay high multiples to buy businesses in parts of the world where they currently have little or no strategic footprint. It is well known that many MNCs have been looking at acquiring Japanese businesses, but generally they have been put off by cultural considerations, in terms both of the ability of management to adapt to new ways of operating and of concerns over the M&A process.

Recent developments in the Japanese MBO market

The prolonged stagnation of the Japanese economy in the 1990s forced the Japanese to challenge many of the traditional aspects of government and business practice. Various changes have resulted.

Government-led reforms

As well as the "Big Bang" reforms introduced to boost competition in the financial sector, the government has introduced a series of measures that have been designed specifically to stimulate M&A and facilitate the growth of the MBO market. These include:

- changes in accounting relating to consolidated accounts and accounting for pension benefits;
- changes in the tax code, which make it possible to offer stock options as incentives to management;
- raising the upper limit for preferred stock issues (important for gearing MBO structures) and stock options;
- introducing a stock swap system to facilitate restructuring and divestment; and
- a change in Japanese law to provide for the use of holding companies as vehicles to buy or hold businesses or operations.

Increased focus on shareholder value

It was commonly discussed in Japan in the late 1990s that a major catalyst was needed to break the Japanese economy out of its

> " The results of freeing Shinsei Bank from the burdens of excess debt and allowing its management to go back to growing business and improving productivity have exceeded my wildest expectations. Private equity can be a positive vehicle for change, a positive lubricant, and can play a positive role in bringing the Japanese economy back to its former pre-eminence in the world economy. "
>
> TIM COLLINS, CEO,
> RIPPLEWOOD HOLDINGS[4]

traditional structure. Many felt that government should provide a stronger lead and facilitate a hard landing, rather than the expected soft landing, for the economy. In the same vein, some observers wished for a Margaret Thatcher type of leader to emerge. The former British prime minister is highly regarded in Japan for having transformed the UK from its structural difficulties of the 1960s and 1970s into one of the more entrepreneurial and open Western economies. In the end, the catalyst came from neither, but was made up of a series of business events that served as both shocks and challenges to the status quo. We will cover three of them briefly. One of these was the announcement of the merger between three significant and hitherto solid banks – Industrial Bank of Japan, Fuji Bank, and Daiichi Kangyo Bank – now operating as Mizuho. This one event publicly signaled the weakness of the banking system, and also cut across the sacred cow of the *keiretsu* business groupings. Another major shock was the announcement in March 1999 that Renault, the French car manufacturer, had purchased a 36.8%, and controlling, stake in the Japanese auto giant Nissan. In the same way that the three banks were seen as financial pillars of the Japanese economy, Nissan had been the most prestigious company in the key automotive sector, with strong links with the government. It was caught by over-expansion abroad after losing market share at home to Toyota, and had experienced continuous losses for the majority of the 1990s. The third event was the filing for bankruptcy of the Long Term Credit Bank and subsequent purchase in March 2000 by Ripplewood, a US private equity firm, which renamed the bank the Shinsei (or "new birth") Bank.

These events – and others like them – helped to start the process of changing mindsets in Japan. The growing enthusiasm concerning the need to restructure was evident by the almost daily press announcements covering the latest restructuring initiative. Old habits, unfortunately, can run very deep and many of these were often simply a soft rearrangement of company structures – otherwise sometimes referred to as a "shuffle of business cards". A senior manager of one major Japanese company proudly announced that the company had restructured into 20 separate business divisions – this seemed a positive move and one that would facilitate easier divestment and allocation of assets. When asked how many of the divisions were core, he replied: "I don't quite understand the point of your question... they are *all* core." The new regulations on consolidation of company accounts prompted a large round of restructurings. For the first time, bad businesses couldn't be hidden off balance sheet and there was a scramble to offload these problem businesses. This type of restructuring, of course, didn't provide a rich source of MBO opportunities and it seemed that in Japan the process of divesting *non-core* businesses really meant divesting *non-performing* businesses. Some corporates, however, were more serious about selling non-core businesses and, as shown in Figure 13.7, Japan has experienced year-on-year growth in numbers of transactions, from 11 reported in 2000 to 67 in 2003.

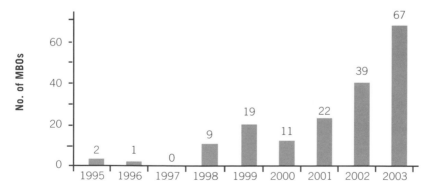

Source: Asia Venture Capital Journal statistics

Figure 13.7 Growth of the MBO Market in Japan, 1995–2003

The increase in MBOs in Japan has been a product of the change in attitudes toward restructuring, but also a catalyst for releasing entrepreneurial drive and shareholder value. Although many of the obstacles to MBOs – particularly the availability of good-quality businesses for sale and well-rounded management teams – can still be a major obstacle, it is very encouraging to see that the numbers of MBOs continue to increase and some attractive exits for investors have already been realized. Much has been achieved in a short space of time. Back in 1997, apart from a few private equity practitioners and those from the financial sector who had spent some of their careers in Europe or the US, most Japanese thought MBO stood for Management by Objectives! Since then, the completion of several high-profile and landmark MBOs has helped to raise awareness of this form of M&A and the acronym is now often seen in the popular press.

One of these landmark MBOs, Vantec Corporation, is profiled as a case study below. Vantec attracted much interest, both inside and outside Japan, as it demonstrated that an MBO with all the key characteristics of strong cash flow, growth opportunity, geared financial structure, and a strong exit could be achieved in Japan. More importantly, it sent a clear signal to other Japanese management teams that they, once independent from the parent company, were quite as capable as their Western counterparts in terms of enterprise and value creation. To this end, they were able to create and realize an attractive return for themselves and their funders.

> " Landmark MBOs by Schroder Ventures of Recruit Building Management in January 2000, Benkan Corp. in October 2001 for 10 billion yen, and by UK-based Private Equity Group 3i, of Vantec in January 2001 for 15 billion yen opened the door to MBOs of non-distressed businesses. "

PRICEWATERHOUSECOOPERS,
"RECENT TRENDS IN PRIVATE EQUITY,"
NOVEMBER 5, 2002

MBO of Vantec Corporation

Vantec Corporation was set up in 1954 to provide logistics services exclusively to Nissan Group. It grew rapidly together with Nissan, and by the late 1990s had become one of the leading businesses of its kind in Japan, with sales of over US$600 million by 1999. Its main business was just-in-time manufacturing logistics, although it also provided packing and export services, as well as managing the Nissan parts center. Vantec, like other support service subsidiaries in Japan, had developed as a budget center rather than a profit center. Hence, its margins were very low compared with independent logistics companies, as its main business objective was to provide a service to Nissan Group rather than to create shareholder value.

In 2000, Renault's newly established president of Nissan, Carlos Ghosn, announced his turnaround plan, which would involve not only severe cost cutting, but also the divestment of non-core businesses. Vantec fell into this category, as Nissan's new French CFO, Thierry Moulonguet, confirmed: "By selling its stake in Vantec, Nissan continues to implement its policy of divesting its non-core activities, including those associated parts and services which are not directly related to designing, manufacturing and selling vehicles."[5]

On the face of it, Vantec exhibited many of the characteristics of similar subsidiaries in Japan's *keiretsu*:

- It was majority owned by its main customer.
- Most of its secondary customers were also from the Nissan Group companies — that is, from within its *keiretsu* group.
- The president was a long-term Nissan Group manager.
- The senior operational management team had long service with Vantec, as did many of the 2,000 employees. There were also many "secondees" from other parts of the Nissan Group.
- Margins were low, with no profit culture.

This combination of characteristics was generally seen as a challenge in terms of being able to develop the business successfully post acquisition.

Establishing a valuation for a business of this nature is also difficult, as the potential risks are high and the quality of information generally poor. Some of the key risks are discussed below.

Key risks

High Dependence on One Customer

Nissan and its group companies historically accounted for a large majority of Vantec sales. Third-party customers were typically a small minority share in such businesses and often taken to fill capacity, rather than to increase profitability.

> ...Vantec has tiny margins and Nissan will demand further price reductions. Vantec will have to develop third party business very quickly to compensate.

FINANCIAL TIMES, JANUARY 15, 2001

Management's Ability to Embrace an Entrepreneurial Culture

With employees and senior managers steeped in years of support mentality and operating under the umbrella of the prestigious Nissan Group, there would be a high risk that breaking away and becoming independent would be too difficult. Adapting to a profit culture would be an even greater challenge. Linked to this was management's will to invest alongside the private equity investor and become shareholders. Existing belief in the market was that this financial commitment would not only be small, but potentially not forthcoming at all, with management more used to low-risk incentives such as "guaranteed bonuses" for achieving their annual soft budgets.

Management Reporting Systems and Culture

After a lifetime of operating budgets and serving the top company's manufacturing operations, these businesses are generally ill-equipped to switch to a product and customer profitability culture. This makes it particularly difficult to carry out due diligence, where there is a need to establish where – and if – sources of profit growth exist.

Ability to Survive as an Independent Business

One of the benefits that vendors hope to gain from the divestment of non-core businesses is the ability first to reduce fixed overheads, but second to pay arm's-length competitive market rates for the service in the future. Clearly, a major part of the due diligence carried out by the acquirer needed to establish the competitiveness of the company's service or product and benchmark it with market rates. While it is unlikely that the major customer would disappear immediately, some comfort had to be gained that the acquired company would be profitable at market rates and also that the customer – in this case, Nissan – would continue in good faith to buy Vantec's services at a fair market rate.

Achieving an Exit

In calculating returns, private equity funds make assumptions on when an exit would be and at what price. In reality, this can prove a challenging assumption. Exit options include a sale to a third-party purchaser, a listing on a public exchange, or some kind of share buy-back. Selling to a foreign trade buyer was generally seen as the most attractive option for such MBOs, but, as discussed earlier, this type of M&A has been rare in Japan. So, for early MBOs in Japan, the exit was somewhat of a leap of faith based on the assumption that the M&A market would continue to develop and create attractive exit opportunities. The potential for exit would certainly be a risk in the case of Vantec.

Vantec becomes independent

After reviewing the interest of several buyers, Nissan eventually sold the business to an MBO consortium which included management, 3i-Kogin Buyouts Ltd. (an MBO private equity fund adviser formed as a joint venture between 3i Group plc and IBJ, a Japanese bank), and a Japanese banking syndicate. Management and the 3i-Kogin Buyouts-led private equity syndicate invested in the equity, and the bank syndicates provided the senior debt. The actual price was undisclosed, although the total deal size was reported to be some US$150 million, making it the largest example of an MBO in Japan at the time. The issue of pricing in Vantec's case sparked much interest in the market. The consortium acquired Nissan Group's super majority stake of 75% using the holding company structure shown in Figure 13.8.

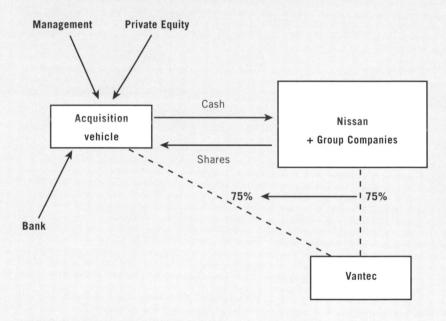

Figure 13.8 Vantec MBO: Acquisition Method

So, what was it about Vantec that made the MBO possible? There were several factors.

A Serious and Willing Seller

Renault's Carlos Ghosn brought a Western focus to the task of restructuring Nissan. This focus succeeded in cutting across layers of management inertia that would have had the potential to make the negotiations and completion of the sale difficult. It also enabled the acquirer to carry out the appropriate due diligence and agree the normal legal documentation.

An Ongoing Relationship with Nissan

As suggested earlier, acquisitions such as Vantec in Japan would involve more complex valuation negotiations, and the final price would depend very much on the value of the ongoing servicing agreement with its vendor and largest company, Nissan, going forward. This was confirmed in a later interview with management and the private equity partner: "There were two sides to the negotiations; one was the price side and the other was setting up a trading arrangement. So Nissan had comfort they would have a supplier and Vantec had comfort they could have sensible margins going forward."[6]

> Some market professionals said the total funding of ¥15bn appeared expensive. 'We estimate the company's price/earnings multiple to March 2000 is near 100. It looks really expensive,' said one partner at a private equity house. 'It should probably cost less than ¥10bn,' agreed a second private equity banker.

INTERNATIONAL FINANCING REVIEW,
JANUARY 20, 2001

This strong relationship with its key customer was to prove hugely beneficial to Vantec in the next few years, particularly as Nissan's own turnaround plans began to bear fruit.

An Entrepreneurial Leader and Committed Senior Team

Initial due diligence revealed that the president, Shinsuke Okuno, and his senior team had already demonstrated their entrepreneurial tendencies before the MBO. Since his

> " ...the management has invested with us in the investment vehicle. The weight of money has come from 3i and banks, but the management has put in substantial sums, which are easily as much as we would expect management to invest in a European MBO.[7] "

appointment as president some 18 months earlier, Okuno had set in place two key programs. The first was one to drive cost reduction, and the second was to increase the proportion of third-party (non-Nissan group) customers. The opportunity to become independent appealed to Okuno, and he and his senior team were keen in the opportunity, becoming at the same time owners in the new business.

Strong Cash Flow and ability to attract Senior Debt

It is understood that there was strong competition to provide long-term banking facilities for the transaction, which eventually was provided by a banking syndicate led by Mizuho Financial Group. The amount of debt used in the transaction – some 50% – with the associated requirement to cover interest and capital repayments gave a clear indication that Vantec also enjoyed a strong and consistent level of cash flow. Without this, as we saw earlier in the chapter, a geared structure and the appropriate equity returns wouldn't be possible.

The Opportunity for Value Growth

The new shareholders believed that the MBO provided Vantec with new opportunities to grow shareholder value. For example, its new independence would enable it to approach potential customers in other *keiretsu* groups, as well as to develop customers outside the automotive sector to reduce its reliance on this area. Management were very confident they could grow the business: "Vantec president Shinsuke Okuno, leader of the management team investing in the company, said the buyout provides an exceptional opportunity to expand the business."[8]

After the MBO

Vantec's performance improved both in terms of sales and margin following the MBO, as can be seen in Figure 13.9. It was reported that Vantec's operating profit margin — very low at less than 1% of sales prior to the MBO — doubled every year following the completion. In addition, the level of sales also grew every year. Its customers include Coca-Cola and UCC Coffee.

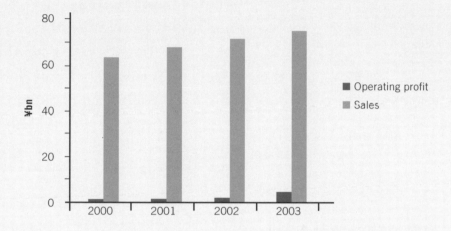

Note: Operating profit for 2003 is estimated

Figure 13.9 Vantec Sales and Operating Profit Performance 2000-2003

In terms of realizing value from the investment — remember that the development of an M&A market to facilitate exits was another concern for developing MBOs in Japan — the original shareholders achieved an exit from the investment in August 2003 at a reported 3x multiple of their original investment. This would imply an internal rate of return (IRR) well in excess of 50%. After an auction believed to have attracted the interest of global logistics companies, the sale became the first example of a secondary MBO[9] in Japan. With the significant overhang of private equity funds looking for quality opportunities in Japan, this type of sale may become commonplace. The contribution of Vantec and other early MBOs to developing the MBO market in Japan has been to demonstrate the benefits of the process to vendors and MBO teams alike, as well as to the economy in general, by promoting the transparency and accountability that goes hand in hand with growing shareholder value.

A Positive Result for the MBO Entrepreneurs

The development of the MBO markets in Europe has shown the positive effect that examples of successful MBO managers can have on encouraging other managers to step forward. Okuno and his team have joined a growing number of Japanese MBO managers who can demonstrate not only that they have succeeded in breaking off from their industrial group and developed a thriving independent business, but also that they have made a very attractive return from their investment. In Vantec's case, the metamorphosis of the salaryman management team into entrepreneurs continues as they reinvest some of their gains in the second MBO, showing ongoing commitment and belief that they can drive the company to further successes.

> " The buyout advances Nissan's supply chain restructuring and gives Vantec independence to pursue third party business aggressively. For the first time, Vantec management will be directly accountable to investors and properly incentivised by the need to service US$65m debt and a stake in the equity upside. This ought to drive efficiency and create shareholder value. "
>
> THE LEX COLUMN," *FINANCIAL TIMES* (UK), JANUARY 15, 2001

Despite the growing numbers of MBOs in Japan, the market remains in an early stage of development. The good news for entrepreneurial managers is that the sheer size of the Japanese economy is likely to provide a steady supply of interesting MBO opportunities for some time to come. The other beneficiaries are the private equity buyout funds, which are already being attracted in numbers to one of the most exciting buyout markets currently. Their very presence will help to grow the market and set global standards.

> **In the four years since** the buyout investment concept began to gain its foothold in Japan, it has not only altered the country's private equity landscape but has led it to a new level. During these four years, Japan has not only advanced to become home to Asia's largest buyout fund pool, close to $5bn with 40 funds, it also now boasts a transaction total that amounts to an awesome aggregate $4.97bn. **"**

"BREAKING DOWN THE *KEIRETSU*," *ASIA PRIVATE EQUITY REVIEW,*

RESTRUCTURING DEVELOPMENTS ELSEWHERE IN ASIA

Other Asian countries have been encouraged by the growing acceptance of M&A and MBOs in Japan and Korea. The next growth areas are likely to be Singapore and India, with China also starting to show promise.

Singapore

The Singapore business landscape is not only one of the more advanced in Southeast Asia, it is also one of the most structured. Traditionally, Singapore has been a popular stepping stone for MNCs wishing to establish operations in Asia. They are attracted by the modern infrastructure and facilities, and by Singapore's position as a multicultural hub. The other key feature in the business landscape is the role of government-linked companies (GLCs) – Singapore's equivalent of Europe's nationalized industries and Japan's *keiretsu*. This has been recognized for some time, and a committee to look at this issue as far back as the late 1980s recommended ways to divest these government stakes. A 2002 article in Singapore's *Business Times* reported that since these earlier recommendations: "…GLCs have in fact grown bigger and more pervasive. Their parent, Temasek Holdings, now has some 80 key companies under its direct control. These companies account for 13% of GDP and at least a third of the stock market's capitalization."[10]

A more recent review of the issues facing the Singapore economy was convened and in 2002 published its recommendations. Again, the proposals were quite categorical regarding GLCs, the key recommendations being as follows:

- Set up and keep GLCs for strategic purposes only.
- Review GLCs constantly and divest non-strategic ones when commercially viable.
- Explore ways of divestment other than through IPOs or trade sales, including using methods such as MBOs with the aim of creating more entrepreneurial local companies.

These recommendations have been welcomed, albeit with much cynicism. This isn't surprising given the natural inertia that can be built into this type of business structure over time. However, the situation facing Singapore is very different now. In the mid-1980s, it didn't face the competitive threat from massive economies such as China and India which, among other effects, has led more recently to a certain amount of hollowing out of manufacturing capability in favor of areas with lower labor costs. Also explicit in the proposals is not only that non-core GLCs should be divested, but also that the core GLC business areas should look to expand and acquire on a global scale and benchmark against the best of class. Later in 2002, the results were published of a study undertaken by the British private equity firm 3i that looked at the potential for MBOs in Singapore from GLCs and other large businesses. The study[11] took a sample of 29 listed businesses and 42 GLCs, and reviewed their subsidiary relationships. After applying a filtering process to remove property, investment companies, and so on, the study identified over 1,500 potentially non-core subsidiaries and divestment candidates. In a similar manner to the METI study in Japan in 1997, this helped to demonstrate the potential for an MBO market in Singapore – although, also like Japan, there needs to be some willing sellers to create the appropriate M&A conditions.

Since 2002, Singaporean companies haven't been in a hurry to embark on a huge "sell-off." Unlike some of their Japanese counterparts, there is no particular financial crisis to encourage quick or fire sales. Despite this, Temasek is clearly looking for opportunities to divest government-linked companies where there is no fit with its core strategies. Some large businesses have already been auctioned off, including CPG (formerly the Public Works Department) to Downer of Australia, and Singapore Yellow Pages as an LBO to a private equity/management consortium. In September 2004, Temasek sold one of its two ground-handling businesses, Changi International Airport Services (CIAS), to Dnata, the Dubai-based airport ground-handling services operator. All these sale auctions attracted both trade buyers and MBO syndicates, which not only demonstrated the appetite of managers and private equity funds to bid for the businesses, but was also an indication that vendors welcomed these syndicates as potential buyers. As other countries have shown, this isn't a quick or straightforward process, but it is believed that Singapore will continue to provide strong opportunities for MBOs going forward.

South Asia

Since 2002, anticipation has been growing in India concerning its development into another potentially large Asian MBO market. This anticipation has been fueled by a number of developments. Indian conglomerates are beginning to sell off some of their non-core businesses, there has been an increase in distress sales, privatization programs are being developed by state governments, and more and more SMEs are looking to bring in professional management to help deal with succession issues. Already, several transactions have been completed, and global private equity funds, including Actis (formerly Commonwealth Development Corporation), Baring Private Equity, Newbridge Capital, Carlyle Group, and Warburg Pincus, are putting resources in terms of funds and investment executives into the region. Like Japan, India has its own set of obstacles that need to be addressed before the MBO market can develop freely. In particular, India has a history of being a complex tax and regulatory environment; however, measures are being taken to cut the red tape and make it easier for foreign funds to support this restructuring. In September 2004, INSEAD held an MBO conference in Mumbai and gathered together over 70 practitioners – both local and foreign – to examine the key priorities in terms of establishing the MBO market in India. The top 15 priorities are set out in Figure 13.10, but it is noticeable that the need to change regulations accounts for a large number of them.

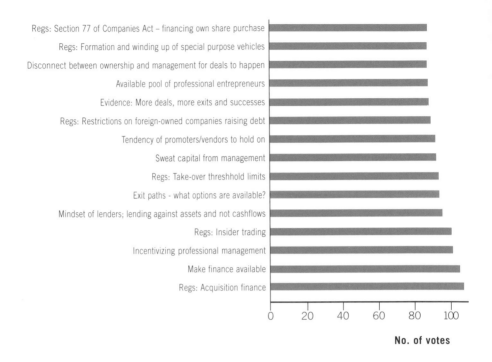

Figure 13.10 Key Priorities for Establishing an MBO Market in India

▶▶ CONCLUSION

In the late 1990s, management buyouts wouldn't have warranted a mention in a book on Asian entrepreneurship. However, MBOs are emerging in Asia as a useful tool for releasing new entrepreneurial activity, and early success is evident in those countries where numbers of large businesses or industrial groupings need to restructure in order to survive in an increasingly open and competitive global economy. Whereas the challenge for early-stage companies is to find capital, there is no shortage of private capital flooding to Asia looking for MBO opportunities with Asian MBOs now recognized internationally as one of the most attractive asset classes. The key challenge for the Asian MBO market going forward is to change entrenched business and management cultures and remove legal, tax, and regulatory obstacles. There is some encouraging momentum already in these respects, and this is expected to gather pace as the benefits of MBOs to Asian economies become more tangible and the practice is adopted more widely as an acceptable means not only to restructure complex business groupings, but also as a method to release government-owned industries and services to the private sector.

ENDNOTES

1   Coller Capital's *Global Private Equity Barometer* (a survey of over 100 international institutional investors in private equity funds), November 22, 2004: www.collercapital.com.

2   *Webster's Dictionary,* 1913.

3   European Venture Capital Association and PricewaterhouseCoopers, *Survey of the Economic and Social Impact of Management Buyouts and Buyins in Europe,* January 2001.

4   Speaking at a JETRO (Japan Export Trade Organisation) conference, March 2002.

5   *Reuters,* January 12, 2001.

6   "Deal of the Month," *Corporate Finance,* February 2001.

7   Ibid.

8   *Asian Wall Street Journal,* January 15, 2001.

9   A secondary MBO is where a new equity consortium backs the existing management team to buy the business from the previous equity partners.

10 *Business Times* (Singapore), May 31, 2002.

11 3i Asia Pacific research project identifying more than 1,500 non-core businesses as possible management buyout opportunities, published November 2002.

SECTION V

Conclusion

*T*o round off the book, we offer some thoughts on a handful of specific topics that we think will be especially prominent in the entrepreneurship scene in Asia-Pacific over the coming decade.

A Look Forward

*O*ver the course of the last few years, the Asia-Pacific region has increasingly emerged as rich in opportunity. This has attracted many emigrants to return home, but it has also attracted the attention of entrepreneurs and financiers the world over.

Much of this attention has centered on technology-related innovations and developments, but we suggest that certain non-technology-related areas will also offer opportunities.

We end with a gallery of young entrepreneurs, representing the new generation of Asian entrepreneurship

A REGION OF OPPORTUNITY

In the survey we carried out in preparation for this book, we found a very high degree of optimism among Asian entrepreneurs – 97% of our respondents described themselves as "somewhat" or "very" positive about prospects for their business over the next five years. In similar vein, the Technology Fast 500 Asia Pacific 2004 CEO survey reported that 99% of CEOs interviewed said that they were "somewhat," "very," or "extremely" confident that their company will sustain its high level of growth over the next 12 months.

> " Asian entrepreneurs are thus very bullish about the near future, and about the opportunities that will exist in this region. "

Asian entrepreneurs are thus very bullish about the near future and about the opportunities that will exist in this region. In the case of the Technology Fast 500 respondents, over half said that they saw the Asia-Pacific region as presenting opportunities for significant growth for their companies over the next five years, more than twice as many as those who said this about North America.

So, in view of this, how do Asian entrepreneurs feel about their competitive position with regard to their regional neighbors? This was a topic explored by the *UPS Asia Business Monitor* and the findings are given in the following box.

Asian SME competitiveness ratings

When asked about the competitiveness of SMEs in other countries relative to those in their own country, respondents overwhelmingly voted for mainland China's SMEs, with three-quarters (73%) of those outside China rating Chinese SMEs as being more competitive. ASEAN countries in particular reserved strong praise for China, with 83% of firms in the Philippines and Thailand, 80% in Indonesia, and 78% in Malaysia considering Chinese firms more competitive than those in their countries, reinforcing the sense of economic threat posed by China to companies in Southeast

Asia. Chinese SMEs scored highest in competitiveness in every economy except South Korea, where they took second place behind Japanese SMEs.

Firms in the developed Asian economies also rated highly in general, with 59% of those outside Japan rating Japanese SMEs as being more competitive than local ones, 55% choosing Hong Kong SMEs, 54% selecting South Korean SMEs, 52% voting for Taiwanese SMEs, and 49% picking Singaporean SMEs. At the opposite end of the scale, just 12% of SMEs outside of the Philippines rate that country's companies more competitive than local ones, and only 17% outside of Indonesia.

Interestingly, within China, a majority of SMEs consider their foreign counterparts to be more competitive than local firms. A full 63% of Chinese SME leaders consider Japanese companies to be more competitive, followed by Hong Kong at 60%, South Korea at 51%, and Singapore at 50%.

Respondents also prioritized the contribution of various factors toward building competitive businesses and rated their own country by whether such factors are present locally. In approximate order of priority, survey respondents felt access to capital to be a very important factor in competitiveness, followed by innovation, access to market intelligence and other business information, access to overseas markets, availability of qualified staff, supply-chain efficiency, labor costs, and legal framework.

In developed and higher-cost markets such as Australia, Hong Kong, Japan, South Korea, Singapore, and Taiwan, labor costs stand out both as highly important as a driver of competitiveness and as an area where these markets have difficulty competing. Innovation also is of major importance, and widely seen as lacking, especially in China, Hong Kong, and Malaysia. Supply-chain efficiency is flagged for attention in China, Indonesia, India, the Philippines, and Thailand. Legal framework is commonly considered to be lacking in China and Indonesia, as is access to market intelligence and other business information. Government support for SMEs is generally considered lacking, particularly in Hong Kong, Indonesia, the Philippines, and Thailand.

Above all other factors, access to capital and funding stands out as a key driver of SME competitiveness, and it more often than not is lacking in the local business environment. More than 80% of respondents in China and the Philippines complained of a lack of adequate access to funds. In only three markets – Australia, Hong Kong, and Taiwan – did fewer than half of all respondents feel they lacked sufficient access to funds for doing business.

Source: UPS Asia Business Monitor, January 2005.

THE RETURNING DIASPORA

This topic follows logically from the preceding one, for clearly, if the perception that most growth opportunities will be situated in Asia-Pacific over the coming few years is shared by expatriate Asians, then a growing number of them will be tempted to return home to share in these opportunities.

The OECD recently published a study[1] describing the results of two specific primary surveys, one of IT professionals in Bangalore and their role in making the city a corridor for international mobility of Indian professionals, and the second of health professionals (doctors and nurses) in New Delhi. In these surveys, highly skilled Indians were asked about their motivations for emigrating, their experiences abroad, their reasons for coming back to India, and their perception of their current situation. These surveys were carried out as a supplement to a study on estimating the stocks, flows, and international mobility of human resources in science and technology in India.

The IT professionals were asked, inter alia, what was the prime stimulus that prompted them to return. Their answers are presented in Figure 14.1. It is clear from these that their return had nothing to do with difficulties experienced in the host country, and everything to do with perceived opportunities in India.

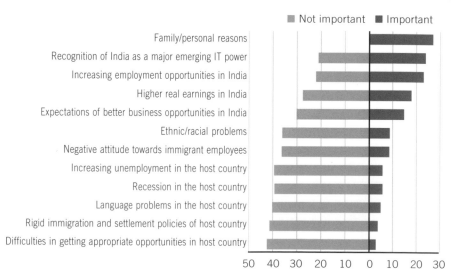

Figure 14.1 Motivating Factors in Return Migration to India

It was also clear from the study that the returnees were very satisfied with their decision:

> When the respondents were asked to speak on the "positive and negative feelings" after coming back home to India, all of them expressed that positive feelings substantially outweigh the negatives. "Physical proximity to the family as well as to the nation" and an independent environment were reported as the most important positive feelings. Several of them expressed their satisfaction on the development of Bangalore as a cosmopolitan city with an increasing number of employment opportunities in almost every emerging field.
>
> [Over half of the] respondents revealed that they had tried to motivate their friends and colleagues and some relatives as well to return to India. However, not all of them were successful in this endeavour. Generation of a fairly large number of good employment opportunities, and many more lucrative opportunities for self-employment, especially in India's IT sector, a sense of feeling at home consequent to a socially comfortable and easy life — were the inducements that were cited by these respondents to their friends and colleagues abroad.

However, it is becoming increasingly evident that returning migrants don't simply participate in better and more numerous business opportunities. Their experiences and opinions gained abroad in various host countries are having an impact on domestic policy-making. A recent article in *India Review*[2] had this to say on the subject:

> Patterns of elite migration, combined with certain features of India's policymaking process and institutional environment, have reshaped the economic preferences of elites, with significant consequences for the trajectory of economic reforms.
>
> ...international migration and return, and the Indian diaspora itself, have emerged as important vehicles for the diffusion of ideas shaping India's economic policies. There is little reason to suspect that they will not continue to do so.

HERE COMES THE REST OF THE WORLD

However, it is by no means that only returning migrants who are heading to Asia to participate in the perceived growth opportunities. Much of the attention of entrepreneurs and financiers around the world is focused on the region. As *Forbes* recently put it:

> Entrepreneurs are going where the growth is and where the smarts are. China has deepening resources, especially in manufacturing. Taiwan and Japan are still hotspots for electronics; Korea is big in online games and broadband ideas; Singapore is a big venture capital player; eastern Europe has crack software engineers; India and Ireland have legions of good programmers; Israel knows security technologies and chip design; Australia has great optics technology and call centers.[3]

> " ... it is by no means only returning migrants who are heading to Asia to participate in the perceived growth opportunities. "

This appeared in an account of a meeting held in New York in late September 2004 attended by 110 entrepreneurs and venture capitalists from 17 cities around the world. Organized by Jerusalem Venture Partners, the meeting was about the opportunities of Asia's tech markets (see box).

The global start-up

VCs who once bragged about never driving more than half an hour to visit a portfolio company are jetting to Australia for optical engineers, Israel for security whizzes, India and Kazakhstan for brute software coding, South Korea for online gaming and Japan for graphics chips. For growth across the board, China is the place to go. IT spending there is expected to hit $48 billion by 2008, a twofold increase, and grow three times as fast as in the U.S. Its mobile phone users are increasing at 25% a year. One of every three cell phones and eight of every ten DVD players in the world are made in China. Shanghai produces 40% of the world's semiconductors. India's communications minister has set a target of up to 250 million telephones by 2007, with what one VC estimates to be a $30 billion investment in the necessary infrastructure.

"VCs in Silicon Valley used to pride themselves on being local," says Margalit, who has $680 million under management. "That was well and good when the U.S. was the mecca for technology, but today the leading markets are China, Japan, Korea, Taiwan. Entrepreneurs need to talk to the people who are determining where the world is going, and they can't do that if everyone around the table is American." [...]

Norwest Venture Partners' Promod Haque, who sits atop *Forbes* Midas List of tech dealmakers, says he won't even consider investing in an entrepreneur unless that person has worked out an international strategy. In June Haque and his partners took executives from eight portfolio companies on a two-week business-building mission to his native India. One of Norwest's companies, Virtela Communications, initiated five new deals on that trip.

A global view is required just to keep pace with foreign firms quick to copy an idea. Yahoo faces serious competition by indigenous copycats in countries such as Korea. Ebay has been scrambling to buy up imitators in Korea and elsewhere. Along with other VCs, Benchmark Capital invested $13 million in online networking outfit Friendster in 2003. William Gurley, a Benchmark general partner, now counts at least three Chinese imitators. "You can't plan U.S. success first and then go global ten years from now. They're all reading the tech business magazines and VentureWire. They know what you're building before you get there," he says.

Silicon Valley Bank, famed as a lender to young U.S. companies, opened offices in London and Bangalore in September. Next year SVB plans to move into China and Israel. The bank is going abroad to get an edge over its US competition, but it isn't lending in Asia – its staff is there to make introductions for entrepreneurs to potential customers, investors and partners. "Venture capital is a global industry. We are going to see more cross-border companies being funded," says Ash Lilani, head of global sales and marketing at SVB, "and the earlier you get to know startups, the deeper the relationships."

Consultancies are seeing a nice boost as well. Kenneth DeWoskin, head of business development for PricewaterhouseCoopers Transaction Services in China, says demand for advice on how to do business in Asia has been so taxing that he has doubled the size of his corps to 6,000 in the last 24 months. He plans to add another 1,000 employees in China next year. "The first thing I tell entrepreneurs is, 'Keep your bags packed at all times,'" says DeWoskin. [...]

Risks will always abound. In China red tape and issues about piracy and intellectual property are obstacles. In India there is a 20% turnover rate at most IT-outsourcing shops and driving to their gated corporate campuses requires navigating streets jammed with beggars, cows and elephants. An engineer for Lumenaré Networks was sitting on a bench outside his office in Noida, in the northern state of Uttar Pradesh. His cell phone rang, and when he picked it up, a monkey leapt at him and bit his hand in an attempt to grab the phone. Not something that Lumenaré's venture backers at Sevin Rosen Funds in Silicon Valley ever had to worry about before.

Source: Forbes, November 29, 2004, p. 161

SECTORS OF ACTIVITY

Technological sectors will inevitably figure importantly in new entrepreneurial ventures – the fruit of the immense amount of creativity and innovation that is happening around the region and which we looked at in Chapter 3. Of these, according to the Technology Fast 500 Asia Pacific 2004 CEO survey, those that have the greatest potential for growth over the next 12 months are wireless communications service, and all internet/IP-related sectors, which between them got 50% of the votes. To put that into perspective, the third-ranked sector – business software – got under 10%.

The move away from a purely low-cost manufacturing area toward direct and intensive involvement in technology development has been perhaps the major phenomenon across Asia over the last few years. It was well summarized by Adam Segal in a recent article:[4]

The attraction of emerging technology clusters in places such as Shanghai, China, Bangalore, India, and Hsinchu, Taiwan, was at first based on their cheap labor supply. But as local technology companies have developed, new research institutes have been founded, and scientists and engineers from such countries have returned home after training and working in the United States, these hubs have started supporting innovation of their own. Craig Barrett of Intel has said that the Chinese are now "capable of doing any engineering, any software job, any managerial job that people in the United States are capable of." And Microsoft has reportedly contracted with the Indian companies Infosys and Satyam not only to do simple software coding, but also to provide highly skilled software architects.

No longer content to dominate labor-intensive manufacturing, Asian governments are also actively promoting technological innovation. Japan and South Korea each currently spend 3 percent of GDP on R&D (compared to 2.7 percent in the United States) and Beijing is trying to reach an R&D spending target of 1.5 percent of GDP in 2005 (up from 0.6 percent in 1996). Asian countries are also trying to take the lead in three areas that are likely to generate the next wave of innovation: biotechnology, nanotechnology, and information technology. Governments have increased their support for all three areas, and Asia now spends as much as the United States and Europe combined on nanotechnology. South Korea, China, and Japan have all established national offices to coordinate research and are spending significant private and public resources on new developments.

In addition to increasing science and R&D budgets, China, India, South Korea, and Taiwan are shifting from top-down, state-directed technology policies to more flexible, market-oriented approaches that foster innovation and entrepreneurship. Regional governments are using tax, education, and fiscal policies to create clusters of domestic start-ups. They are encouraging students, scientists, and technology managers to return from Silicon Valley to set up their own companies in Shanghai or Bangalore.

> **The move away from a purely low-cost manufacturing area toward direct and intensive involvement in technology development has been perhaps the major phenomenon across Asia over the last few years.**

However, we have the feeling that some non-technological "niche" sectors will also grow in importance – for instance, education, "boutique" tourism and leisure, and environmental and "socially useful" ventures. As examples of these, we offer a brief gallery of young entrepreneurs and their ventures scattered around the region.

Education

- Pine Tree Institute, Beijing. Ninie Wang's new venture builds on the fact that in China currently, there are no social services that promote and facilitate continuous learning for people of all ages. Pine Tree Institute fills part of this gap by providing a first-class learning experience to urban Chinese over 50 years of age.
- Ali Syedain of Karachi recently completed the acquisition of an entity that owns and runs five schools in Karachi. It has a staff of 250 and has some 2,800 students. The objective is to run the schools to a much higher standard but at affordable prices, thus raising the reference level for education in the city.
- Gerald Cai's Singapore-based venture, Questation, revolves around the use of a proprietary virtual classroom learning platform that allows students to connect to teachers via the internet and learn through speaking, talking, and typing. The initial focus is Singapore-standard mathematics classes targeted at pupils in the United States.

Tourism and leisure

- Parik Laxminarayan and Alex Metzler recently launched Enchanting India, a high-end travel and tourism service initially aimed at the German market.
- Currently in launch phase in Singapore is Hian Goh's Asian Food Channel (AFC), a new niche pay TV channel focused on the Asia-Pacific market. Providing food content for the Asian audience, AFC will contain a mix of Eastern and Western content in a variety of formats and genres, from cooking and variety shows, to education and restaurant guides.

Environmental and socially useful

- Matrika, Singapore. Hiran Vedam launched this venture to develop and market a locating device for people at risk, generally very old or very young people, who are more susceptible to getting lost.
- Sulax Shah, along with six other young co-founders, launched Shri Kamdhenu Electronics in Vallabh Vidyanagar, a small town in India, to satisfy an existing and unmet need in the rural Indian marketplace – that of automating milk collection processes to make them more efficient and to enable faster and more accurate payments to farmers. This particular need had gone unfulfilled largely because the market segment comprising local dairy cooperatives was ignored by larger companies, perhaps in part on the assumption that it would be difficult for rural and often illiterate farmers to accept and use high-tech solutions.
- A young group of entrepreneurs is planning to build world-class hospitals in China. They have already identified an attractive site in Shanghai to build their first hospital, and are in discussions with several local groups to provide hospital management services as well. They have also identified one of the top US teaching hospital groups to be their partner in this venture.

▶▶ CONCLUSION

The common characteristic linking all these entrepreneurs is their youth – at the time of finishing this book only two are over 30 years old. They are all, thus, representative of Asia-Pacific's new generation of entrepreneurs. It is a fairly safe bet that young people such as these – in six out of the eight cases, the lead entrepreneur has postgraduate-level academic qualifications – from even the immediately preceding generation would not have been likely to choose the entrepreneurial route. They will form the foundation of a more widely perceived and appreciated entrepreneurial culture that will in turn engender new generations of entrepreneurs.

> ❝ ... young people such as these will form the foundation of a more widely perceived and appreciated entrepreneurial culture that will in turn engender new generations of entrepreneurs. ❞

A living symbol of this process is Kanags Surendran, a 26-year-old Indian. Kanags is developing for launch in the near future an internet-based series of educational materials and courses, designed to provide for a wide audience in Asia the essentials of what needs to be known in order to have a reasonable chance of successfully launching a new business.

In doing this, he is directly addressing the needs of the hundred or so young men and women in Mumbai, and Linan Zhu's Chinese entrepreneurs, with whom we started this book.

ENDNOTES

[1] Binod Khadria, "Migration of Highly Skilled Indians: Case Studies of IT and Health Professionals," OECD Directorate for Science, Technology and Industry Working Paper 2004/6.

[2] Devesh Kapur, "Ideas and Economic Reforms in India: The Role of International Migration and the Indian Diaspora," *India Review*, 3(4), October 2004, pp. 364–84.

[3] Forbes, November 29, 2004, p. 161.

[4] Adam Segal, Is America Losing Its Edge?, *Foreign Affairs*, 83(6), November/December 2004, p. 2.

Index

3i Group 316
3i-Kogin Buyouts Ltd 316

Accounts payable 121, 125
ACNielsen 217
Acquisition 57, 86, 112, 135,
    144, 187-188, 195-196,
    198, 200, 224-225, 228,
    248, 274, 283, 296, 298-
    299, 301-302, 308, 313,
    316-317, 324, 338
Actis Private Equity 323
Air Asia 154
Andhra Pradesh 41
ASEAN 30, 153, 224, 238, 330
Asian Food Channel 338
Asset 15, 46, 103, 117, 129,
    131, 141, 182, 194, 244,
    251, 311, 324
Astra 224
Auckland 110
Audit committee 180, 253-254
Australasia 197, 271-273
Australia 9-12, 17, 27, 30-32,
    34, 52, 54, 132, 151, 158,
    160, 162, 165, 176, 178-
    179, 185, 227-228, 230,
    238, 323, 331, 334

Bangalore 45, 59, 60-62, 66-
    67, 74, 102, 165, 332-
    333, 335-337
Bangladesh 17, 42
Bank debt 192-193, 196, 244,
    289, 296-297
Bank overdraft 134
Barter 133
BarterAsia.com 133-134, 147
Beijing 4, 40, 55, 102, 217,
    235, 260, 337-338
Benchmark Capital 335
"Big Bang" reforms 309
Benkan Corp. 312
Biopolis 41
Board structure 143, 247
Branson, Sir Richard 154
Brunel, Isambard Kingdom 38
Bubble burst 88
Burn rate 70, 71, 88
Business angel 18, 66, 67, 82-
    84, 95, 97, 99, 101-103,
    110, 188-189, 249
Business Angel Network South
    East Asia (BANSEA) 102
Business process outsourcing
    (BPO) 13, 61-62, 70, 73,
    77

Cai, Gerald 338
California 19, 51, 102, 110,
    252, 277
Cambodia 17, 124, 127, 153
Cantillon, Richard 150
Capital 4, 7, 18, 40, 42, 44,
    46, 57, 63, 66, 73, 76-79,
    81-84, 86, 88-92, 95-99,
    103, 105-108, 111-113,
    117-119, 126-127, 129-
    131, 133-135, 141-142,
    150, 155, 159-160, 174-
    175, 181, 187-189, 191-
    192, 194-196, 198-199,
    201-202, 206-212, 221-
    222, 225, 229, 235, 241-
    243, 245, 247-249, 252,
    254, 256-259, 261-263,
    274, 284, 289-290, 295,
    300, 303, 318, 321, 324,
    326, 331, 334-335
Carlyle Group 323
Cash collection 121
Cash flow 21-22, 27, 65, 67,
    74-76, 83, 105, 118-120,
    130, 135, 138, 141, 145,
    187, 189, 193, 206, 210,
    211, 233, 265, 277, 279-
    281, 296, 298, 300, 302,
    308, 312, 318
Cash management 22-23, 60,
    76, 117, 121-122, 125,
    128, 143, 146, 193
Celestial Nutrifoods Limited
    260
Chaebol 7, 112
Changi International Airport
    Services (CIAS) 323
Chareon Pokphand 228

Chemdex 37
Cheung Kong Holdings 269
Chew, Elim 154
Chief executive officer (CEO) 4,
    15, 34, 59, 121, 139-140,
    142, 144-145, 161, 171-
    175, 177-178, 185, 215-
    216, 231-232, 261, 268,
    270, 274, 282-284, 307,
    311, 330, 336
Chief financial officer (CFO)
    119, 125, 127, 137-138,
    140, 142-146, 299, 313
China 4-5, 9-12, 17-18, 25-27,
    29-32, 34, 40, 42, 51-53,
    55, 80-81, 92, 93, 96,
    110, 115, 121-122, 124,
    126, 130-131, 135, 137,
    141, 151-153, 155, 162,
    165, 179, 185, 187-188,
    202, 208-209, 211, 216-
    217, 225, 227, 232, 234-
    236, 238-242, 244, 252-
    253, 256, 258-263, 269,
    277, 321-322, 330-331,
    334-339
China Securities Regulatory
    Commission 259
Chinese Academy of Sciences
    40
Citibank 224
CLSA Private Equity 204
Coca-Cola 133, 319
Coface 121, 126-127, 135
Collateral 125, 128-129, 131,
    192, 194-195, 205, 245
Collins, Tim 311
Commitment money 291

Conglomerate 288, 293, 295, 303, 323
Contract enforcement 124
Core strategies 288, 323
Corporate disclosure 252
Corporate governance 23, 29, 126, 143, 145, 177-180, 185, 205, 239, 242, 246-247, 249, 251-254
Corporate manager 287-288
Countertrade 133
CPG 323
Creative Technologies 163
Credit agencies 126
Credit collection 121, 125
Credit histories 135-136
Credit insurance 135, 195
Credit rating 126, 137
Credit record 133, 136
Credit risk 126, 132-133, 136-137
Creditor 119, 122, 252
Croatia 11, 165
CSMC Technologies Corp 202, 209
CSRC 259, 262
Cyberjaya 40

Daiichi Kangyo Bank 310
Daqing 260
Datsun 39
de Meyer, Arnoud 43, 55, 224, 238
Dealflow Connection 102
Debt 123-124, 189-190, 196, 245, 249, 295-299, 302, 308, 316, 318

Decision-making 101, 109, 113, 137, 252, 273, 278, 285, 293
Definition of entrepreneurship 291
Dehradun 203
Delhi 202, 332
Deloitte Touche Tohmatsu 174
Dequan, Ming 261
"Descending from heaven" 306
Dhaka 42
Diaspora 341
Dilution 68, 201, 246-247
Divesting 293, 311, 313
Dnata 323
Dot.com 4-5, 12, 37, 62-63, 67, 150, 176, 180, 262, 277
Downer 323
Dream Gate 160
Dubai 42, 323

E-commerce 138
Early stage 63, 67, 82-83, 91, 101, 103, 171-172, 207, 219-220, 291, 320
Early-stage investing 84-85, 90, 92-93
EasyJet 154
Ebay 37, 335
Education 5, 14-16, 32, 48, 156-157, 160, 227, 272, 337-338
Eiffel, Gustave 38
Enchanting India 338
Enforcing contract 123
Enterprise Investment Initiative 97
Enterprise New Zealand 157

Enterprise New Zealand Trust
(ENZT) 156-158
EntrePass 6, 153
Equity capital 134, 198, 202,
248
Equity funding 187, 194-197,
201-202, 302
Europe 15, 24, 26-27, 38, 44,
61, 84, 94-95, 101, 106,
110-111, 120, 132, 135,
178-179, 183, 197, 223,
225-228, 230, 232-234,
236, 239-241, 269, 271-
274, 283, 287, 289-290,
292-293, 295, 302-303,
309, 312, 320, 326, 334,
337
European Business Angels
Network (EBAN) 101
European Venture Capital
Association (EVCA) 293,
326
Exit 87, 89, 91, 101, 108-110,
121, 124, 144-145, 207-
208, 210-211, 221, 249,
265, 275, 283, 296-300,
308, 312, 315, 319, 324
Expansion capital 83, 187,
189, 198-199, 201, 203,
206-207, 209, 211

Factoring 130-134, 136, 142,
145, 191, 195, 244
Families 252, 291
Family and friends 82, 84, 95,
188-189
Family business 178, 249,
265, 267, 271-276, 280-
281, 284-285

Fernandes, Tony 154
Finance manager 138-144,
299
Financial engineering 295
Financial officer 117, 244
Financial structure 252, 295,
300, 302, 312
Flextronics 228
Forbes 155, 334-336, 341
Formal venture capital 78, 92,
97-99
Founding entrepreneur 267,
274
France 9, 11, 233-234
Frankfurt 110
Friendster 335
Fuji Bank 305, 310
Fund carry 89-90
Fund life 107-108
Funding 4-6, 16, 18, 29, 60,
63, 68-69, 77-78, 82-83,
86-88, 90-92, 97, 99, 105,
113-114, 132, 134, 140,
142, 187, 189-202, 204,
208, 210-212, 249, 258,
261-262, 270, 277, 283,
293, 296, 299, 301-302,
308, 317, 331
Fundraising 64, 66, 68, 77, 79,
87, 191, 204

Garg, Sam 43, 55
Gates, Bill 154
Gates Electronics 254
GE Capital 224
Gearing effect 296
General Electric 173
Genome Valley 41
Germany 234

Ghosn, Carlos 313, 317
Global Entrepreneurship
    Monitor (GEM) 3, 9-12,
    14-15, 18-19, 96-98, 135,
    149, 153, 157
Goh, Hian 338
GOME Electrical Appliances
    217
Governance Metrics
    International (GMI) 179,
    185
Government 5, 7-8, 23-24, 26,
    29, 40-41, 55, 80-84, 102,
    113-114, 138, 149-152,
    156, 158-159, 161-165,
    177, 188-191, 201, 212,
    221-222, 230-231, 252,
    259, 300, 309-310, 321,
    322, 325, 331
Government-linked companies
    (GLCs) 321-322
Grant Thornton 197, 271-272
Guangdong 217
Guangyu, Huang 217
Guangzhou 102, 137
Guaning, Su 43
Gurgaon 203

Haidan Science Park 40
Haier 216
Haji-Ioannou, Stelios 154
Haque, Promod 335
Hashimoto, Masujiro 38
Heilongjiang province 260
Hicom 224
Ho Chi Minh City 42

Hong Kong 9-12, 17, 19, 27-
    32, 34, 93, 96, 102, 110,
    122, 124, 126, 132-133,
    160, 162, 165, 179-180,
    185, 199, 204, 210, 215,
    217, 228-233, 235-236,
    240, 243, 245, 253, 258-
    260, 268-269, 275, 331
Hong Leong 228
Hoogewerf, Rupert 155
Hsinchu 40, 336
Hutchinson 228
Hutchison Whampoa 269
Hyderabad 41
Hyundai 217

IBJ Research 268
Ibuka, Masaru 38
ICICI Knowledge Park 42
iGlobe Partners Pte Ltd 110
Independent director 143, 180,
    247, 252-254, 256-257
India 4, 5, 9, 10, 11, 12, 13,
    17, 18, 24, 25, 30, 31, 32,
    34, 41, 45, 53, 55, 60, 61,
    62, 70, 77, 81, 92, 93, 96,
    110, 121, 122, 124, 126,
    130, 131, 152, 154, 155,
    156, 162, 180, 185, 187,
    188, 199, 202, 203, 205,
    206, 208, 227, 228, 236,
    253, 321, 322, 323, 324,
    331, 332, 333, 334, 335,
    336, 337, 338, 339, 341
Indian Institute of Management,
    Lucknow 62, 165
Indian Institute of Technology,
    Bombay 46, 55, 165

Indian Institute of Technology, Kanpur 155
Indonesia 17, 28-31, 34, 53, 122, 124, 127, 158, 162, 179, 185, 224, 253, 330-331
Industrial Bank of Japan 310
Informal venture capital 95-97, 99
Information and communications technologies (ICT) 39-40, 225
Information technology (IT) 13, 40, 42, 46, 61-62, 77, 111, 154-156, 228, 235, 276, 292, 332-334, 336-337, 341
Infosys 154, 155, 216, 337
Initial public offering (IPO) 23, 82-83, 89-91, 108, 110, 177, 190, 198, 204-205, 207-208, 210, 239-242, 245, 247, 251, 254-255, 257, 261-262, 296
Innovation 23, 33, 35, 39, 43-44, 54-55, 97-98, 159-160, 182-183, 217, 329, 331, 336-337
INSEAD 15, 43, 55, 182, 183, 185, 223, 227, 238, 323
Institutional buyout (IBOs) 289
Institutional investor 89, 242, 252, 290, 326
Intel 111-112, 184, 336
International Angel Investment Institute (IAII) 101-102
International Enterprise Singapore 231

Investors 18, 29, 33, 57, 63, 77-78, 82, 84-92, 97, 99-113, 115, 118, 135, 142-143, 174, 189, 198, 201, 205, 207-208, 210-212, 240, 242, 246, 249-254, 256-257, 263, 269, 290, 307-308, 312, 321, 326, 335
Invoices 131-132
Ireland 334
IRR 297, 319
Israel 4, 41, 334-335

Japan 9-12, 14, 17, 28, 30, 34, 38, 43, 52-54, 102, 110, 112, 122-124, 126, 132, 138, 159-160, 165, 179, 185, 199, 223, 225-226, 252, 268, 287, 289, 292-293, 295, 303-313, 315-317, 319-323, 326, 331, 334-335, 337
Jerusalem Venture Partners 334

Ka-shing, Li 268-269, 275
Kaliakoir 42
Karachi 338
Karnataka 154
Kauffman Center 15
Kazakhstan 334
Keiretsu 112, 295, 305, 310, 313, 318, 321
Kenmark Industrial Co., Ltd 131-132
Keystone Management Services 176, 185

Korea 4, 7, 9-12, 14, 17, 19, 29-31, 34, 96, 102, 112, 122, 124, 126-127, 151, 162, 165, 179, 185, 199, 224, 238, 253, 287, 321, 331, 334-335, 337

Korean Small and Medium Business 231

Laxminarayan, Parik 338
Lee Kuan Yew 229, 238
Legend Capital 4
Letters of credit (LC) 129
Leveraged buyouts (LBOs) 289, 323
Li, Victor 269
Limited partner 90, 105-108
Liquidity 207, 256, 259, 274, 285
Liquidity preference 87
Listing expenses 251, 255, 260
Long Term Credit Bank 311
Lumenaré Networks 336
Luthra, Vandana 201-202

Malaysia 8, 17, 19, 29-30, 34, 39-40, 53, 93, 99, 110, 114, 122, 124, 126, 130, 132-133, 151, 154, 160, 162, 165, 179-180, 185, 224, 244-245, 253, 258, 277, 330-331
Malaysian SME Information & Advisory Centre 231

Management buyout (MBOs) 54-55, 90, 94, 198, 201, 265, 270, 285, 287, 289-298, 300-303, 305-306, 308, 311-313, 315, 319-326
Manila 50, 236
Market share 216, 304, 310
Matching principle 195-196
MBO consortium 297, 299-300, 316
McDonald's 38, 49-51
Mergers and acquisitions (M&A) 200, 274-275, 285, 289, 293, 299-300, 303, 304, 307, 308, 309, 312, 315, 319, 321, 322
MeritTrac 60, 63-67, 69-71, 73-75, 77-78, 95, 104, 118
Metzler, Alex 338
Microsoft 108, 337
Middle East 126, 203, 233
Milestone 68, 70, 84, 86-88, 90, 104-105
Ministry of International Trade and Industry (METI) 159-160, 268, 322
Mizuho 310
Mizuho Financial Group 318
MNCs 7, 70, 85, 122, 133, 144, 224, 284, 309, 321
Morita, Akio 38
Moulonguet, Thierry 313
Multimedia Super Corridor (MSC) 8, 39-40, 55
Multinational 7, 40, 62, 64, 70, 75, 150, 224-226, 230, 309

Mumbai 4, 18, 54-55, 61, 102, 165, 216, 277, 323, 340
Murphy, Glen 217
Murthy, Mahesh 216
Murthy, Narayana 154-155, 216, 238
Myanmar 127, 153

Nanfou Batteries 137
Nanyang Technological University 43
Nasdaq 47, 85, 155, 240, 262
National Commission on Entrepreneurship 164
National Entrepreneurship Network (NEN) 156
Nationalized industries 288, 293, 300, 321
New Delhi 332
New York 240-241, 334
New Zealand 9-12, 17, 27, 54, 99, 132, 156-157, 160, 162, 165, 179, 185, 231
New Zealand Trade and Enterprise 231
Newbridge Capital 323
Ningbo Bird 216
Nissan 39, 305, 310, 313-318
Noida 336
Non-core businesses 293, 303, 311, 313, 315, 323, 326
Non-executive director 247, 274
Norin Optech 137
North America 111, 197, 230, 271, 273-274, 285, 287, 290, 330
North Asia 96

North Korea 4, 127
Norway 240
Norwest Venture Partners 335

OECD 123-124, 332, 341
Okuno, Shinsuke 317, 318
Open book accounting 129
Ordinary share 296
Outblaze 231-234, 238
Own money 4, 82, 102-104, 188, 305
Owner-manager 268, 272

Padaki, Madan 62
Pages, Erik 164
Pakistan 17, 27-28, 42, 55, 102, 122, 124, 127, 160, 162
Panda 216
Partner 26-27, 43, 49, 57, 82-83, 90, 99-101, 104-111, 132, 135, 153, 156, 164, 169, 171, 174, 180-181, 183, 201, 204-205, 224, 243-246, 255, 269, 278, 302, 317, 326, 334-335, 339
PassionFund 216
Peking University 40
Penang 6
Personal guarantee 190-191, 193, 246, 249-250, 274
Perth 176
Peru 233
Philippines 17, 26, 28, 30-32, 34, 50-52, 110, 122, 124, 126, 180, 185, 245, 253, 330-331

Pine Tree Institute 338
Pipeline 89-90, 242, 262
Pre-IPO 89-90, 110, 208
Preference share 204, 296
Price-earnings multiple 246
PricewaterhouseCoopers 55,
    199, 240-241, 307, 313,
    326, 335
Private equity 82, 95, 142,
    144, 187, 189-191, 194,
    196-201, 204-205, 207-
    208, 210-213, 245, 249,
    262, 265, 270, 283, 288-
    291, 293, 295, 297, 301-
    302, 305, 307, 311-317,
    319-323, 326
PSA 228
Public listing 103, 142, 144,
    191, 198, 205, 239, 246,
    299
Putrajaya 40

Quang Trung Software Park 42
Questation 338

Receivable 120, 131, 133, 193
Recruit Building Management
    313
Renault 310, 313, 317
Restructure 265, 288, 293,
    311, 324-325
Retirement 159, 265, 267,
    271, 273

Return 5, 29, 47, 49, 63, 65-
    67, 70, 82, 84, 86-87, 91-
    92, 101, 103, 105-107,
    109, 111, 113-114, 134,
    141, 175, 180, 189, 194-
    196, 198, 207-208, 210-
    211, 219, 227, 239, 242,
    249, 277, 282-283, 295-
    302, 308, 312, 315, 318-
    320, 329, 332-337
Ripplewood 311
Risk 15, 26, 44, 51, 62, 66,
    86, 88-89, 91-92, 97, 102-
    103, 107, 126-127, 131-
    134, 136-137, 142, 145,
    160, 174, 183, 189, 193-
    196, 198, 204-206, 208,
    211, 221, 234-235, 245,
    249, 255, 269, 278, 282,
    291-292, 298, 301, 314-
    315, 336, 339
Russia 9, 165

Salaryman 291-292, 305, 307,
    320
Samsung 44, 217
Sapp, Bob 160
SARS 23, 25, 27, 126, 128,
    187, 240, 277
Scalability 63
Schroder Ventures 313
Schumpeter, Joseph 38, 150
Secured instruments 82
Security 129-130, 189, 191,
    194, 244-245, 250, 254,
    300-302, 308, 334
Seed phase 95
Senior debt 295-296, 298,
    302, 316, 318

Shacho 306-307

Shanghai 102, 217, 230, 240, 259-262, 335-337, 339

Shareholder 23, 69, 71, 78, 86-89, 91, 100, 104, 113, 142-144, 177, 179-180, 192-194, 196, 205, 207, 210, 247, 249, 251, 269-270, 289, 293, 295, 297, 299-301, 304, 307, 309, 312-314, 318-319, 321

Shareholder value 143, 177, 293, 295, 304, 309, 312-313, 318-319, 321

Shell 224

Shenzhen 4, 240, 260, 262

Shinsei Bank 311

Silicon Valley 4, 6, 18-19, 35, 39-41, 54-55, 335-337

Sim Wong Hoo 154, 163, 165

Simpson, Steve 176, 185

Singapore 6-7, 9-14, 17, 27-30, 32, 34, 38, 41, 44, 48, 52-53, 55, 93, 96-97, 99, 102, 106, 110, 122, 124, 126, 130, 132, 150-151, 153, 155, 160-163, 165, 177-180, 185, 200, 224, 228-229, 231, 238, 243-247, 252-262, 321-323, 326, 331, 334, 338-339

Singapore Stock Exchange 254, 257, 260-262

Singapore Straits Times Index 257

Singapore Yellow Pages 200, 323

Singh, K. Natwar 152

SingTel 224

Siu, Yat 231-232

Small- and medium-sized enterprises (SMEs) 7, 26, 31-32, 34, 80-81, 120-122, 125-126, 128-129, 135-136, 140, 142-144, 151, 153, 162, 164, 191, 193, 195-197, 200, 212, 218-219, 223, 231, 234, 239, 248, 252, 254-256, 258-259, 262, 268, 323, 330-331

Small-cap company 239

Sony 38, 226

South Korea 26, 29, 31, 34, 96, 102, 112, 122, 124, 126, 151, 159, 162, 165, 179, 185, 217, 224, 238, 253, 287, 331, 334, 337

Southeast Asia 113, 227, 243, 321, 330

SP Jain Institute of Management 62

Sri Lanka 17, 29, 122, 124, 127, 133

Starbucks 38

Start-up 9-10, 16, 45, 54, 59-65, 79, 83-84, 92, 94-95, 97, 100, 102, 105, 110, 112, 157, 159, 161, 165, 174-176, 180, 184, 187-189, 193, 198, 200, 206-208, 265, 290-291, 334, 337

State-owned enterprises (SOEs) 225, 259

Stock option 173, 289, 309

Strategic partner 27, 82-83, 164, 174, 180

Subordinated debt 296-297
Succession 23, 33, 265, 267-271, 273-275, 278, 280-282, 284-285, 323
Surendran, Kanags 340
Switzerland 240
Syedain, Ali 338
Syria 233

Taiwan 7, 9-12, 17, 19, 30, 32, 34, 40-41, 96, 102, 110, 122, 124, 126, 132, 165, 179-180, 185, 209, 224, 228, 240, 253, 275, 277, 331, 334-337
Taiwan Semiconductor 228
TCL 216
Technology Fast 500 Asia Pacific 2004 330, 336
Temasek Holdings 321
Terrorism 23, 25, 27, 226
Thailand 7-12, 17, 19, 26, 29-30, 32, 34, 53, 122, 124, 126, 130, 159, 162, 165, 179, 185, 201, 224, 228, 244, 253, 330-331
Thatcher, Margaret 310
TiE 4, 18-19
Toyota 224, 226, 310
Track record 108, 124, 136, 141, 193, 206, 246, 262
Trade credit 133-134
Transparency 26, 30, 123, 126, 143, 177-178, 225, 242, 247, 249, 302, 307, 319
Tsinghua University 40

UCC Coffee 319
Uganda 9, 11
UK 6, 41, 44, 54, 154, 178, 203, 210, 223, 227, 230, 288, 293, 295, 310, 313, 321
Undercapitalization 194
United Arab Emirates 203
United States (US) 5, 9-12, 14, 17, 21, 24-29, 40-41, 43-44, 46-48, 52, 54, 61, 84, 94, 96, 101-102, 106, 110, 123-124, 132, 154, 163, 178-179, 183, 209, 217, 223, 226-227, 230-233, 236, 239-241, 268-269, 277, 283, 288, 290, 292-293, 303-304, 307, 309, 311-312, 335-339
University of Mysore 155
Uppsala 219-220, 232
UPS 22-23, 25-28, 30-31, 34, 330-331
UPS Asia Business Monitor 26, 34, 330-331
Uttar Pradesh 336

Valuation 67-68, 86-91, 103, 126, 162, 189, 193, 208, 246-247, 279-280, 297, 314, 317
Vantec Corp. 312, 313
VC investment 92, 94
Venezuela 9
Venture capital (VC) 4, 18, 47, 63, 66, 77, 84-94, 96-97, 99-100, 105-115, 150, 175, 201, 208, 245, 249, 290, 334-335

Vietnam 17, 42, 122, 124,
        127, 153, 159, 165, 228
Virtela Communications 335

Wadhwani Foundation 48, 156
Wadhwani, Romesh 48, 156
Walden International 110, 210
Wang, Ninie 338
Warburg Pincus 323
Welch, Jack 173
Williamson, Peter 182-183,
        224, 238
Working capital 66, 73, 77,
        117-119, 127, 129-131,
        133-135, 192, 195, 221-
        222, 243, 245, 247-248
WTO 224

Yoost, Dean 307
Young Enterprise Scheme (YES)
        156-158

Zhu, Linan 4, 18, 340